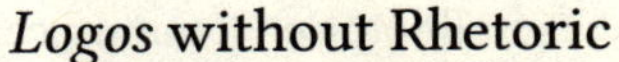

Logos without Rhetoric

Studies in Rhetoric/Communication
Thomas W. Benson, Series Editor

Logos without Rhetoric

The Arts of Language before Plato

Edited by
Robin Reames

Afterword by
Edward Schiappa

The University of South Carolina Press

Published by the University of South Carolina Press
Columbia, South Carolina 29208

www.sc.edu/uscpress

Manufactured in the United States of America

26 25 24 23 22 21 20 19 18 17
10 9 8 7 6 5 4 3 2 1

Library of Congress Cataloging-in-Publication Data
can be found at http://catalog.loc.gov/

ISBN 978-1-61117-768-8 (cloth)
ISBN 978-1-61117-769-5 (ebook)

This book was printed on a recycled paper with
30 percent postconsumer waste content.

It is perhaps a true proverb, which says that the beginning of anything is the most important; hence it is also the most difficult. For, as it is very powerful in its effects, so it is very small in size and therefore very difficult to see. When, however, the first beginning has been discovered, it is easier to add to it and develop the rest. This has happened, too, concerning rhetorical speeches, and also practically all the other arts.

Aristotle
On Sophistical Refutations

Contents

Series Editor's Preface

What are the origins of rhetoric in Western culture? To this day most students new to the study of the history of rhetoric are introduced to the story of Corax and Tisias, who were said by the Greeks to have written the first handbooks on oratory in the fifth century B.C.E. in Sicily and whose teachings quickly migrated to Athens. But earlier practices of argument and persuasion reach back to the origins of literacy and beyond in the mists of memory in oral culture. Against this tradition of gradually developing practice and increasingly self-conscious practice, Edward Schiappa, writing in the 1990s, offered a contrasting view. In 1990, Schiappa argued that it was not until fourth-century Athens, with Plato's dialogue *Gorgias,* that the term rhetoric (*rhētorikē*) was coined, and that the naming of the art enabled the foundation of what may truly be called rhetorical theory.

In Logos *without Rhetoric: The Arts of Language before Plato,* Robin Reames and the contributors she has brought together consider the intellectual and material history of rhetoric, eloquence, and oratory before Plato. The result is a fascinating, vivid, and learned journey, guided by scholars of distinction and originality—Terry L. Papillon, Robert N. Gaines, Carol Poster, Thomas Rickert, Marina McCoy, David C. Hoffman, and Michael Svoboda, along with Robin Reames as editor and contributor and an afterword by Edward Schiappa.

The intellectual delights of this richly documented and theoretically dazzling volume are augmented by a spirit of intellectual generosity that shines through every contending theoretical and historical argument. The result is a work that is important, original, and at the same time lucid and accessible—a model of scholarly eloquence.

Thomas W. Benson

Preface and Acknowledgments

The idea for this volume began as a panel on Heraclitus that I organized for the Rhetoric Society of America biennial conference, which included presentations by Jason Helms, David Hoffman, Carol Poster, and myself. I am grateful to the lively discussion of the panel presenters and the attendees for inspiring the larger work of this volume, which aims to gather and reconsider some of the intellectual antecedents for the ascendance of rhetoric in fourth-century B.C.E. Greece. Although originally the discussion focused exclusively on Heraclitus, and considered the hermeneutic traditions that exclude his thought from the history of rhetoric, our considerations led us to entertain more broadly how these hermeneutic traditions constrain our view of many other figures as well, where strict and firm distinctions between "poets," "philosophers," "sophists," and "rhetoricians" anachronistically dictate how and to what extent these thinkers are viably associated with the birth of rhetoric and rhetorical theory. I am grateful to all of the contributors, whose enthusiasm for this theme brought the project into being.

In addition the contributors, I wish to thank Jim Denton, Linda Fogle, and the editorial staff at the University of South Carolina Press, whose hard work has made this volume possible, and to the eagle-eyed copyeditors who see the errors of our ways. We the authors are grateful to the anonymous reviewers who offered invaluable feedback and commentary at earlier stages of the project. I also wish to thank Bentley University; the Jeanne and Dan Valente Center for Arts and Sciences at Bentley, and its director, Christopher Beneke. The center's generous support made beginning the work for this volume possible. I am grateful as well to the librarians and library services at Harvard's Widener and Houghton libraries, whose outstanding collections are nothing less than inspirational. Thanks also are due to my colleagues and students at the University of Illinois at Chicago, in particular Ralph Cintron, Monica Westin, and Nathan Shephard, as well as William McNeill of DePaul University, all of whom participated in a roundtable discussion of this and other work. And of course, heartfelt thanks goes to Edward Schiappa, whose scholarship on the beginning of rhetorical theory in Greece laid a firm foundation on which to build this work, and whose interest in this project is generously offered in the afterword.

Finally, I wish to thank my partner, Drew Dalton, whose support, encouragement, generosity, and vast knowledge of the history of philosophy make my work both more possible and more worthwhile, and my daughter, Thea, whose laughter, love, and patience make all of it more fun.

Earlier versions of two of the essays in this volume appeared previously as journal articles. An early version of my essay on Heraclitus appeared as "The *Logos* Paradox: Heraclitus, Material Language, and Rhetoric" in *Philosophy and Rhetoric* 46:3, 328–50 (© 2013 Pennsylvania State University Press), and a previous version of Thomas Rickert's essay on Parmenides appeared as "Parmenides, Ontological Enaction, and the Prehistory of Rhetoric" in *Philosophy and Rhetoric* 47:4, 472–93 (© 2014 Pennsylvania State University Press). Although the essays included here differ substantially from those earlier versions, they are used with the permission of the Pennsylvania State University Press.

A Note on Translations

The authors of these essays have consulted various translations for the primary ancient texts. For this reason, the primary texts are cited throughout the volume and in the bibliography by the translators' last names. Primary ancient texts that are not specifically quoted, either in the original Greek or in translation, are not listed in the bibliography. All complete works by ancient authors referenced but not quoted in this book (for example, Homer, Hesiod, Aristophanes, Thucydides, Plato, Xenophon, Aristotle, Cicero, and Diogenes Laertius) are available in the Loeb Classical Library published by Harvard University Press. Partial works and fragments of ancient authors are available in Barnes (1982 and 1987) and Sprague (1972). The authors include the original or transliterated Greek text where they feel it would be valuable for readers of Greek.

Introduction

There are primarily two ways of accounting for the beginning of rhetoric: one we might call the narratological account and the other the nominal account. We inherit the narratological account from the ancient rhetoricians themselves, who told stories of the beginning of their craft. In this account, the art of rhetoric was introduced to Athens in the fifth century B.C.E. by the Sicilians Corax and Tisias, who, we are told, were the first to write handbooks on the subject and brought those handbooks with them to Athens. According to the nominal account, by contrast, rhetoric only truly emerged as a distinct art once it was deliberately and self-consciously named *rhētorikē* (by Plato, in the *Gorgias* dialogue) as a means of separating it from other "language arts" or *logōn technē.* By the former view, rhetoric began with the material introduction of a new cultural habit—a habit that would eventually require a systematic theory and a name to correctly identify its function in the *polis* and in education. This would have evolved gradually during a period of time when Athens was both expanding her imperial reach and opening herself to the suasory techniques of eloquent foreigners. By the latter view, the naming of the practice was precisely what created the boundaries that distinguished rhetoric from both eloquence in general and other language arts, including dialectic and sophistry, in particular. And, moreover, this occurred radically and abruptly, spurred by the radical and abrupt changes that were wrought on the Greek culture once literacy became widespread.

The question of when and how rhetoric began is by no means new. It is reflected, among other places, in the fourth century B.C.E. in Aristotle's *On Sophistical Refutations.* For Aristotle, the beginning of anything, including rhetoric, is "the most important" and therefore the most powerful because, in true Aristotelian form, it is the most rarified and the most potent when it is inscribed with the most potentiality. Neither was Aristotle the last ancient commentator to raise the question of rhetoric's beginning. It appears again in the first century C.E. with Quintilian, who, in considering whether rhetoric is a knack or a systematic art (yet another recurring question since antiquity), wrote:

> To this is added the quibble that nothing that is based on art can have existed before the art in question, whereas men have always from time immemorial spoken in their own defence or in denunciation of others: the teaching of rhetoric as an art was, they say, a later invention dating from about the time of Tisias and Corax: oratory therefore existed before art and consequently cannot be an art. . . . It is sufficient to call attention to the fact that everything which art has brought to perfection originated in nature. . . . If therefore any kind of speech is to be called eloquence, I will admit that it existed before it was an art. If on the other hand not every man that speaks is an orator and primitive man did not speak like an orator, my opponents must needs acknowledge that oratory is the product of art and did not exist before it. (*Inst. Or.* II.7–11; Butler, 329–31).

In essence, Quintilian was articulating an ancient version of the difference between the narratological and nominal accounts of rhetoric's beginning: what are we to call the practices or eloquence and oratory before they were formulated explicitly by the art called *rhētorikē*? And conversely, how do we account for rhetoric as an art if its by-products emerged naturally, prior to the development of the explicit art?

For the ancient testimony of rhetoric's beginning, the story of Corax and Tisias—described by Quintilian as an account that places the development of rhetoric at an improbably late date—serves to fill a small part of the chasm of Greece's unwritten history, a canyon in which echo numerous questions about the past, reverberating only with the timbre of the poet's voice. In the early and late fifth-century B.C.E. historical narratives of Herodotus and Thucydides, for example, we bear witness to the presence of a dual anxiety: on the one hand, an anxious desire to put in writing the things that had happened in Greece's wars with Persia and Sparta, and on the other hand, an anxious suspicion of the unwritten accounts that were handed down through the oral tradition from time immemorial, which cannot be confirmed through firsthand experience.[1] In both Herodotus and Thucydides, there is an apparent fear that if their accounts are not committed to writing they are in danger of being lost forever, along with a corresponding suspicion of word-of-mouth accounts. This general attitude helps to explain the prominence of the story of Corax and Tisias throughout the ancient testimonies of rhetoric's beginning: they are by all accounts credited with beginning the art because they put their art in writing and in so doing separated it from a less technical form of eloquence and oratory that lacked any documentary history.[2] In the same way that the histories of Herodotus and Thucydides manifest a relatively new concern with documentary evidence about the past, according to which what counts as "history" must be written and its source must be identified, the ancient testimony from Aristotle to Quintilian manifests a desire to mark the beginning of the history of rhetoric at the moment that the art was first committed to writing.

Contemporary scholarship in the history of rhetoric, particularly that of Thomas Cole and Edward Schiappa, offers sound reason for marking the beginning of rhetoric's history in this way, although this leads them to date rhetoric's beginning much later than Aristotle and Quintilian do. In their view, rhetoric, as a self-conscious study of language and its effects and as a meta-discursive practice that is both more systematic and more self-aware than merely intuitive eloquence, could only have truly taken shape with the externalization of language in literacy. Cole wrote:

> For the rhetorician's preoccupation with controlling the medium of transmission to come into play, two developments had to take place, neither of which would have occurred when it did without the contribution of Plato and Aristotle. First, audiences and composers had to acquire the habit of abstracting essential messages from verbal contexts: the informative core of any piece of communication from its non- or extra-informative—that is, rhetorical—residue. . . . Second, a "written" eloquence had to come into being—that is, a body of prose texts which might be read or delivered verbatim and still suggest the excitement, atmosphere, and commitment of a spontaneous oral performance or debate. Plato—along with, to a lesser degree, the other Socratics and the orator Isocrates—was the first to compose such texts. Without such texts there would have been no satisfactory data base on which to conduct the detailed precise analysis of the verbal medium that is characteristic of rhetoric. (1991, x)

For Cole, the "absolute separability of a speaker's message from the message used to transmit it" (12) doesn't appear in ancient literature before the *Phaedrus* dialogue (35), in which Plato deliberately displays the interconnectedness of a written speech and the development of a theoretical vocabulary based on its analysis. Prior to this, Cole argues, there is a glaring "absence of detailed analysis . . . everywhere in protorhetoric" (111). This leads to the conclusion "that the metalanguage that would have made analysis possible simply did not exist at the time to any significant degree" (111).

Perhaps the most crucial element of such a metalanguage is the term *rhētorikē* itself, which, Schiappa has argued, was most likely coined by Plato in the fourth-century *Gorgias* dialogue, and, he suggests, this likelihood affects how we understand and describe texts that predate the appearance of the term (1990, 457). As though in direct response to Quintilian's first-century insistence that rhetoric "existed before it was an art" (*Inst. Or.* II.11; Butler, 31), Schiappa contends, by contrast, that "humans can get quite good at doing various things long before developing abstract theories and specialized vocabularies about what it is that we are doing" (1999, 110), and although eloquence may have existed in practice, the term *rhētorikē* demarcates a distinct set of theoretical practices that simply did not and could not exist in the absence of the "terministic screen" to define those practices. "Prior to the coining of *rhētorikē*," Schiappa wrote, "the verbal arts were understood as less differentiated and more holistic in scope than they were in the fourth century" (23), and while it may be "possible to cull an 'inferred' or 'implied' theory or set of rules out of such texts . . . it is potentially anachronistic and misleading to call it a theory of rhetoric" (109). Unlike Quintilian, Schiappa prefers to limit the term *rhetorical theory* "to texts containing explicit discussion of rules and principles of rhetoric which may or may not influence the compositional practices of others" (109). In other words, he only applies the term to texts from the fourth century and later because, prior to Plato's terminological innovations and Aristotle's classifications, there is no "explicit discussion of rules and principles of rhetoric" (109).

This crucial work in the history of rhetoric by Cole and Schiappa in the 1990s ultimately dictates a set of scholarly standards that both directs and, in some ways, is problematized by the studies in the present volume. In the wake of the studies by Cole and Schiappa, it is no longer viable to think in general terms of rhetoric-writ-large that "could never have lain too far below the surface of the Greek consciousness" (Cole 1991, 23). On the contrary, investigation into rhetoric's history must be as dubious of the lore of rhetoric's beginning—including the tale of Corax and Tisias—as it is of any generalizations that do not attend carefully to precise technical vocabulary and key terms (Schiappa 1999, 11), the *ipsissima verba* of the authors themselves in surviving works (10) as opposed to testimony, fragments, and reports of works that are now lost. However, as the essays in this volume demonstrate, this creates problems for historians of rhetoric who would hope to gain a view of the full scope of rhetoric's history, including its prehistory.

Key terms of rhetorical theory in early texts are frequently obscured from view either because they are mistaken for nontechnical vocabulary or because they are anachronistically over-prioritized and vested with far too much metaphysical, philosophical, or theological weight—*logos* would be a prime example of a term that suffers simultaneously from both of these obscurities. Likewise, the *ipsissima verba* of works that exist only as fragments in the works of others—if they are truly and thoroughly "given priority over accounts of those theorists by later authors" (Schiappa 1999, 10)—are reduced to quotes taken out of context when stripped of the invaluable commentary offered by those later authors who, unlike us today, had access to the entire works. And while it may be true that "inferring rhetorical theory from practice is difficult business" (Timmerman and Schiappa, 170), it is by no means an impossible business, particularly when careful attention to practice reveals a self-conscious manipulation of the medium that can only be explained through recourse to theory, even if that theory is no longer materially extant. Furthermore, it is often more difficult to draw a firm distinction between theory and practice than it is to derive theory from practice, as Gorgias' *Encomium* and Plato's *Phaedrus* undeniably demonstrate. Perhaps most important, however, is the recognition that, if we are to "avoid the vocabulary and assumptions about discourse theories and rhetorical practice imported from the fourth century when analyzing fifth-century [or earlier] texts" (Schiappa 1999, 115), then we must likewise avoid the anachronistic over-prioritization of *rhētorikē* as a key term when that prioritization is itself informed by the later academic "disciplining" of rhetoric which gained prominence only in late antiquity and the medieval era.[3]

This book comprises eight specific case studies, each of which attempts to intervene in one or more of these problems by examining the status of rhetorical discipline prior to and therefore in the absence of the influence of Plato and Aristotle's full-fledged development of rhetorical theory in the fourth century B.C.E. Although some of the essays concern figures who would have been contemporaries of Plato, and therefore chronologically not "before Plato" but "with Plato," each study is concerned with the arguable presence of rhetorical theory that demonstrably existed prior to Plato's coining of the term (before "*rhētorikē*," in other words) and therefore in the absence of his influential contribution to the development of the discipline. To varying degrees, the studies are in accord with the idea that rhetoric should not be uncritically conflated with eloquence. Rather, in each study, it is a given that "the self consciously manipulative character of the process distinguishes rhetoric from eloquence" (Cole 1991, ix). Accordingly, we follow Schiappa's recommendation that any study of rhetoric's beginnings should proceed as "individualistic studies that provide an alternative to the standard account of early Greek rhetorical theory" (1999, 80). Hence, the essays are a series of individualistic studies, dealing with individual thinkers, texts, and rhetorical practices that offer evidence of self-conscious manipulation and abstract theorization in texts that predate the fourth-century ascent of Plato's concept of *rhētorikē*.

These essays collectively make a case for understanding rhetoric's development as an evolutionary, gradual process and argue for a more porous boundary between theory and practice in how we think about rhetoric's beginning. This proceeds in part not through wholesale suspicion and dismissal of *testimonia*, but through a more careful analysis of what both the *testimonia* of ancient authors and the material conditions that primed the ascent of sophistry and rhetoric contribute to our knowledge of the technical content of pre–fourth-century rhetorical texts. And while rhetorical theory cannot always be extracted from rhetorical practice, it often can, particularly when that practice deliberately highlights its own theory-derived patterns or matches precisely the testimony of rhetorical theory that is no longer extant. Furthermore, while it is true that the early texts considered here do not explicitly identify their vocabulary as technical terms of rhetorical theory, hermeneutic tendencies often block our view of how the vocabulary may rightly be understood as rhetorical theory. These tendencies dictate, for example, that Plato and Aristotle's account of Theodorus' parts of speech be viewed with suspicion, that Parmenides' and Heraclitus' thought was primarily philosophical and therefore irrelevant to the tradition of rhetoric, that Homer's thought could only have indicated a mythopoetic and therefore nonrational and nontechnical discourse, and so on.

By reconsidering these interpretive habits in light of rhetorical theory, the terms, vocabulary, genres, and general thought-worlds of these early texts are no longer confined strictly to proto-theology, proto-philosophy, myth, poetry, or satire. Rather, they are rightly understood as the rhetorical theory that was present in rhetoric's beginning, before the terms themselves came to be named *rhētorikē.* It is possible to consider, without anachronistically broadening the concept of rhetoric, the specific terminology that was not only prioritized and prominent prior to the prioritization of the term *rhētorikē,* but also indispensible for the full-fledged development of rhetorical theory proper. This articulates an important difference between, on the one hand, anachronistically imposing late vocabulary on early texts and, on the other hand, resisting interpretive grooves that obscure our view of the longer genealogy of rhetorical theory.

The first three essays of the volume each consider the ancient testimony of fifth-century sophists: Isocrates, Gorgias of Leontini, and Theodorus Byzantius. In "Unity, Dissociation, and Schismogenesis in Isocrates," Terry Papillon analyzes Isocrates' notions of political unity and hostility in the light of the changing rhetorical and political situation in Greece, specifically in contrast to Thucydides' treatment of Pericles and the Peloponnesian War. According to Papillon, "Isocrates recognized the dangers of schismogenesis in Greece and sought to reunite her. . . . In this he seems to elevate his discourse to a higher plane than Pericles, to the level of inter-*polis* unity instead of intra-*polis* concord. He may have been a new man with new and frightening ideas, but still perhaps only a product of his age, a new century in which new senses of unity were thrust upon the Greeks. This resulted from the nature of the political realities of the day and the political individuals of the day, such as Philip and the leaders of Persia" (**18**).

In "Theodorus Byzantius on the Parts of a Speech," Robert Gaines disputes the standard view that late–fifth-century sophist Theodorus recognized only five parts of speech. Rather, Gaines examines the ancient testimony, particularly the testimony of Plato and Aristotle, to conclude that Theodorus recognized twelve parts of speech. Gaines finds this conclusion corroborated by his analysis of Lysias 6, a forensic speech dated only a few years after Theodorus' prime. Through the analysis of the testimony and the speech, Gaines ultimately provides technical and textual support for Aristotle's own account of the gradual evolution of rhetoric in the century prior to Plato and Aristotle, as opposed to its radical revolutionary emergence in the fourth century. Consequently, Gaines argues, "the case of Theodorus offers a credible instance of a fifth-century theory about the parts of practical speeches, where technical vocabulary has been devised in elaboration of the theory, the theory is conveyed in a book purportedly aimed at instruction, and the practice of speechmaking was evidently influenced by the theory. Moreover, the case itself is based on direct textual evidence from roughly contemporary authors and indirect textual evidence from an extant speech delivered in the Attic courts. The existence of this example necessarily complicates any attempt to deny evolution in the art of speechmaking before Plato. It also supports the idea that we should take Aristotle seriously when he asserts that Theodorus contributed to the early development of rhetoric" (29).

In the third essay, Carol Poster offers a comprehensive study of the ancient testimony about Gorgias in order to intervene in the debate over whether Gorgias' "On Non-Being" should be interpreted as sophistical satire or as philosophical ontology. Ultimately, Poster concludes that "asking whether we should understand Gorgias as 'a sophist,' 'a philosopher,' or 'a rhetorician' is simply a badly phrased question. He was a person who at various times in his life engaged in certain *activities,* some that would later be termed philosophic (studying with Empedocles, writing a treatise on metaphysics), some sophistic (display oratory, teaching), and others rhetorical (teaching, possibly—but not probably—compiling some sort of handbook)" (45–46). Poster argues that the ancient testimony not only does not support a satirical reading of "On Non-Being," it also (and perhaps more importantly) suggests a gradual shift in Gorgias' intellectual development from his early focus on ontology and physics ("On Non-Being") to a later interest in rhetoric. The chronological shift in Gorgias' attention from ontology to rhetoric, supported by Poster's examination of the ancient testimony, is synecdochic for the large-scale gradual developments that led up to the explicit development of rhetorical discipline in the fourth century.

In the fourth essay, "Parmenides: Philosopher, Rhetorician, Skywalker," Thomas Rickert considers the evidence that Parmenides theorizes explicitly on rhetorical themes, and therefore cannot unambiguously be categorized as a "Presocratic philosopher" rather than a "Preplatonic rhetorician." Considering him exclusively as a philosopher and "the father of Western rationality" necessarily "delimits fuller understanding of his work and its relation to Greek thought and culture" (49). Parmenides' emphasis on rhetorical themes, his association with a cult of priest-healers, and his obvious impact on the thought of the sophist Gorgias all indicate, Rickert argues, bodily, nonrational, and rhetorical sources for Parmenides' thought, later attributed exclusively (and wrongly) to pre-Socratic philosophy and rationality. In particular, Rickert explains that the "'logical' 'Aletheia' section of 'On Being' cannot only be a first example of philosophical argumentation. It develops the proem's proto-rhetorical thematics, including its incantatory and transformative aspects. . . . Persuasion is not simply present as a technique; Parmenides knits persuasion and deception into his philosophy, and . . . his ontology. In this sense, rhetoric takes new bearings from Parmenides; and, if these bearings are picked up and not opposed by those who follow him, including Zeno, Empedocles, and Empedocles' student, Gorgias, then there is significant revision to be made to our rhetorical histories" (59).

"Heraclitus' Doublespeak: The Paradoxical Origins of Rhetorical *Logos*" is my own. In this essay I consider Aristotle's testimony regarding Heraclitus' thought and the paradoxical play on words contained in his use of the term *logos* in the opening lines of his book on nature. Drawing on Martin Heidegger's analysis of *logos* in fragment 50, I argue that Heraclitus' *logos* was a technical term, intended to draw conscious attention to the two-sidedness of discourse and speech and, therefore, an early example of a self-conscious theory of discourse. While I tend to agree with Schiappa "that the two-*logoi* fragment is a Protagorean development of Heraclitus' worldview" (2003b, 92), I am less convinced that Protagoras' two-*logoi* fragment contributes such a novel contribution to the history of rhetoric and philosophy as Schiappa claims it does. Rather, it seems that the basic content was already present (albeit in a riddling form) in Heraclitus, who, like Protagoras, theorized both world and word. This contradicts Schiappa's contention that "Protagoras was the first recorded Greek thinker to treat language per se as an object of study" (97). Rather, it might be more accurate to claim that he was the first thinker to use uncritically the nascent prose conventions that valued a-mythical directness and clarity in his treatment of language as an object of study. In this way, Protagoras' thought (and particularly the two-*logoi* fragment) is not so much "an extension of Heraclitus' thought into the realm of what we would now call linguistic theory" (98) as it is an extension of what we might now call Heraclitus' linguistic theory and cosmological ontology into the contemporary prose conventions of the fifth century.

The sixth and seventh essays investigate the status of rhetoric as opposed to eloquence in the Homeric epics. Both Marina McCoy and David Hoffman suggest that the rhetorical displays by Homer's characters (the embassy to Achilles, the Ithacan assembly, and Odysseus' rhetoric in the catalog of the shades), on the one hand, soften the rigidity of the distinction between preliterate *mythos* and literate rationality (Hoffman), and, on the other hand, reveal a self-conscious manipulation of persuasive means and rational strategies that are more explicitly worked out in later rhetorical theories (McCoy). In "Rhetoric and Royalty: Odysseus' Presentation of the Female Shades in Hades," Marina McCoy identifies in the Odyssean "catalog of women" evidence of techniques that require self-conscious awareness of the technique in order to be used *as* techniques. McCoy suggests that Homeric scholarship has emphasized the catalog's purpose as a poetic device used by the author Homer, and not, for example, a rhetorical device used by the character Odysseus. According to McCoy, the use of the catalog of women for Odysseus' purposes within the plotline of the story indicates the poet's awareness of the possibility of the use of specific techniques of persuasion by a speaker. These techniques are more likely to be the product of theoretical knowledge when they are not only displayed repeatedly but also adjusted for particular circumstances with each repeated use. McCoy suggests that "Odysseus' capacity to apply the same kind of strategy across multiple instances, and even to two different audiences (Arete and Alkinoos) suggests knowledge that can apply across kinds of cases and can respond to novel situations. If a person is persuasive once, it may simply be a chance occurrence. . . . But Odysseus is far more skillful, and displays knowledge of how to influence his listener's disposition (*diathesis*) and to create a favorable view of his character in the eyes of his audience (*ethopoiēsis*) in multiple ways" (**83**). Repetition and adjustment stand in the place of explicit theory, thereby making more porous the supposed boundary between what Schiappa calls "nontheoretical texts," "undeclared theory," and "rhetorical theory" (1999, 109).

In "*Mētis, Themis,* and the Practice of Epic Speech," David Hoffman examines how two of Homer's assemblies demonstrate, through the terms *mētis* and *themis,* the presence of a temporally situated "strategically rational" discourse that is later echoed in Isocratean rhetoric. This analysis runs counter to the view that the agonistic discourse in Homer's epics are "quarrels" as opposed to strategically or systematically rational discourse. Consequently, Hoffman's analysis suggests that the distinction between a nontechnical or nontheoretical and technical or theoretical understanding is harder to maintain when the former so blatantly displays "the practice of carrying on an argument by (a) being familiar with a body of 'lore' consisting of customs (later laws), examples, maxims, and anecdotes, and (b) having the knack for evoking the right bit of lore at the right time. The lore may be variously called *themis* or *philosophia* or *historia,* and the knack for invoking it may be called *mētis* or *kairos.* Although the rules of this sort of game are simple enough at this most abstract level, there is great complexity in the actual play, as is demonstrated both by our ancient examples from the *Iliad* and the *Odyssey,* and by contemporary 'theorists of practice'" (**112**). Consequently, Hoffman suggests, "there is a strong thread of continuity that runs from the *basileus'* practice of bringing that past into meaningful contact with the present, through the Isocratean approach to rhetoric, right up to our own lived experience in the contemporary world" (**112**).

The final essay, "It Takes an Empire to Raise a Sophist," serves as a capstone for these individual studies. Michael Svoboda suggests that drastic material and political changes in Greece prior to the fourth century had enormous implications for what we take for granted about the later "disciplining" of rhetoric. While literacy and the practices made possible by literacy (such as the analysis of written speeches) profoundly influenced the rise of rhetoric, Svoboda suggests that their importance should not eclipse the effect that political and material transformations would have had on the formation of rhetorical discourse. Historical studies by scholars such as David Tandy, Karl Polanyi, Moses Finley, Karl Bucher, Edouard Meyer, and Paul Cartledge have attempted to reconstruct the radical material changes in Greece starting at the beginning of the eighth century.

These changes include a massive growth in population, a replacement of the gift economy with a trade economy, the reversal of the relationship between status and wealth (a family no longer had wealth because of their status; they gained status because of their wealth), and the introduction of "unobligated wealth" (Tandy 1997, 231). Svoboda contends that these drastic changes in material and political conditions also drastically changed the role of discourse in economic exchange. Following the work of Tandy, who observed how the discourse of the poets was instrumental in defining new relationships between status and wealth, Svoboda suggests that the verbal wares the sophists supplied were offered in response to conditions quite different from those in fourth-century Athens. Consequently, "the sophists attacked by Isocrates, Plato, and Xenophon are not in the vanguard of a new economy; they are fighting a rearguard battle against Athenians who are creating a new postwar economy. . . . The schools of Plato, Isocrates, and others are innovations rather than throwbacks, innovations made necessary by the collapse of the imperial economy and the destruction of so much private wealth, both encumbered and unencumbered" (129). Svoboda attempts to temper the emphasis of writing and literacy on the development of fourth-century rhetorical theory by turning greater attention to the material conditions that gave rise to the sophistic movement in the fifth century.

These essays are arranged counter-chronologically, beginning at the end and ending at the beginning. In the end, we are left to consider how true Aristotle's words might still be for the history of rhetoric—its beginning is powerful and at the same time difficult to see. But when the beginning is discovered, it somehow enlarges and comes more clearly into view. And with that clearer perception, we begin to see that the beginning was only the end of previous beginnings.

Unity, Dissociation, and Schismogenesis in Isocrates

Terry L. Papillon

In a 1991 article in the *Quarterly Journal of Speech,* "Schismogenesis and Community: Pericles' Funeral Oration," James Mackin Jr. talked about the danger of promoting schismogenesis, the creation of schisms of rival groups, by using antithesis in discourse.[1] He pointed out the artistry and success of Pericles' funeral oration in bringing the Athenians together and in promoting the deliberative aim of continuing the struggle against the Peloponnesians. Mackin showed how Pericles' use of antithesis sets the ideal of Athens against the image of Sparta in order to solidify the Athenian community. The result of this success, however, was to cause a greater divide between Athens and Sparta and to exacerbate the hostilities still further. There could be no turning back from the war, and in the end, there could be no reconciliation.[2]

Thus Pericles successfully unites the people of Attica in their effort, but it causes the Athenians to ignore the wider ramifications of their actions. As Mackin puts it in his ecological approach: "We are all systems embedded in a hierarchy of systems that constitutes our ecosystem. In solving local needs, producers cannot attend to a single entity or process and ignore its relationship to the larger ecosystem without eventually causing ecological damage. Communicative systems are susceptible to the same type of damage. In rhetoric, the ecological problem is not the building of community at one level, but the failure to recognize and nurture community at other levels" (260).[3] The difficulties of Athens' "will to power" as described in the pages of Thucydides have been discussed on many prior occasions.[4] The antagonism between Athens and other *poleis* during the war resulting from such an attitude is a major theme in Thucydides' acute portrayal in *The Peloponnesian Wars.*[5] Mackin offered a fresh approach to this issue by focusing on the type of discourse that, in offering a solution to the immediate rhetorical situation, creates huge difficulties for a larger and less proximate situation.

We are helped in understanding how Isocrates operated in the fourth century by using the anthropological framework of schismogenesis and the rhetorical notion of dissociative arguments, the actualization of which was modeled on fifth-century patterns of thinking. That is, we can think of Isocrates as "pre-Platonic" if we think of his dependence on earlier traditions and how we now understand those traditions. Thus Isocrates represents one example of a common construction tactic; he was not necessarily copying Thucydides, he and Thucydides both employed techniques that already existed. There were commonplace arguments before there was any categorization of commonplaces; otherwise there would be no commonplaces to gather.

Such an approach helps us to appreciate the contributions of Isocrates as a rhetorical actor, but it also helps us to think about his debt to prior traditions. In a period of work parallel, and at times responding, to Plato, there were pre-Platonic influences on Isocrates. That Isocrates has worked in the tradition of the Greek poets has been shown (Papillon 1998). That he followed some of the earlier sophistic notions has also been argued widely.[6] Looking back to the historians and their sources, I will examine the phenomenon that Mackin pointed out in Thucydides. With all these roots, however, the debt is not so much to a specific earlier author, but to ideas percolating already in the fifth century. H. L. Hudson-Williams made this point as long ago as 1948: "To trace similarity between two authors who follow the same rhetorical conventions is not difficult. To prove that one was directly influenced by the other is almost impossible. This is particularly true of writers like Thucydides and Isocrates, but to a lesser extent it is true of Greek literature as a whole. For in this, as in other ways, the rhetoricians and their pupils laid emphasis on what was already a characteristic of Greek literature. Greek writers in general were not afraid of the trite and the commonplace, but they were very much concerned with the form in which it was expressed" (81).

There are fourth-century rhetorical techniques that owe their inspiration to a time before Plato, and before the conceptualization of ideas that comes with Plato. And we are aided by the use of modern theoretical constructs, schismogenesis and dissociation, to gain some understanding of a process that has its roots prior to the nominal existence of the process.

How to Create a Schism

The notion of schismogenesis comes out of the anthropological writings of Gregory Bateson, such as *Naven*.[7] Bateson defines schismogenesis as "a process of differentiation in the norms of individual behaviour resulting from cumulative interaction between individuals" (1958, 175). He distinguishes two major types of schismogenesis: symmetrical differentiation and complementary differentiation. Both of these types lead to separation into groups.

Symmetrical differentiation includes two groups who have the same aspirations and behavior patterns: Group One shows a behavior (A) toward Group Two. Group Two shows the same behavior pattern (A) back toward Group One. Bateson discusses the possibility of "progressive differentiation" (1935,

181) where the symmetrical pattern becomes more extreme. Thus, if Group One boasts and Group Two boasts back, the boasts will grow louder on both sides.

Complementary differentiation has two groups who show different behavior patterns. Group One shows one behavior pattern (X) consistently to Group Two, while Group Two shows a different behavior pattern (Y) consistently back toward Group One. Complementary differentiation can lead to progressive unilateral distortion of each group, where Group One shows a greater or more extreme version of their pattern (X) and Group Two shows a greater or more extreme version of its own pattern of reaction (Y). Thus with two groups where the relationship is assertion-submission, the assertive behavior will become stronger for Group One, and Group Two will become more and more submissive.[8]

The list below shows examples of different kinds of behaviors that can be categorized (based on Bateson 1935, 182):

Symmetrical	Complementary
Boasting	Assertion-Submission
Commercial rivalry	Exhibition-Admiration
Desire to command	Fostering-Feebleness

Bateson believed that cultural situations exhibiting one form of schismogenesis can be controlled by the admixture of a small bit of the other type.[9] This would keep schismogenesis from becoming extreme and leading to the downfall of the social structure. In the complementary pattern, the group that becomes increasingly submissive, for example, would have to assert itself eventually or finally be destroyed. In symmetrical schismogenesis, as the boasting continues to grow on both sides, eventually one side would need to show some sense of submission or the boasts would grow to a hostile degree and lead to the destruction of one or both sides. This latter example may be the pattern leading up to the outbreak of the Peloponnesian War. Furthermore, such lack of moderation may have been the case in the later events of the fourth century in Greece, where rival states continued to vie for control.

As set out by Bateson, schismogenesis occurs in a cultural context; that is, it is a behavior that happens among people. It can also be political, occurring on the state level as well as the individual or tribal level (Richardson 1939). In rhetorical terms, dissociation serves as a technique that might have some effect upon schismogenesis (promoting it or reducing it, for example). Perelman and Olbrechts-Tyteca used the term *dissociation* most famously in their study *The New Rhetoric: A Treatise on Argumentation* (1969, 411–59).[10] Edward Schiappa summarizes this approach as "a strategy whereby an advocate attempts to break up a previously unified idea into two concepts; one which will be positively valued by the audience, and one which will be negatively valued" (1985, 73). Since this assumes the separation of ideas that were formerly thought of as a unified concept, such an argument can have a profound impact on the culture (Perelman and Olbrechts-Tyteca 1969, 411–12).

Isocrates, Schismogenesis, and the Politics of Fifth- and Fourth-Century Athens

These concepts of schismogenesis and dissociation help us understand Isocrates' approach to the political situation in contrast to Pericles' reaction to the politics of the prior generations. According to Mackin's persuasive argument, Pericles encouraged schismogenesis on the *polis* level during the Peloponnesian Wars of the fifth century. In the funeral oration, for example, Pericles contrasts what is true government, true military readiness, or true education with what is not; that is, he contrasts the Athenian way with the Spartan way:

> We have a form of government that does not emulate the practices of our neighbors, setting an example to some rather than imitating others. In name it is called democracy on account of being administered in the interests not of the few but the many. . . . In our approach to warfare, we also differ from our opponents, in the following ways. We leave our city accessible to all and do not, by *xenelasia,* prevent anyone from either listening or observing, although some enemy might benefit by seeing what we do not hide, because we do not put more trust in contrivance and deception than in the courageous readiness for action, which comes from within. As for education, starting as children they pursue manhood with laborious training, but with our more relaxed way of life we are no less willing to take on equivalent dangers. (2.37, 39; Lattimore 1998, 92–93)

The concept of government and especially military readiness is broken into what we, the Athenians, do (correctly) and what others, the Spartans, do (incorrectly). This helped to solidify the Athenians against the Spartans and helped promote symmetrical schismogenesis, but did not look to the future when the Athenians might once again have to work with the Spartans. Even in Pericles' plans, where there would be an Athenian victory, the Athenians would need to work with the conquered, and his rhetorical strategy of dissociation to solidify Athens against Sparta would have inhibited this. In the early part of the Peloponnesian Wars, neither side considered the need to work with the vanquished to be a real issue; both sides seemed to view the enemy as just that—an enemy to be treated however the victor wished. This may be a result of the imperial thoughts of both sides.

The political situation in the fourth century was different, and Isocrates recognized this, even if the *poleis* did not. Greece experienced a very frustrating period when different *poleis* struggled against each other for control. Athens would assert itself in the latter part of the fifth century and then fall in 404; Sparta would assert itself and then back away in 371 after the battle of Leuctra; Thebes would assert itself and then back away in 362 after the battle of Mantinea; Athens would reassert itself, but then back off as a result of the social wars of the 350s. And it would all become a moot point in 338 when Philip II of Macedon would defeat a united Greek force at the battle of Chaeronea and take political control.

Isocrates narrated this situation more eloquently when he focused on Athens and Sparta in his treatise *On the Peace*: "Did we not choose to do things that made Sparta the rulers of the Greeks, and did they not as rulers manage things so badly that a few years later we rose back to the top and took control of their security? Did not the meddlesomeness of Athens' supporters make cities go over to Sparta, and the arrogance of Sparta's supporters compel those same cities to go back to Athens?" (8.107–8; Papillon 2004, 159). Isocrates saw things on a different plane than Pericles. From early to late in his career Isocrates argued for a unity of the Greek states in a joint conflict against Persia. He would change from the dissociative arguments of Pericles to a more unified approach based on *eunoia* or goodwill.[11] Or to say it more accurately, he changed from encouraging schismogenesis between *poleis* to encouraging a higher-level schismogenesis between the Greeks and the Persians. The separation still happens, but it happens on a higher, ethnic level. He borrowed the rhetorical argument seen in the fifth-century example of Pericles in the pages of Thucydides and adapted it to the realities of the fourth century. This, in turn, was based on the earlier traditions (Papillon 1998). In both Thucydides and Isocrates, the rhetorical move occurs without the introspection, abstraction, or vocabulary characteristic of Platonic assessment (Schiappa 1999). His rhetorical argumentation, however, did not necessarily keep up with his political views, and it took some time before his dissociative arguments matched his political aims in a neat way.

Isocrates used dissociation first on the *polis* level in the *Panegyricus*. He certainly wanted to join the Greek states together, but he has to deal with the question of leadership. At the time of this discourse, about 380 B.C.E., the idea of asserting Athenian leadership was very difficult, given its still weakened position under Sparta. As a result, Isocrates argued ostensibly for a joint command under Athens and Sparta; all the while, however, he still argued for Athens' superiority. That is, he argued for a unified Greece but still used dissociative arguments to separate Athens from Sparta. At this point he was more "Periclean" in his rhetoric, trying to assert Athenian superiority even while arguing for unity:

> Now, some of the Greeks follow us, others follow the Spartans, and the governments by which they manage their cities have divided most of them along these lines. Thus, whoever thinks that the others will accomplish anything good before the two leading cities are reconciled is quite naive and out of touch with the situation. But someone who is not only seeking to make a display, but also wishes to accomplish something, must look for the kind of arguments that will persuade these two cities to share equally with each other, to take up joint leadership, and to gain advantages from the Persian King that

> they currently want to get from the other Greeks. It would be easy to get our city to take this approach, but the Spartans are still hard to persuade, since they have accepted the false argument that it is their ancestral right to lead. Nevertheless, if someone should point out to them that this right is ours rather than theirs, they might perhaps give up arguing and consider their own advantage. (4.16–18; Papillon 2004, 32)

He begins with unity, but cannot resist pushing Athens ahead with a dissociative argument. This is not a good marriage. His call for the unity of the Greeks came at a very bad time, especially when he wanted a particular *polis* to lead. The Greeks were in the midst of this sixty-year period of wrangling about who should lead. Isocrates showed his very Greek sensibilities by arguing in this early discourse that there must be a leader. He will decide eventually that the coalition does not need a leading *polis,* but a leading individual. He will move to this approach, and his discourses will have a rhetorically stronger focus as a result. He can argue his political goal, a unified Greece in opposition to Persia, without the difficulty of having to argue for one Greek *polis* over another. The discourse *To Philip* in 346 B.C.E. shows this stronger approach: "Therefore, I think that it will be advantageous for you, since everyone else is so cowardly, to take the lead in this war against the [Persian] King. And just as it is fitting for all the other descendants of Heracles and those who are tied to a particular government and its laws to love that city in which they live, so it is fitting for you, who were born free of worldly concerns to think of all Greece as your homeland, as did your ancestor, Heracles, and to take risks on its behalf, just as you would for everything that is especially important to you" (5.127; Papillon 2004, 103). He did not seem to be able to maintain this, however, as his bias toward Athens led him to contrast Athens and Sparta again in the *Panathenaicus* of 339.[12]

Mackin criticizes Pericles/Thucydides for causing a much larger rift in the social fabric, though Mackin then tries to defend Pericles and Thucydides (258). Such a rift would not occur to a Greek, since they were "caught in *polis* thinking" in the late fifth century, in spite of the unifying effects of the Persian wars and the Delian league earlier in the fifth century. That things have changed in the fourth century is clear, allowing us to take Mackin's point seriously, only to see that the focus has also changed for Isocrates. Isocrates saw the change and the need to recast the community in terms of Greeks, not individual city-states. Isocrates' interest in Philip later on shows the real extreme to which Isocrates' vision of a new dichotomy goes.

A key for Isocrates comes from Bateson: "It is certain that either type of schismogenesis between two groups can be checked by factors which unite the two groups either in loyalty or opposition to some outside element. Such an outside element may be either a symbolic individual, an enemy people, or some quite impersonal circumstance. But it must be noted that where the outside element is a person or group of persons, the relationship of the combined groups A and B to the outside group will always be itself a potentially schismogenic relationship of one or the other type" (1935, 183). Isocrates of course, just like Pericles before him, does not think of the dangers of schismogenesis on an even higher plane, for Isocrates would never see a need for the Greeks to work together with the hated Persians.

In arguing for a united Greece against a common enemy (Persia), Isocrates offers a new sense of Greek culture and politics.[13] He uses the sense of unifying good-will (*eunoia*) to be his motivating force, rather than Thucydides' interest in fear (*phobos*). We see this as he tries to unify the Greeks and especially when we see him systematically trying to find a leader for his new coalition. He moves from traditional *polis* thinking—*we must have a city to lead our unified peoples and so how can I argue for Athenian superiority?*—to a more federated sense with an autocratic ruler—*who will lead our unified Greeks? Will it be Dionysus?* (368 letter) *Archidamus?* (356 letter) *Philip?* (discourse in 346, letters in 342 and 338). Isocrates came to see that the notion of individual *poleis* was passing away and that a new sense of Greece was emerging.

Conclusion

Perelman and Olbrechts-Tyteca had argued that dissociation can cause great stress in a community because it redefines old concepts, taking something that was a single notion and breaking it up. Isocrates, in arguing for a united Greece under one leader, redefined the notion of politics, and in an interesting inversion, tried to move the Greeks from a plurality to a unity. In this sense he may have been more insightful than his political rival Demosthenes, who sought to maintain the old system. This idea of independent *poleis* was, after all, a notion very strongly ingrained in the Athenians, and one that neither Demosthenes nor most Athenians could give up. Isocrates may not have realized what he bargained for when he wished Philip to take a leadership role, at least if we are to believe the tradition that he was disappointed to see what Philip did and died just after Chaeronea.[14]

On the other hand, Isocrates may be less capable than Demosthenes in that he is not able to maintain his interest in a leader. He had moved from Athenian leadership in the *Panegyricus* of 380 to his interest in Dionysius in 368, Archidamus in 356, and Philip in 346. He returns to Athenian leadership in 339 with the *Panathenaicus*, but moves back to Philip in 338 in the last of his writings. His inability to stay his course (and settle on a leader) may be his final and fatal weakness. Yet even if he was unable to carry out his vision, the fact that he had envisioned such a possibility marks him as a man with a new and frightening sense of how the world worked in the fourth century.

By thinking in terms of schismogenesis, and specifically schismogenesis on different planes, we gain some clearer understanding of the situation. Isocrates attempted to recognize the danger of schismogenesis and turn it to a more fruitful end for the Greeks. He recognized the dangers of schismogenesis in Greece and sought to reunite her, to value *eunoia* over *phobos*. He continued the pattern, though, by using such antithesis-for-unity in his argument that Greece needed to unite against Persia. In this he seems to elevate his discourse to a higher plane than Pericles, to the level of inter-*polis* unity instead of intra-*polis* concord. He may have been a new man with new and frightening ideas, but still perhaps only a product of his age, a new century in which new senses of unity were thrust upon the Greeks. This resulted from the nature of the political realities of the day and the political individuals of the day, such as Philip and the leaders of Persia.

In following Pericles and bringing dissociative argument from the late fifth into the fourth century, Isocrates shows us a practical example of an early rhetorical practice. The schismogenic approach of Pericles was fundamentally a tribal approach to politics. This would not stand in the fourth century. Ironically, given the foundational differences between Isocrates and Plato, Isocrates moved toward the Platonic notion of an autocratic ruler. He too would look around to see who could best lead. Without Plato's sense of epistemology or self-conscious language, however, Isocrates could only grasp at earlier pre-Platonic techniques at unity.

All of these fourth-century voices—Isocrates, Plato and Demosthenes—failed, but for different reasons. Demosthenes clung to an outdated sense of Athenian superiority, though with a rhetorical skill that would set the oratorical world aflame. Plato could not inculcate his new ideas of knowledge and action into a disheartened and pragmatic people—there would be no philosopher-king—though he did so with a vigor that would set the philosophical world aflame. Isocrates did not recognize that his ideas of communication and community would allow a political game wherein the most powerful and ruthless win, though he set the intellectual and educational world aflame. That none could succeed in the fourth century should not dissuade us from recognizing that all three gave great gifts to later centuries. It is for us to assess and to actualize what will set the post-Platonic world aflame.

Theodorus Byzantius on the Parts of a Speech

Robert N. Gaines

Theodorus Byzantius, who flourished in the late fifth century B.C.E.,[1] is recognized by several ancient authors as having contributed to the early development of rhetoric.[2] We know that Theodorus composed books on the art,[3] and we have Aristotle's report that Lysias recognized Theodorus' superiority as a teacher of rhetoric and so turned his own efforts toward writing speeches for others.[4] Of the contents of Theodorus' books on the art we have five specific indications. Two brief notices in Aristotle's *Rhetoric* comment on doctrines concerning a sort of argument based on "errors committed" (2.23.28, 1400b) and "novel expressions" of a paradoxical nature (3.11.6, 1412a). Other indications concern Theodorus' conception of the parts of a speech.[5]

What we should make of the evidence on Theodorus' theory of speech parts is not obvious. Ancient sources provide support for a Theodorean scheme of at least twelve speech parts.[6] However, the standard view—as propounded by Hamberger and Solmsen—is that Theodorus recognized five speech parts: proem, narration, proof, refutation, and epilog. Both commentators arrive at their interpretations by subsuming Theodorean speech-elements under speech parts recognized by other theorists.[7] In opposition to the standard view, I contend that a twelve-part scheme of speech parts was recognized by Theodorus. On behalf of this contention I offer two lines of argument. The first is that the evidence of Theodorus' near contemporaries—Plato and Aristotle—is more decisive than previously assumed. In discussing Theodorus, these authors are not simply rehearsing terminology for identifiable components of speeches; rather, both are documenting what they considered to be an over-complicated theory of the distinct parts in the arrangement of a speech. The second line of argument is that a conception of twelve speech parts is consistent with the structure of the pseudo-Lysianic *Oration* 6: *Against Andokides for Impiety*.[8] This fragmentary forensic speech—dated about 400 B.C.E.—provides direct evidence of oratorical practice around the time of Theodorus.[9] It thus offers a suitable artifact in relation to which the plausibility of Theodorus' scheme of speech parts may be tested.

Theodorus and the Parts of a Speech: Testimonia

Plato's comments on Theodorean speech parts arise in *Phaedrus* 265d–267d, just after his proposal of dialectic as the heuristic for invention and arrangement of speech materials. Within the dialogue he has Socrates ask whether there can be anything of importance to the rhetorical art that lies outside the dialectical processes of collection and division. Phaedrus replies (at 266d) that Socrates has not discussed "the things that have been written in books on the art of speeches" (τά γ' ἐν τοῖς βιβλίοις τοῖς περὶ λόγων τέχνης γεγραμμένοις).[10] Socrates immediately responds with a summary, and he represents the theory of speech parts at 266d–267d:

> ΣΩ. . . . προοίμιον μὲν οἶμαι πρῶτον ὡς δεῖ τοῦ λόγου λέγεσθαι ἐν ἀρχῇ· ταῦτα λέγεις—ἦ γάρ;—τὰ κομψὰ τῆς τέχνης;
>
> ΦΑΙ. Ναί.
>
> ΣΩ. Δεύτερον δὲ δὴ διήγησίν τινα μαρτυρίας τ' ἐπ' αὐτῇ, τρίτον τεκμήρια, τέταρτον εἰκότα· καὶ πίστωσιν οἶμαι καὶ ἐπιπίστωσιν λέγειν τόν γε βέλτιστον λογοδαίδαλον Βυζάντιον ἄνδρα.
>
> ΦΑΙ. Τὸν χρηστὸν λέγεις Θεόδωρον;
>
> ΣΩ. Τί μήν; καὶ ἔλεγχόν γε καὶ ἐπεξέλεγχον ὡς ποιητέον ἐν κατηγορίᾳ τε καὶ ἀπολογίᾳ, . . .
>
> ΣΩ. . . . τὸ δὲ δὴ τέλος τῶν λόγων κοινῇ πᾶσιν ἔοικε συνδεδογμένον εἶναι, ᾧ τινες μὲν ἐπάνοδον, ἄλλοι δ' ἄλλο τίθενται ὄνομα.

> SOC. . . . You mean that there must be an introduction first, at the beginning of the discourse; these are the things you mean, are they not?—the niceties of the art.
>
> PHAED. Yes.
>
> SOC. Second is some kind of narration and testimonies are after it, third are indications, fourth are probabilities; and I believe confirmation and additional confirmation are mentioned by the man from Byzantium, that most excellent artist in words.
>
> PHAED. You mean the worthy Theodorus?
>
> SOC. Of course. And he tells us how refutation and additional refutation must be accomplished, both in accusation and defense, . . .
>
> SOC. . . . But all seem to be in agreement concerning the conclusion of discourses, which some call recapitulation, while others give it some other name.[11]

Here Plato associates at least ten parts of a speech with Theodorus.[12] *Proem* (προοίμιον), *some sort of narration* (διήγησις τις), *indications* (τεκμήρια), and *probabilities* (εἰκότα) are numbered ordinally in the exposition to stress their distinction and sequence in a speech. Also, *testimonies* (μαρτυρίαι) are set apart from narration and placed just afterwards, suggesting that testimonies too constitute a separate speech part. *Confirmation* (πίστωσις) and *additional confirmation* (ἐπιπίστωσις) are linked syntactically with the foregoing, and this implies that they participate in the same distinction and sequence. *Refutation* (ἔλεγχος) and *additional refutation* (ἐπεξέλεγχος) are added next, and, in parallel with *confirmation* and *additional confirmation,* they are evidently joined to the sequence. Finally, Plato closes the exposition of speech parts with a general attribution of the *speech-conclusion* (ἐπάνοδος *vel* ἄλλο ὄνομα) to all who theorize about the art of speeches, including Theodorus. Now, there is wide agreement among scholars that Plato's handling of Theodorean speech parts is at least partly satirical.[13] Something important about this satire is that for a knowledgeable reader it works best if Theodorus actually held the views for which he is ridiculed. Accordingly, given Plato's critical objectives, it is quite plausible that Plato's account of Theodorus as an authentic—if unsympathetic—attempt to enumerate speech parts according to Theodorus.[14]

Aristotle mentions Theodorus in his general account of speech parts at *Rhetoric* 3.13.4–5 (1414b). Here Aristotle insists that speech parts should include none other than proem, statement, proof, and epilogue, and he criticizes those who propose *refutation* and *comparison* as additional parts. Aristotle extends this critique with a sharp complaint against Theodorus at 3.13.5 (1414b12–16):

> ἔσται οὖν, ἄν τις τὰ τοιαῦτα διαιρῇ, ὅπερ ἐποίουν οἱ περὶ Θεόδωρον, διήγησις ἕτερον καὶ ἡ ἐπιδιήγησις καὶ προδιήγησις, καὶ ἔλεγχος καὶ ἐπεξέλεγχος. δεῖ δὲ εἶδός τι λέγοντα καὶ διαφορὰν ὄνομα τίθεσθαι·
>
> Therefore, if one divides these sorts of things as the Theodorean school does, there will otherwise be narration and after-narration and pre-narration, as well as refutation and additional refutation. But it is necessary to posit a name of a thing only when speaking with reference to a certain species and a differentia.[15]

In this passage, Aristotle volunteers details of Theodorean theory in a polemical context where the efficacy of his polemic depends upon the accuracy of his report. Clearly, the subject at stake is the theory of speech parts, and Theodorus is criticized because he proposes speech parts that cannot—in Aristotle's view—be distinguished with recourse to species and differentia. Given this context, we have no choice but to interpret Aristotle as here attributing five distinct speech parts to Theodorus. Two of these, namely refutation and further refutation, confirm Plato's report in the *Phaedrus.* Three of the parts, narration, after-narration, and pre-narration, elaborate Plato's report. I say "elaborate" because the language of Plato's report does not foreclose the possibility of multiple forms of narration. In fact, at *Phaedrus* 266e2, Plato refers to διήγησίν τινα, and this phrase permits the interpretation that Plato means "some kind of narration (among several)."[16] Thus, while Plato and Aristotle do not provide identical reports on Theodorus regarding narrative speech parts, their accounts are not inconsistent on the possibility of multiple forms.

The Platonic and Aristotelian evidence concerning Theodorean speech parts supports the conclusion that Theodorus recognized twelve parts organized in something like the order represented in Table 1.

Table 1: Speech Parts of Theodorus Byzantius

Speech Part	**Source**
προοίμιον (proem)	Pl. *Phdr.* 266d–267d
προδιήγησις (pre-narration)	Arist. *Rh.* 3.13.5 (1414b14)
διήγησις (narration)	Pl. *Phdr.* 266d–267d; Arist. *Rh.* 3.13.5 (1414b13–14)
ἐπιδιήγησις (after-narration)	Arist. *Rh.* 3.13.5 (1414b14)
μαρτυρίαι (testimonies)	Pl. *Phdr.* 266d–267d
τεκμήρια (indications)	Pl. *Phdr.* 266d–267d
εἰκότα (probabilities)	Pl. *Phdr.* 266d–267d
πίστωσις (confirmation)	Pl. *Phdr.* 266d–267d
ἐπιπίστωσις (additional confirmation)	Pl. *Phdr.* 266d–267d
ἔλεγχος (refutation)	Pl. *Phdr.* 266d-267d; Arist. *Rh.* 3.13.5 (1414b14)
ἐπεξέλεγχος (additional refutation)	Pl. *Phdr.* 266d–267d; Arist. *Rh.* 3.13.5 (1414b15)
τέλος τοῦ λόγου: ἐπάνοδον *vel* ἄλλο ὄνομα (end of the speech: recapitulation or some other name, i.e., conclusion)	Pl. *Phdr.* 266d–267d

The utility of this information has been obscured in the past by a lack of sources that elaborate or even corroborate its elements (cf. Hamberger, 75–76). This has led to considerable speculation, particularly about the definition and relationship of parts in Theodorus. The problem with such speculation is that there has been little basis for judging among competing views. In such a circumstance, it seems reasonable to attempt an enlargement of the scope of evidence.

Pseudo-Lysias Oration 6 and Theodorean Speech Parts

My approach is to compare Theodorus' twelve-part scheme of speech arrangement with the speech known as pseudo-Lysias, *Oration* 6: *Against Andokides for Impiety.* This comparison seems appropriate because Theodorus' speech parts are apparently designed for forensic speaking, and *Oration* 6, a forensic speech, was composed around 400 B.C.E.—within a few years of the intellectual acme of Theodorus.[17]

My contention is that the structure of *Oration* 6 is explicable with reference to Theodorus' scheme of speech parts, although this contention is subject to a pair of limitations. The first is that *Oration* 6 is incomplete. The most inclusive text survives in *Palatinus Graecus* 88, and this manuscript is missing folios that affect *Oration* 6 in two places (Sosower, 10; Carey 2007, xviii). Specifically, before our text of the speech begins, somewhere between 100 and 660 words are missing (Todd 2007, 386); also, near the end of the speech, between the sections now numbered 49 and 50, approximately 400 to 575 words are missing (Todd 2007, 408, 471–72). Accordingly, our current text of *Oration* 6 represents only about 69–85 percent of the original speech.

The second limitation is that *Oration* 6 is a supporting speech (or συνηγορία). Ancient Athenian court cases were complex actions that frequently involved multiple litigants on each side—particularly in public trials. In fact, Rubinstein has shown that, within the thirty-six Athenian public trials for which we have evidence, twenty-eight (or 78 percent) involved supporting speakers (συνήγοροι) distinct from the main prosecutors or defendants in the case (62). The public prosecution of Andokides (ca. 400 B.C.E.) was not an exception to this general tendency, and it appears that in *Oration* 6 the supporting speaker joined the prosecution as a kind of religious authority who could provide arguments that lay outside the qualifications of his co-prosecutors (Rubinstein, 142; cf. Usher 1999, 113–14). The specialization involved in serving as a supporting speaker often meant that the speaker was not expected to present arguments concerning the main charge or even a speech with a typical introduction and narration (Todd 2007, 406; Rubinstein, 59–60). This fact complicates any attempt to understand the structure of a supporting speech. And in the case of *Oration* 6, the complication is intensified by loss of materials at the beginning and near the end of the text.

Still, despite limitations associated with *Oration* 6 as a critical object, significant, nearly continuous material survives from the speech, specifically fifty-four sections in 2,744 words (Todd 2007, 408). This material supports a useful comparison with Theodorus' arrangement scheme, so long as we remember that the speech is missing its earliest elements and might not have included all typical speech parts in the first place. In this context, then, our current text of *Oration* 6 falls rather neatly into Theodorus' last five speech parts, namely confirmation (§§1–19), further confirmation (§§20–34), refutation (§§35–45), further refutation (§§46–49), and conclusion (§§50–54).

The impetus for *Oration* 6 was to support a prosecution of Andokides for impiety. Andokides, an Athenian orator and politician, had been implicated in two forms of impiety during 415, profanation of the Eleusinian Mysteries and mutilation of Herms. In return for his information against others, Andokides had secured freedom in exile, though his possible return to Athens had been all but precluded by the decree of Isotimides (presumably in 415; see, for example, Clinton, 35), which forbade anyone who admitted impiety from entering the *agora* or sacred sanctuaries (Ps. Lys. 6.9, 24). Later, after the Amnesty of 403/2, Andokides returned to Athens with the intention of resuming his political career. In about 400, however, Kephisios prosecuted him for impiety based on his participation in the Eleusinian Mysteries earlier in the year. The argument apparently was that Andokides' participation violated the decree of Isotimides (And. *Mys.* 1.8).

Oration 6 followed a more robust accusation by one or more members of the team prosecuting Andokides. The text—as we have it—begins in the middle of an example the point of which is to illustrate the danger of impiety. Dishonor to divinities can lead to a terrible death (§1).[18] This lesson is associated in a general way with Andokides in the next section, where he is characterized as deserving destruction (§2). But the lesson is also applied to Andokides' jury in §3 as follows:

> ἀδύνατον δὲ καὶ ὑμῖν ἐστι, περὶ τοιούτου πράγματος φέρουσι τὴν ψῆφον, ἢ κατελεῆσαι ἢ καταχαρίσασθαι Ἀνδοκίδῃ, ἐπισταμένοις ὅτι ἐναργῶς τὼ θεὼ τούτω τιμωρεῖτον τοὺς ἀδικοῦντας· ἐλπίσαι οὖν χρὴ πάντα ἄνθρωπον ὄντα καὶ ἑαυτῷ ⟨ἃ⟩ καὶ ἑτέρῳ ἔσεσθαι.
>
> It is impossible for you on your part, as you cast your votes, to show either pity or favour to Andokides, because you know how actively these two goddesses punish wrongdoers; so one must expect, being human, that everything will happen to oneself which will happen to someone else as well. (trans. Todd 2007, 413, 415)

In the first three sections of *Oration* 6, then, we find an argument where divine punishment follows impiety, the justice of Andokides' execution is asserted, and the jury is warned away from alignment with the defendant, lest it offend "the goddesses," Demeter and Persephone, who are honored in the Mysteries.

To me at least, this argument seems to be aimed at confirming the charge against Andokides, and my understanding of the next sixteen sections is that they contain arguments with the same function. At §§4–7 the jury is told that it cannot escape negative judgment from the Greeks if it favors Andokides, because he is well known for impiety and otherwise infamous for annoying many cities in his travels. Likewise, at §§8–12 the jury is warned that it cannot preserve both the ancestral laws and Andokides, since he disrespects the law in his violation of it and in his gestures toward its enforcement. In the next two sections, §§13–14, the argument addresses a claim that Andokides is likely to make—he should not suffer more than others against whom he informed for impiety. The reply is this: leniency to the others before was impious, and leniency to Andokides now will be impious, particularly since Andokides admitted profaning the Mysteries, while the others did not. At §15 the jury is admonished that, if anyone acts criminally toward statues of gods, they—the jury—should restrain that person from entering religious sanctuaries and exact punishment for any violation of the restriction. At §§16–18 a flurry of arguments insists that the jury should enforce Athenian laws of piety more vigorously than other cities do, penalize citizens who transgress (such as Andokides) more than foreigners (such as Diagoras of Melos), and pursue religious criminals who are present more zealously than those who are absent. Finally, in §19, it is urged that Andokides does not honor gods, because he engaged in sea travel and sea commerce with no fear of divine punishment. All of these arguments either assert, assume, or reason for Andokides' impiety in 415, his culpability for more recent actions, or the legal and religious duty of the jury to punish him. Accordingly, I recognize the arguments in §§1–19 as a confirmation of the current charges against Andokides.

The arguments are related but quite different in the next segment of the speech (§§20–34). Here Andokides' impiety is amplified, but the immediate charges against him are not generally at stake. Rather, beginning at §20, the speech chronicles misfortunes divinely imposed upon Andokides to punish him at length for impiety before his inevitable destruction. In §§21–23 the chronicle starts with a reference to Andokides' impiety of 415 and proceeds to discuss the immediate results, namely his imprisonment and denunciation of friends and relatives. At §§24–25 Andokides' denunciations lead to death of those most dear to him, and when he is released from prison, he is excluded from the *agora* and sanctuaries. Andokides migrates to Kition in §26, but he soon finds himself imprisoned again, this time for treason. In §27 he escapes Kition and seeks refuge in Athens, but is imprisoned. In §28 he migrates to Cyprus, but is imprisoned for a crime. In §§29–30 it is recounted that, since fleeing Cyprus, he has returned to Athens twice: first he was expelled; now he is greeted by two indictments. The religious significance of the turmoil in Andokides' life is elaborated in §31:

> καὶ τὸ μὲν σῶμα ἀεὶ ἐν δεσμοῖς ἔχει, ἡ δὲ οὐσία αὐτοῦ ἐλάττων ἐκ τῶν κινδύνων γίγνεται. καίτοι ὅταν τις τὸν αὑτοῦ βίον τοῖς ἐχθροῖς καὶ τοῖς συκοφάνταις διανέμῃ, τοῦτ' ἔστι τὸ ζῆν βίον ἀβίωτον. ἃ τούτῳ ὁ θεὸς οὐκ ἐπὶ σωτηρίᾳ ἐπινοῶν δίδωσιν, ἀλλὰ τιμωρούμενος τῶν γεγενημένων ἀσεβημάτων.

> He has his body always in chains, and his property is becoming diminished as a result of his perils. But when somebody divides up his own livelihood among enemies and sykophants, this is to live a

> life that is not worth living. God realised this, and gave it to him, not as a way of preserving him, but as punishment for past impieties. (trans. Todd 2007, 427)

This theme of divine punishment is continued in §32, where Andokides hands himself over to the jury through a divine compulsion. In §§33–34, Andokides' shameless pursuit of political power is contrasted with his religious disability—the gods will not be pleased if Andokides continues to give advice about sacrifices, processions, prayers, and oracles. Finally, the speech returns to the case at hand in the last sentence of this segment (§34): "He has continued now to commit offences against you, and has not escaped notice, but he will be punished as soon as he is put on trial" (§34). Within §§20–34, *Oration* 6 presents arguments that are pertinent to the judgment of Andokides, though they do not support or even specifically mention the particular charges upon which the jury is to render verdict. These sections of the speech depict Andokides as beset and perhaps even maddened by the gods as punishment for his original impieties. At the same time, they position the jury as the instrument of the gods' ultimate destruction of Andokides; for a god has driven Andokides to them, and his final punishment may be achieved through a guilty verdict. Since these arguments relate generally to the judgment of Andokides and yet differ substantially in focus from those presented in the *confirmation,* it is reasonable to classify §§20–34 of *Oration* 6 as an *additional confirmation.*

At the beginning of §35, the direction of argument in *Oration* 6 changes abruptly—here the text reads: "He in his turn will rely on the following argument; for it is necessary to explain to you what things this man will say in his defense, so that having heard both sides, you might give a better judgment" (ἰσχυριεῖται δὲ καὶ τούτῳ τῷ λόγῳ· ἀναγκαίως γὰρ ἔχει ὑμᾶς διδάσκειν ἃ οὗτος ἀπολογήσεται, ἵν' ἀκούσαντες παρ' ἀμφοτέρων ἄμεινον διαγνῶτε).[19] There actually follow in §§35–45 four anticipations of defenses that Andokides will raise, each with a response from the speaker (cf. Todd 2007, 463–68). First, at §§35–36, Andokides will claim his denunciations ended disruption, but in reality he disrupted Athens and "you" (jury members) restored it. Second, at §§37–41, Andokides will claim that political agreements are valid for him, but he has no part in them; the agreements were for people of the city and of the Peiraieus, not for Andokides, who was absent. Third, at §42, Andokides will accuse Kephisios of corruption, and he may have a point, but there will be another time to consider Kephisios; now is the time to judge Andokides. And fourth, at §§43–45, Andokides will argue that if he is punished it will discourage informers, but Andokides was rewarded for informing and is only at risk because he broke the immunity decree; besides, informers should not be immune from new crimes, but punished, and while they are counted as Athenian citizens when away from the city, when they are in Athens they are counted as criminals. The four arguments in §§35–45 are self-consciously refutative, and they seem to constitute a distinct speech part that may be recognized as a *refutation.*

Following refutation of Andokides' anticipated defenses, *Oration* 6 turns in §§46–49 to considerations unrelated to the specific charges that might nevertheless motivate acquittal. Here through responses to rhetorical questions, the argument entertains five possible reasons that the jury might want to acquit Andokides. At §§46–48 the question is posed, "Is it because he is a brave soldier?" (πότερον ὡς στρατιώτης ἀγαθός; trans. Todd 2007, 435). The answer is that he has not served, even though other exiles have done so. Likewise, at §49 the question arises, "What contribution [has he made]?" (ποίαν εἰσφορὰν . . .).[20] He did not import grain when the city was in danger, even though foreigners did so. Finally, just before a gap of 400 to 575 words, §49 presents three questions: "But as for you, Andokides, what service have you performed? What sorts of crimes have you remedied? What sort of nourishment have you repaid?" (σὺ δὲ τί καὶ ἀγαθὸν ποιήσας, ὦ Ἀνδοκίδη, ποῖα ἁμαρτήματα ἀνακαλεσάμενος, ποῖα τροφεῖα ἀνταποδους . . . ; trans. Todd 2007, 437). We may assume the answer in each case was none. And although we do not have the complete text for this segment of the speech, its surviving structure and content strongly suggest that it was meant to refute and perhaps preclude considerations apart from specific charges that might be considered during jury deliberations. Given the nature of this sort of refutation and its evident difference from that carried out by the speech part *refutation,* it is not inappropriate to conceive §§46–49 of *Oration* 6 as an *additional refutation.*

The final segment of *Oration* 6, §§50–54, is obviously devoted to a *conclusion.* At §50 the jury is told to remember what Andokides has done and the import of Eleusinian Mysteries in Athens. In §§51–52 Andokides' deeds are summarized: He imitated sacred rites, showed them to noninitiates, spoke the ritual words, mutilated gods of Athenian worship (for which he was cursed), and admitted all these things. He broke the law excluding him from holy places—he came to the city, sacrificed on altars, entered sanctuaries, and washed himself in the Eleusinion. In §53 the jury is admonished not to favor Andokides in secret, only to be hated by the gods in public; the jury should realize that punishing Andokides will purify the city. At the end, §54 contains an emotional plea—the jury must not be misled by Andokides. The jury knows what to do. Andokides is guilty of impiety. Death is a just punishment.

Conclusion

Distinguishable elements of the speech generally correspond with the last five speech parts recognized by Theodorus Byzantius. Thus, Theodorus' complex scheme of speech arrangement is now partly instantiated—and explicated—by an extant forensic speech in the Attic corpus. *Oration* 6 is structured so that confirmatory and refutative arguments are represented in separate units that relate either directly or only incidentally to the specific charge in the forensic case. Such a structure suggests an intelligible and practical rationale behind Theodorus' proposal of separate speech parts devoted to *confirmation, additional confirmation, refutation*, and *additional refutation*. And the availability of such a rationale supports the plausibility of a Theodorean twelve-part arrangement scheme, particularly against the presumption that its complexity makes it impractical.

While *Oration* 6 helps explain Theodorus' theory of speech parts, the reverse is also true. For some time, commentators have complained about the disorganization of this speech.[21] But when the main content of *Oration* 6 is understood to represent confirmations and refutations distinguished by their direct and indirect relation to the charge at hand, the order of materials in the speech is rationalized.[22] The novelty of this rationalization strongly suggests that the composer of *Oration* 6 was following Theodorus' scheme or a scheme very much like it. And, given that we have no evidence for such a scheme outside the Theodorean school, it seems almost certain that the composer is applying Theodorus' theory of speech parts.

If this much is correct, then Theodorus may take center stage in a controversy about the origins of rhetoric. For a long time historians have accepted an evolutionary view of early development in the rhetorical art. This view was founded upon a comparison of the origins of rhetoric and logic volunteered by Aristotle in *On Sophistical Refutations* 24 (183b23–36):

> μέγιστον γὰρ ἴσως ἀρχὴ παντός, ὥσπερ λέγεται. διὸ καὶ χαλεπώτατον· ὅσῳ γὰρ κράτιστον τῇ δυνάμει, τοσούτῳ μικρότατον ὂν τῷ μεγέθει χαλεπώτατόν ἐστιν ὀφθῆναι. ταύτης δ' εὑρημένης ῥᾷον τὸ προστιθέναι καὶ συναύξειν τὸ λοιπόν ἐστιν· ὅπερ καὶ περὶ τοὺς ῥητορικοὺς λόγους συμβέβηκε, σχεδὸν δὲ καὶ περὶ τὰς ἄλλας ἁπάσας τέχνας. οἱ μὲν γὰρ τὰς ἀρχὰς εὑρόντες παντελῶς ἐπὶ μικρόν τι προήγαγον· οἱ δὲ νῦν εὐδοκιμοῦντες, παραλαβόντες παρὰ πολλῶν οἷον ἐκ διαδοχῆς κατὰ μέρος προαγαγόντων, οὕτως ηὐξήκασι, Τεισίας μὲν μετὰ τοὺς πρώτους, Θρασύμαχος δὲ μετὰ Τεισίαν, Θεόδωρος δὲ μετὰ τοῦτον, καὶ πολλοὶ πολλὰ συνενηνόχασι μέρη· διόπερ οὐδὲν θαυμαστὸν ἔχειν τι πλῆθος τὴν τέχνην. ταύτης δὲ τῆς πραγματείας οὐ τὸ μὲν ἦν τὸ δ' οὐκ ἦν προεξειργασμένον, ἀλλ' οὐδὲν παντελῶς ὑπῆρχεν.[23]
>
> Just as it is said, the beginning of anything is the most important. Hence it is also the most difficult; for, as it is very powerful in its effects, so it is very small in size and therefore very difficult to see. When, however, the first beginning has been discovered, it is easier to add to it and develop the rest; this very thing has happened concerning rhetorical speeches, and also practically all the other arts. Those who discovered the beginnings <of the art> carried them forward quite a little way, whereas the famous modern professors of the art, entering into the heritage, so to speak, of a long series of predecessors who had gradually advanced it, have brought it to its present

> perfection—Teisias following the first inventors, Thrasymachus following Teisias, Theodorus following Thrasymachus, while many others have made numerous contributions; hence it is no wonder that the art possesses a certain amplitude. Of our current inquiry, however, it is not true to say that it had already been partly elaborated and partly not; nay, it did not exist at all.[24]

Within this comparison Aristotle evidently asserts that rhetoric developed gradually over a considerable period with many contributors. Following this assertion as a kind of heuristic, traditional historians attempted to work out how rhetoric evolved in consequence of the principles, practices, and intellectual relations that arose among such contributors. These attempts have lately been challenged by revisionist historians, who insist that rhetoric did not evolve gradually; rather, they say, rhetoric was invented by Plato and Aristotle.[25] The main arguments in this challenge have been that (1) traditional origin-narratives of rhetoric are doubtful, particularly in connection with Corax and Tisias,[26] and (2) the technical term ῥητορική was not invented until the 380s B.C.E., and only after this innovation was it possible for Plato and Aristotle to conceive and develop the rhetorical discipline.[27] This antievolutionary position has not escaped critique,[28] but it has posed a lingering problem for the evolutionary view, namely an apparent lack of direct evidence for specialized theoretical instruction in speechmaking before the second decade of the fourth century B.C.E.[29]

Here we have sources roughly contemporary with Theodorus who provide direct evidence for his having conceived and published specialized theoretical precepts regarding a twelve-part scheme for the arrangement of speeches. Moreover, in pseudo-Lysias, *Oration 6,* we have a forensic speech in the Attic courts dated about 400 B.C.E., wherein the parts of the speech (as we have them) follow a scheme of arrangement consistent with that evidently proposed by Theodorus. The partial instantiation of Theodorus' scheme in *Oration* 6 supports the plausibility of a complex Theodorean theory of speech arrangement. At the same time, however, it also demonstrates that the composer of the speech has employed such a theory to inform his oratorical performance. Thus, the case of Theodorus offers a credible instance of a fifth-century theory about the parts of practical speeches, wherein technical vocabulary has been devised in elaboration of the theory, the theory is conveyed in a book purportedly aimed at instruction, and the practice of speechmaking was evidently influenced by the theory. Moreover, the case itself is based on direct textual evidence from roughly contemporary authors and indirect textual evidence from an extant speech delivered in the Attic courts.[30] The existence of this example necessarily complicates any attempt to deny evolution in the art of speechmaking before Plato. It also supports the idea that we should take Aristotle seriously when he asserts that Theodorus contributed to the early development of rhetoric.

GORGIAS' "ON NON-BEING"

Genre, Purpose, and Testimonia

Carol Poster

Full fathom five [the sophist] lies;
Of his bones are coral made;
Those are pearls that were his eyes:
Nothing of him that doth fade
But doth suffer a sea-change
Into something rich and strange.

Shakespeare
The Tempest, Act 1, Scene 2

George Kennedy once called "On Non-Being" (*Peri Tou Mē Ontos*) Gorgias' "only definite philosophical work" (1972, 30).[1] In it Gorgias famously proposes "first and foremost, that nothing exists; second, that even if it exists it is inapprehensible to man; third, that even if it is apprehensible, still it is without a doubt incapable of being expressed or explained to the next man" (Sextus Empiricus *Adv. Math.* 7.65; Kennedy 1972, 42). Whether this proposition should be taken as serious philosophy, satire, or display oratory has been the subject of much dispute. Rather than use "On Non-Being" as a lens through which to examine the ancient relationships between philosophy and rhetoric, I will instead examine how reception of the text in philosophically and rhetorically oriented testimonia can be used to provide generic context for its interpretation. What is at stake in the question of how we should interpret "On Non-Being" are our assumptions about the relationship of sophistic to philosophy. Essentially, if "On Non-Being" is a satire of Parmenides or if it is a serious, but juvenile, piece of ontological speculation that Gorgias retracted in some manner later in his career, we can preserve a distinction between pre-Socratic nature philosophers and older sophists on the basis of whether they discussed such matters as physis and cosmos. However, if such speculations are indifferently characteristic of both sophists and philosophers, the distinction between the two categories becomes rather more complicated.[2]

Problems and Questions

"On Non-Being," like many other remnants of pre-Platonic thought, is particularly resistant to the ordinary forms of historical scholarship applied to most later works. The text itself is both badly preserved and strikingly decontextualized. On a purely textual level, the version of "On Non-Being" found in Sextus Empiricus is overtly described as a paraphrase, and the version in the pseudo-Aristotelian *MXG* descends from a text that the copyist himself describes as frequently illegible or incomprehensible. Moreover, the two versions are somewhat inconsistent with one another. On the level of context, we have no information on how "On Non-Being" was originally circulated (spoken or written), its audience (insiders among a specific philosophical circle? a broader community of experts? students?), its intentions (attacking Parmenides? display of Gorgias' expertise on recondite questions? teaching students abstract argument? defending Parmenides against the pluralists?), or even its genre. The question of whether we should read "On Non-Being" as parody, serious *reductio ad absurdum,* or straightforward proof depends, to a large degree, on what we presume about the relationships between ancient rhetoric and philosophy (or even if they were sufficiently distinct for such a phrase to be meaningful). The wide variety of scholarly opinions about the purpose and genre of "On Non-Being" demonstrate that internal evidence does not suffice to settle these questions.[3]

Judging whether "On Non-Being" should be read as satire depends on possession of both general cultural background and specific biographical knowledge. Knowing that eating babies was unacceptable in eighteenth-century Britain suffices to warn us that Jonathan Swift's "Modest Proposal" was not intended seriously. More subtle satire, which relies on political, ideological, or subcultural assumptions, is harder to gauge. Edward Copleston's *Advice to a Young Reviewer with a Specimen of the Art* (1807), which illustrates how a Scottish reviewer might savage *Paradise Lost* were it a new poem, was, as his pupil Richard Whately lamented, often read seriously. Whately's own *Historic Doubts Relative to Napoleon Buonaparte,* a *reductio ad absurdum* of Hume's attack on the veracity of the New Testament miracles, can be mistaken (by, among others, a not insignificant number of Canadian undergraduates) as a serious disproof of Napoleon's existence. Given the undisputed existence of Flat Earthers, UFO enthusiasts, Birthers, and all manner of conspiracy theorists, even the sheer absurdity of a position is no guarantee of its parodic nature. In the case of "On Non-Being," whether, in fact, we should reconstruct the treatise as asserting a position inherently absurd or not depends to a great degree on what we interpret the treatise to be claiming; its putative "absurdity" is one possible end point of interpretation, not a self-evident starting point.

Although no testimonia explicitly address the question of the genre and purpose of "On Non-Being," analysis of the contexts and patterns of reception of Gorgias shows how his work was embedded in ancient understandings of "rhetoric" and "philosophy." The unfortunately scant biographical tradition supplies, as well, predominately negative information concerning whether "On Non-Being" should be read as a sort of conversion narrative from philosophy to rhetoric, inverting the more common ancient narrative of conversion from rhetoric to philosophy or religion (Porphyry, St. Augustine, and so forth).[4]

The references to Gorgias of Leontini, despite being overwhelmingly concerned with his portrait in Plato's dialogues, can be analyzed categorically to show how patterns of reception can provide a context for reading "On Non-Being."

Gorgias' Biography According to the Major Sources

Below, the major testimonia concerning Gorgias' biography are summarized as a rough timeline. For the extended record, including the specific references to the major sources, see appendix A.[5]

Gorgias was born in approximately 480 B.C.E. Several sources describe Gorgias as a student or follower of Empedocles. Isocrates, Sextus Empiricus, Olympiodorus, and MXG attest to Gorgianic authorship of "On Non-Being." Olympiodorus dates the treatise to the eighty-fourth Olympiad (444–41), which is suspiciously close to Gorgias' flourishing (assuming a 480 birthdate) and unconfirmed by other sources. Given that the treatise engages Eleatic ontology, it is probable that it was written in Italy sometime between Gorgias' early studies and his embassy to Athens; the eighty-fourth Olympiad would indeed fall in the middle of that period.

Little is known of Gorgias' activities, other than his association with Empedocles, prior to his arrival in Athens. His being selected for such an embassy may have been due to his reputation as an eloquent speaker, but distinction in wisdom (*sophos* in its archaic sense), rather than specific oratorical talent, was a traditional criterion for such roles.[6] Diodorus (DK82a4) is the main source for Gorgias' distinction as a speaker before 427, but this may imply a reputation for eloquent speech on philosophical topics rather than strictly "rhetorical" activities if, in fact, subject matter rather than occasion or approach can serve to define a speech as "rhetorical" or "philosophical." As there is no report of a distinctive break with Empedocles or a "conversion" to sophistic, Gorgias' pre-427 activities could have been purely "philosophical" (albeit distinguished for eloquence), or shifting gradually from youthful studies in philosophy to rhetoric/sophistic, or combining the two in some manner.

Diodorus Siculus discusses Gorgias' role in the embassy from Leontini to Athens in 427 B.C.E. (corroborated by epigraphical evidence), describing Gorgias as already eminent as an orator, and much admired in Athens for the novelty of his style. Dionysius of Halicarnassus corroborates Diodorus' account of the embassy and Gorgias' impact on Athenian audiences without mentioning the specific date of the embassy, as does Plato. Diodorus stated that Gorgias returned home to Leontini after the Athenian embassy, which, if accurate, would require a second visit to Athens at a later date to account for activities described by other sources.

There are numerous references to Gorgias having become wealthy through his activities as sophist or rhetorician. Isocrates mentions that Gorgias charged his students one hundred minas. (Whether the precise sum is trustworthy, the general impression of high fees is well confirmed.) Xenophon implies a substantial fee paid by Proxenus to Gorgias. The solid gold statue Gorgias erected of himself at Delphi is frequently cited as evidence of the extent of his wealth (DK82a7). Our sources testify unanimously to Gorgias' longevity, some of which claim he lived to the agė of 105. Numerous followers, admirers, pupils, and imitators of Gorgias are mentioned in testimonia. Philostratus mentions that Gorgias was admired both by young (Critias, Alcibiades, Agathon) and old (Pericles, Thucydides).[7]

The Platonic Gorgias

Given that Plato was at least fifty years younger than Gorgias, and that Gorgias probably resided in Thessaly during much of Plato's adulthood, it is unlikely that the two were well acquainted, although it is possible that a wealthy and intelligent young man like Plato might have encountered Gorgias at some point.[8]

The dialogues portray Gorgias exclusively as a sophist or rhetorician. Plato has Gorgias refer to himself as a specialist in "rhetoric" (*Gorgias* 449a), but as chronology precludes Plato having been present at any such meeting, the precise terminology suggests more about Plato's concepts of education than about Gorgianic vocabulary. References to Gorgias in Plato (*Gorgias, Meno, Apology,* and *Phaedrus*) are consistent in portraying Gorgias primarily as a well-remunerated expert in the practice and pedagogy of verbal skills, a portrait consistent with most of our other sources. One of the most interesting features of the Platonic account of Gorgias, though, is not what is present, but what is absent, in particular the non-presence, as it were, of Non-Being.

Two of Plato's dialogues, *Sophist* and *Philebus,* include extended discussions of the sophist as one who discusses what is not. It is surprising that Gorgias' treatise is not mentioned in Plato's discussions of sophists and non-being. One possibility is that Plato was not acquainted with the treatise. By the time of Plato's activity as a writer, Gorgias was most distinguished for his activity as a sophist/rhetorician, and not for his treatise "On Non-Being." Even had Plato chanced upon the treatise sometime in his youth, he may have either forgotten it or considered it unlikely to be familiar to his audience when composing *Sophist* and *Philebus* (probably after 360 B.C.E.), as it would have been, by that time, a relatively obscure eighty-year-old treatise of only antiquarian interest. That Aristotle was also apparently unaware of the treatise would strengthen the hypothesis that the work was simply not known in academic circles.[9] It might, however, also be the case that the relevant passages in *Sophist* and *Philebus* in fact are evoking Gorgias indirectly, deliberately not mentioning his name as a clever play on the non-being of the individual sophist as well as of the subjects addressed by sophists (a sort of disrespectful inverse of the respect that leads the Philosopher to remain undiscussed in *Theaetetus*). Unfortunately, without definitive external evidence, it is not possible to determine whether the omission of explicit mention of Gorgias' "On Non-Being" from *Sophist* and *Philebus* was due to Platonic ignorance of or lack of interest in the treatise, or deliberate rhetorical strategy. Isocrates, for example, simply refers to Gorgias as "him who chose to write of Helen" (10.14–16, Van Hook, 67), leaving the reader to supply the name of the author. Plato also uses this strategy elsewhere. This lack of explicit naming, therefore, may signal either the fame or the obscurity of the work or figure not named, but without additional contextual information, it is impossible to determine which was actually the case.

Particularly puzzling is the *Philebus,* in which, although not mentioning "On Non-Being," Plato does name Gorgias three times:

> Protarchus: I have often heard Gorgias constantly maintain that the art of persuasion surpasses all others; for this, he said, makes all things subject to itself not by force, but by their free will, and is by far the best of all arts, so now I hardly like to oppose him or you. (*Phil.* 58a–b; Fowler and Lamb, 1962, 367)
>
> Socrates: . . . [Y]ou will not make Gorgias angry with you if you grant that his art is superior for the practical needs of men, but say that the study of which I spoke is superior in the matter of the most perfect truth. . . . (*Phil.* 58c; Fowler and Lamb, 1962, 367, 369)
>
> Socrates: Then we must dismiss the thought of you and me and Gorgias and Philebus and make this solemn declaration on the part of our argument. . . . That fixed and pure and true and what we call unalloyed knowledge has to do with things which are eternally the same without change or mixture. . . . (*Phil.* 59b–c; Fowler and Lamb, 1962, 371)

The final reference (59b–c) is particularly interesting in that it dismisses Gorgias from the discussion just as Socrates insists that the object of knowledge must be changeless and unmixed, in other words being rather than becoming, mingling with non-being, or pure non-being. Without better evidence concerning Plato's knowledge of Gorgias, it is difficult to decide whether this should be read as a clever dismissal of "On Non-Being" or as evidence that Plato, being unaware of the treatise, missed what would otherwise have been an excellent potential transition from a sophistic to an ontological theme.

Isocrates

That Isocrates was a pupil of Gorgias is well attested in the biographical tradition.[10] Although well placed to discuss Gorgias, Isocrates mentions him only infrequently. His portrait is radically different from the Platonic one, emphasizing

Gorgias primarily as the author of "On Non-Being" and as characteristically concerned with abstruse physical or metaphysical speculation. Isocrates mentions Gorgias by name only three times (10.3, 15.155, 15.268) and indirectly references him as the author of *Encomium on Helen* once.

Two Isocratean passages place Gorgias in a rhetorical/sophistic tradition. In *Antidosis* (15.268), Isocrates discusses Gorgias as the wealthiest of the sophists. In *Helen,* after a rather extended diatribe against sophists, criticizing them for their involvement in idle speculations about natural phenomena, Isocrates distinguishes the utility, difficulty, and grandeur of his own themes from both sophistic speculative philosophy and trivial encomia (for example, praise of salt and bumblebees, 10.11–12). Isocrates contrasts his own approach to praising Helen with that of an unnamed author (most probably Gorgias): "This is the reason why, of those who have wished to discuss a subject with eloquence, I praise especially him who chose to write of Helen, because he has recalled to memory so remarkable a woman. . . . Nevertheless, even he has committed a slight inadvertence—for although he asserts that he has written an encomium of Helen, it turns out that he has actually spoken a defence of her conduct! . . . [But the two genres differ];[11] for a plea in defence is appropriate only when the defendant is charged with a crime, whereas we praise those who excel in some good quality" (Isocrates, *Helen,* 10.14–16; Van Hook, 67, 69).

Of Isocrates' praise of Gorgias here, it would be possible to say that it is neither paean nor defense, but vituperation. After arguing that most "sophists" choose overly abstruse or trivial subjects for their discourses, he introduces Gorgias to suggest that even when sophists choose a good topic they treat it badly. By claiming that Gorgias' attempt at encomium is actually a defense, as might be given in a law court, Isocrates not only accuses Gorgias of ignorance of technical rhetoric, as exemplified by Gorgias' not deploying proper encomiastic *topoi,* but also suggests that Gorgias, while pretending to engage in the more elevated activities of ceremonial oratory, cannot avoid descending into the far less dignified habits of courtroom squabbling, which, in Isocrates' account, is similar to philosophical eristic, in that it requires merely superficial cleverness rather than the skills and knowledge needed for dignified speech on serious subjects (10.10–11). This particular conflation of physical speculation and trivial display oratory as characteristic of sophistic suggests that the formulation of "older philosophical rhetoric" that Philostratus uses to describe Gorgias and Protagoras may well be a more accurate framework for investigating Gorgias than the "ancient quarrel" account of the Platonic tradition.[12]

Isocrates' two passages (*Helen* 10.3 and *Antidosis* 15.155) that appear to refer to "On Non-Being," do, in fact, associate speculative physics with sophistic. Both attempt to distinguish Isocratean discourses, which are of public and private utility, and concerned with important political and moral issues, from the idle and useless speculations of everyone else. Isocrates uses the terms "philosophy," "sophistic," and "eristic" indifferently to castigate those who waste their time with "absurd and self-contradictory subjects" that are "entirely useless" (*Helen* 10.1; Van Hook 61). Isocrates emphasizes that such faults are not unique to his contemporaries, but were prevalent among the older sophists as well: "Protagoras and the sophists of his time have left to us [similar] compositions. . . . For how could one surpass Gorgias, who dared to assert that nothing exists of the things that are, or Zeno, who ventured to prove the same things as possible and again as impossible, or Melissus who, although things are infinite in number, made it his task to find that the whole is one!" (*Helen* 10.2–3; Van Hook 61, 63).

The beginning of Isocrates' *Helen* refers to Protagoras, Zeno, Melissus, and Gorgias as "sophists" but criticizes them for the uselessness of their "philosophy" (10.6). Their works are described as diatribes (10.1), eristic (10.6), or more commonly, speeches (*logoi*).[13] In this passage, Isocrates conflates what are, to modern scholars, distinct disciplines of philosophy and rhetoric. This seems, based on an implicit argumentative method of collection and division similar to that used by the interlocutors of the Platonic *Sophist* to track down their quarry.[14] The quibbling eristic-philosopher-sophists, as it may be best to term them in light of Isocrates' interchangeable use of the terms, are synthesized in a unified class in opposition to Isocrates, who stands as a singular good exemplar; the oppositions occur in parallel:

	Eristic-Philosophic-Sophists	**Isocrates**
Money	Get rich exploiting the young.	Makes a modest amount of money educating the young in useful knowledge.
Subjects	Idle abstractions and cleverness.	Politics, morality, practical-wisdom paradoxes, physics, metaphysics, and pure theory.
Epistemology	Seek absolute truth.	Concerned with probabilities.
Civic matters	Pure theoretical discussion.	Active practical engagement.
Skills	Verbal and intellectual agility.	Practical wisdom and moral seriousness.

Were this portrait of older sophists uniquely Isocratean, it could be dismissed as a sort of caricature serving as special pleading for Isocrates' own educational system. A very similar view, however, is found in Xenophon. Moreover, the characterization of Socrates and his *Phrontesterion* in Aristophanes' *Clouds* contains a quite similar conflation of verbal agility, speculation concerning nature, and exploitation of rich young men. Although the protagonist of *Clouds* appears to be a composite portrait of Socrates and Protagoras, the comic force relies on its audience's familiarity with (and antagonism to) a certain type of "sophist" engaged in a variety of activities involving verbal and intellectual skills, which appeared, to the man in the street, as "too clever by half," simultaneously impractical and unscrupulous.

The treatment of Gorgias in *Antidosis* is quite similar to that found in Helen, invoking the same opposition between the barren speculations of "sophists" including Gorgias, Melissus, and Parmenides, and Isocrates' own concern with useful subjects:

> I would therefore advise young men to spend some time on these disciplines, but not to allow their minds to be dried up by these barren subtleties, nor to be stranded on the speculations of the ancient sophists, who maintain, some of them, that the sum of things is made up of infinite elements; Empedocles that it is made up of four, with strife and love operating among them; Ion, of not more than three; Alcmaeon, of only two; Parmenides and Melissus, of one; and Gorgias, of none at all.[15] For I think that such curiosities of thought are on a par with jugglers' tricks which, though they do not profit anyone, yet attract great crowds of the empty-minded, and I hold that men who want to do some good in the world must banish utterly from their interests all vain speculations and all activities which have no bearing on our lives. (*Antidosis* 15.268–69; Norlin 1929, 333, 335)

The passage suggests that metaphysical treatises, like display oratory, attracted "great crowds." While intuitively, modern scholars might consider a performance of "On Non-Being" between athletic contests at festivals quite as improbable as Hilary Putnam being asked to lecture on logic on "Hockey Night in Canada," even allowing for some Isocratean exaggeration, we cannot discount the possibility that clever speculations on nature attracted proportionately larger audiences than their modern equivalents.[16]

Isocratean evidence, on the whole, suggests a less narrowly rhetorical context for Gorgias than the Platonic account. In both *Antidosis* and *Helen,* Isocrates contextualized Gorgias within Eleatic philosophy, listing him alongside Zeno and Melissus in *Helen* and with Empedocles, Parmenides, and Melissus, among others, in *Antidosis.* Gorgias' "On Non-Being" is treated as no more or less serious than the works of the other thinkers mentioned. Isocrates, equally dismissive of them all, nowhere suggests that, while Parmenides and Melissus make serious (if absurd) claims, Gorgias is satirizing Italian physics. Had Isocrates considered the treatise satiric, he could well have cited it as supporting his own condemnation of the absurdities of natural philosophy instead of grouping it among those absurdities.

Rather, however, than distinguish Gorgias from what he considered the abstruse and absurd speculations of the Eleatics, Isocrates portrays the intellectual pyrotechnics of the Eleatics and the verbal agility of the sophist as a unified activity of crowd-pleasing entertainment by display of combined verbal and intellectual skill. Historically, given that both Xenophanes and Empedocles performed poems on abstruse areas of natural philosophy to interested audiences, and that the symposiastic tradition might include serious philosophical discourse as well as flute girls, Gorgias' "On Non-Being" appears less of an idiosyncratic early work, and more of an exemplary case of what Philostratus was to call "the ancient philosophical rhetoric," which combined significant analysis of what were to become "philosophical" issues with elements of verbal ornament and a quasi-popular audience.

Xenophon

Xenophon falls chronologically and ideologically between Plato and Isocrates, both in his reception of sophistic and his views on education. Chronologically, all three were born, approximately, within the same decade (436–25 B.C.E.) and died within three years of one another (350–47 B.C.E.). All three, therefore, were some fifty years younger than Gorgias. Had Gorgias been allotted an average four score years and ten, there would have been little overlap between the adulthood of these three figures and Gorgias, but Gorgias' extraordinary longevity results in some chronological overlap. Of the three, Xenophon is the least likely to have had extended personal contact with the elderly sophist, having left Athens in 401 B.C.E., and subsequently traveling as a mercenary or settling in Sparta, Scillus, and perhaps, at the end of his life, Corinth. It is not possible to rule out that Xenophon, whose estate in Scillus was relatively close to Olympia, may have heard Gorgias speak at Olympia at some time, but neither do we have any evidence to support such an assertion. Since Xenophon's estate in Scillus was located in Elis, and Gorgias wrote an "Encomium of the People of Elis," it is not improbable that Xenophon would have been acquainted with the encomium, or at least cognizant of its existence, but it is not cited within the Xenophontic corpus.

Xenophon contributes in two ways to the reception of Gorgias, first by direct mentions of the sophist and second by a general portrait of sophistic education. Xenophon mentions Gorgias by name in three places, *Symposium* 1.5 and 2.23 and *Anabasis* II.6.16. The least significant of the three is the aside in which Socrates refers to an unusual expression as "Gorgianic" (*Symp.* 2.23). More significant is the comment Socrates makes to Callias near the beginning of Xenophon's *Symposium*: "You have paid a good deal of money for wisdom (*sophia*) to Protagoras, Gorgias, and Prodicus, and many others, while you see that we are what you might call self-taught (*autourgos*) in philosophy (*philosophia*)" (*Symp.* 1.5).[17] In response, Callias refers to displaying his skills at the dinner in speaking at length and with wisdom (*polla kai sopha legein*). This passage is of interest in that it seems to use the terms *sophia* as taught by the sophists and *philosophia* interchangeably, distinguishing instead those who learn from professionals from those who are self-taught. Here, Socrates ironically invokes the prejudice against autodidacts and adult learners as counterpoint to the putative professionalism of the sophists. Neither Socrates nor Xenophon finds this professionalism an indication of pedagogical skills or outcomes, as is seen in Xenophon's account of Proxenus in *Anabasis*:

> Proxenus the Boeotian cherished from his earliest youth an eager desire to become a man capable of dealing with great affairs [*ta megala prattein*], and because of this desire he paid money to Gorgias of Leontini. After having associated [*sunegeneto*] with Gorgias, and reaching the conclusion that he had now become competent to rule, and through friendship with the foremost men of his day, to hold his own in conferring benefits [*euergetōn*], he embarked upon this enterprise with Cyrus, expecting to gain therefrom a famous name, great power, and abundant wealth; but while vehemently desiring these great ends, he nevertheless made it evident that he would not care to gain any of them unjustly. . . . He was qualified to command gentlemen [*kalōn men kai agathōn*], but he was not capable of inspiring his soldiers with either respect for himself or fear. . . . (*Ana.* II.6.16–20; Brownson, 407)

Xenophon's portrait of Gorgias and his student Proxenus here differs from the one Plato provides us of Gorgias and Polus. First, while Plato portrays Gorgias as himself morally upright, but reluctant to teach ethics, and thus his student Polus, and by implication the successors to the older sophists, ending up self-serving and amoral, here Proxenus, through association (*sunousia*) with Gorgias, is seen as having become devoted to justice, but despite his advanced studies, moral probity, and fitness to lead gentlemen—expected outcomes from the traditional model of *sunousia*—he lacks precisely that which the Platonic Gorgias claims to impart, namely technical skills in persuasion (ability to evoke emotions or respect and fear in his soldiers).[18] In other words, Xenophon in this passage, as Isocrates in the passages discussed above, considers Gorgias an eristic-philosopher-sophist whose idle speculations, unlike the useful morality and hardy, thrifty example of Socrates, do not prepare students for practical life.

The attitude towards Gorgias that Xenophon displays in passing in *Anabasis* is paradigmatic of the more extensive points he makes about sophistic education elsewhere, particularly in *On Hunting* (*Cynegeticus*) and *Memorabilia.* The sophist Antiphon is criticized for valuing external goods and contrasted with Socratic indifference to luxury (*Mem.* I.6.11). Euthydemus is portrayed as having amassed a large collection of books by sophists and philosophers (*Mem.* IV.2.1), but nonetheless still lacking in practical wisdom; his investing money in associating with the writings of sophist and philosophers, like that of Proxenus in associating with the living Gorgias, does not actually buy practical expertise. Unlike the sophists, Socrates does lead his associates to practical wisdom, because of his focus on morality and daily life: "He did not even discuss that topic so favoured by the others, 'The Nature of the Universe': and avoided speculation on the so-called 'cosmos' of the sophists, and how it works, and on the laws that govern the phenomena of the heavens. Indeed, he would argue that to trouble one's mind with such things is sheer folly" (*Mem.* I.1.11; Marchant 1923). Xenophon's account of the sophists, whom he describes as talking about all nature (*pantōn phuseōs*) like the Isocratean account, emphasizes multiple ontological accounts: "Some hold that 'what is' is one, others that it is infinite in number; some that all things are in perpetual motion, others that nothing can be moved at any time: some that life is birth and decay, others that nothing can ever be born or ever die" (*Mem.* I.1.14; Marchant 1923). Although no specific sophists are mentioned by name, and Xenophon seems less well acquainted with individual theories, names, and technical terminology than Isocrates, "On Non-Being" would certainly fit within the genre of sophistic metaphysical speculation being condemned in the passage, and the image of clever speaking about abstruse and useless matters fits well with Xenophon's account of the education of Proxenus, the follower of Gorgias described in *Anabasis.*

Xenophon's most extended critique of sophistic education is found in the final two chapters (XII and XIII) of his treatise *Cynegeticus* ("On Hunting"), where he associates physical well-being, good health, and military prowess with concern for human affairs and avoidance of intense metaphysical speculation, an association very similar to that expressed by the Better Argument in Aristophanes' *Clouds*; similarly, the Xenophontic condemnation of sophistic echoes many of the themes satirized in the portrait of the Worse Argument.[19] Xenophon accuses sophists of not instilling the love of toil and true wisdom in students, but instead merely writing about "frivolous subjects" in far-fetched language, offering students empty pleasures but no wholesome maxims, and no useful knowledge or good habits (*Cyn.* XIII.1–6). Interestingly, Xenophon here draws a clear distinction between philosophers and sophists: "Nor am I singular in thus reproaching the modern type of sophist (not the true philosopher, be it understood); it is a general reproach that the wisdom he professes consists in word-subtleties, not in ideas" (*psegousi de kai alloi polloi tous nun sophistas kai ou tous philosophous, hoti en tois onomasi sophizontai kai ouk en tous noēmasin*) (*Cyn.* XIII.6; Dakyns, 123). This general portrait of sophistic, combined with the brief specific mentions of Gorgias, suggests that Xenophon, like Isocrates, would have considered "On Non-Being" part of Gorgias' characteristically sophistic activities rather than opposed to them.

Sophistic/Rhetorical Activities

Before Gorgias' activities should be categorized as "sophistic," "rhetorical," or "philosophical," something which depends on having clear prior concepts of the uses and referents of those terms, it is worth surveying what actual activities are attributed to Gorgias in the testimonia.

Teaching: Gorgias was distinguished as a teacher of public speaking. The tradition is unanimous in describing him as a renowned and well-paid teacher. According to Plato, his teaching was distinguished by a narrow focus on verbal skills.

Display Orations: Gorgias' reputation for traveling extensively and giving display orations which were stylistically distinctive and made strong impressions on his audience is well attested, as is his penchant for extemporaneous orations on subjects proposed by the audience.

Writing Rhetorical *Technai:* Plato (*Phaedrus* 267a) places Tisias and Gorgias among those who have written arts (*technai*) of speaking (*logos*). Quintilian considered Gorgias as following his fellow Sicilians Corax and Tisias in authoring a rhetorical art (*Inst.* III.I.8–9).

Other (Philosophical) Writings: "On Non-Being," especially in light of Isocrates' testimony (see above), fits in a pattern of composing treatises on nature, common in the philosophical schools.

Forensic and Deliberative Oratory: Whether Gorgias engaged in forensic or deliberative oratory in Leontini is unknown. Outside his own *polis* he would not have had standing to participate in civic affairs, and we have no record of his working as a logographer.

Reception as "Sophist," "Rhetorician," or "Philosopher"

The uses of the terms "sophist" and "rhetorician" in antiquity were both inconsistent and contested. Questions of whether Gorgias was a sophist or a rhetorician cannot be addressed with any precision unless rephrased in the form "Did X consider Gorgias a sophist?" or "Was Gorgias a rhetorician according to Y's definition?" Harrison, for example, in an article titled "Was Gorgias a Sophist?" actually addresses not the precise question of her title, but rather the more specific issue of whether Plato considered Gorgias a sophist or a rhetorician. She has argued convincingly that Plato's emphasis on the sophistic and rhetorical activities of Gorgias and Protagoras varies with the argumentative purposes of his dialogues.

Typical categorizations of Gorgias in the testimonia include "rhetorician" (Plato, Diogenes Laertius), "sophistic rhetorician" (Philodemus), "philosophical rhetorician" (Philostratus), "sophist" (Isocrates), "orator," and "teacher." Aristotle, for example, treats Gorgias primarily as a stylist distinguished in display oratory, eight out of twelve authentic Aristotelian mentions of Gorgias appearing in book 3 of the *Rhetoric.*

Philodemus groups Gorgias with Isocrates and Lysias (II.122. fr. 4) as among those who did not claim rhetoric to be a science, but nonetheless argues that their "sophistic rhetoric" (epideictic display) actually was grounded in scientific principles. As the physical text is badly preserved, and Philodemus himself is not compiling a disinterested history, but rather special pleading for a particular position concerning rhetoric in an ongoing debate within the Epicurean schools, it would be unwise to draw extensive conclusions about the relationship of "rhetoric" to "sophistic" in classical Athens from this fragment. The conjunction of Gorgias with Isocrates and Lysias does cohere with evidence suggesting that in this context Philodemus was interested in Gorgias primarily as a distinguished orator and teacher.[20]

Both Dionysius of Halicarnassus and Philostratus, however, sustain the Isocratean and Xenophonic theme of placing Gorgias on an indistinct boundary between natural philosophy and sophistic. Philostratus, in fact, looks back nostalgically on older sophistic as an exemplar of the unified Hellenic *paideia* he himself wants to advocate, with sophistic, philosophy, art, history, and poetry all being part of a cosmopolitan Greek culture, combining intellectual sophistication with graceful expression.[21] Philostratus begins his account of the history of sophistic by stating: "We must regard the ancient sophistic art as philosophic rhetoric [*Tēn archaian sophistikēn rhētorikēn hēgeisthai chrē philosophousan*]. For it discusses the themes that philosophers treat of, but whereas they, by their method of questioning, set snares for knowledge . . . the sophist of the old school assumes a knowledge of that whereof he speaks" (*VS* 480; Wright, 5). Philostratus continues by saying that "the sophistic method resembles the prophetic art of soothsayers and oracles" (*VS* 481; Wright, 5). Though for Philostratus the major concern is stylistic, his description of the type of rhetoric founded by Gorgias seems in line not only with Gorgias' "Helen" and "On Non-Being" but also, perhaps even more strongly, with the texts and descriptions of Empedocles. In subject matter, this older rhetoric not only covered general themes of the virtues and gods and heroes, but also physics (*VS* 481).

Dionysius of Halicarnassus offers a view quite similar to that of Philostratus of the situation of sophistic in the time of Gorgias, albeit sharing in Isocrates' disparaging rather than Philostratus' laudatory attitude: "Gorgias, Protagoras and the sophists had reduced the study of *logos* to a state of confusion. Isocrates took it over from them and was the first to set it on a new course, turning away from treatises on eristics and natural science [*eristikōn te kai physikōn*] and concentrating on writing political discourses and political science itself" ("Isocrates" 1; Usher 1974, 105).[22]

Given that this passage occurs in an essay on Isocrates, it is not unexpected that it would follow an Isocratean account. However, Dionysius and Philostratus are not alone in their treatments of Gorgias as natural philosopher as well as clever speaker.

Sextus Empiricus, in fact, is interested in Gorgias almost exclusively as a natural philosopher. He mentions "On Non-Being" twice in passing in his "Outlines of Pyrrhonism" (II.57 and II.59), but his most detailed discussion of Gorgias occurs in "Against the Logicians," the text in which he summarizes "On Non-Being." Sextus introduces his summary of "On Non-Being" merely by mentioning that Gorgias, like Protagoras, was among those who abolished the traditional criterion of wisdom or *sophos*, albeit taking a different approach from the Protagorean.

Another doxographical tradition appears in a scholion on Iamblichus' *Life of Pythagoras* (267), which provides possibly useful, mingled with obviously erroneous, information on the intellectual tradition of which Gorgias was part: "That Parmenides of Elea was also a Pythagorean; from which it is evident that Zeno 'the double-tongued' was too, he who also provided the foundations of dialectic. So that dialectic began with Pythagoras, and similarly rhetoric. For Tisias, Gorgias, and Polus were students of Empedocles the Pythagorean" (Inwood, 159).[23] The scholiast is a late and not entirely reliable source, being, like Iamblichus, mostly concerned with claiming for the Pythagorean school as many notable figures and achievements as possible; nonetheless, he does (albeit weakly) confirm that Gorgianic rhetoric was, at least within part of the doxographical tradition, not in opposition to Eleatic philosophy, but instead was part of a tradition founded by Parmenides, and continued through Zeno, Melissus, Empedocles, and Gorgias, combining speculation on natural subjects with innovative modes of speech.

The Neoplatonic rhetorical tradition supplies other testimonia. Gorgias is mentioned in passing as rhetorician in Syrianus' commentary on Hermogenes. In Themistius, Gorgias appears as a seller of wisdom (*Or.* 23.286) who accumulated significant wealth (*Or.* 23.294), and, unlike Socrates, charged for "extravagantly wrought" orations (*Or.* 24.300). Themistius summarizes the description of the generic sophist as a mercenary who exploits wealthy young men and forms opinions about the nonexistent (*Or.* 23.288) in Plato's *Sophist,* but, like Plato, does not mention Gorgias' "On Non-Being." Aristides, like Themistius, echoes a Platonic view of Gorgias, as does Proclus.

Olympiodorus, who brings forward Gorgias' authorship of "On Non-Being" in the eighty-fourth Olympiad as evidence of Plato and Gorgias being contemporaries, argues at length that Gorgias should be considered a sophist rather than a rhetorician or orator (14.10). Jackson, Lycos, and Tarrant suggest that Gorgias' "On Non-Being" was of interest to the Neoplatonists due to its use of an Eleatic style of argument, and that it being most readily classifiable as sophistic led to their assessment of Gorgias as a sophist (134n307).[24] Olympiodorus clearly characterizes Gorgias as a sophist at 14.10 and 43.6. Like Philostratus and others of the second sophistic, he tends to distinguish the sophists who specialized in declamation, as teachers and practitioners, from the considerably less distinguished rhetoricians who were concerned with the less visible and more basic pragmatic arts of courtroom oratory.[25]

There is no clear chronological shift in contextualization of Gorgias in the testimonia. Instead, how he is characterized appears to depend on the individual knowledge, interests, and aims of particular sources.[26]

Rhetoric as Activity, Not Essence: Biographical Context for "On Non-Being"

The greatest problems with descriptions of the form "Gorgias was a sophist" or "Gorgias was a rhetorician" is that they transform activities into states of being. Describing Gorgias as a featherless biped identifies a consistent and defining characteristic of Gorgias. "Rhetoric," "philosophy," and "sophistic," however, when attributed to people rather than to abstractions, refer not to immutable characteristics but to types of activities. No matter how frequently Gorgias gave display orations, nor how impressive his eloquence, orating is still an activity performed on limited occasions, unlike being mammalian, which is an essential characteristic. Although some activities, like eating, drinking, sleeping, and breathing, must be done regularly over a human lifetime, rhetorical, philosophical, and sophistic activities are performed intermittently. Just as Gladstone at various times served as member of parliament and prime minister and wrote books on Homer and Moses, so too Gorgias could have engaged in philosophical, rhetorical, and sophistic activities at different times. Rather than an account of Gorgias in the form of a copula of a timeless present (for example, "Gorgias is a sophist" or "Gorgias is a rhetorician"), it would be more accurate to describe a sequence of activities performed over time. One need not be a strong developmentalist or claim insight into his internal psychological evolution to map out his activities over time. Rather than ask whether Gorgias was a "sophist" or a "rhetorician" or "a philosopher," instead it is less misleading to investigate at which periods in his life he appeared to be engaged in such activities as teaching public speaking, giving epideictic displays, or composing works of natural philosophy.

The ancient biographical traditions concerning Gorgias, although lacking in chronological precision, provide a relatively consistent portrait of Gorgias' life and the position of "On Non-Being" within it. Gorgias, born in Leontini around 480 B.C.E., is shown as actively involved in the intellectual culture of his period and connected with Empedocles in some way. He had strong verbal skills and probably fairly broad-ranging interests.[27] "On Non-Being" was probably written in Sicily, and responded to Parmenides' influential treatise. Gorgias had achieved some degree of distinction, either for general wisdom or specific eloquence, in Leontini sometime before 427. Especially after his arrival in Athens, Gorgias became famous as a ceremonial speaker and teacher of speaking, known for a distinctively poetic prose style and for accumulating great wealth from his activities as a speaker and a teacher.

Nothing in the extant testimonia suggests a sharp break with the Italian philosophical tradition. Unlike accounts portraying Aristotle as "the foal who kicked his mare," portraits of Gorgias suggest a gradual shift of focus from an early interest in physics to a later focus on rhetoric. There is no reason to presume a distinct ideological rupture; instead, Gorgias seems to have discovered that teaching the art of speaking to rich young men paid substantially better than composing abstruse treatises on metaphysics, and given a desire for wealth and his striking talents in the oratorical arts, he eventually focused his energies exclusively on the more lucrative activities.

Although many testimonia concerning Gorgias focus on his rhetorical and stylistic achievements, a quite substantial number of sources place him within a tradition of Eleatic philosophical sophistic. Moreover, there is some evidence that, rather than separating Gorgias' activities into "sophistic" and "philosophical," at least certain elements of Gorgias' reception point to his practicing what, for lack of better term, might be called "philosophical sophistic."

This notion of philosophical sophistic, which applies complex and highly technical verbal tools to highly abstract general problems such as the nature of being, might account for an interesting historical claim found in both Sextus Empiricus and Diogenes Laertius that is normally dismissed as inaccurate or confused by modern scholars. Sextus claimed that Aristotle said that "Empedocles first cultivated the art of rhetoric, to which dialectic is antistrophic. . . . And it would seem that Parmenides was not unversed in dialectic, since Aristotle, again, regarded his friend Zeno as 'the pioneer of dialectic'" ("Against the Logicians" I.5–8; Bury, 5). Similarly, according to Diogenes, "Aristotle, in his *Sophist,* calls Empedocles the inventor of rhetoric as Zeno of dialectic" (*VP* VIII.57; Hicks, 435). If we posit Eleatic development of verbal techniques that could be applied to any topic to produce conceptual clarity (or, at a minimum, disprove falsehoods and show many conventionally accepted truths to be illusory), then Gorgias, who could speak on any subject, whether having to do with nature or justice, should be regarded as extending rather than opposing the Eleatic project. Such an Eleatic verbal method would originate in the prosaic poetry of Parmenides and divide in two streams, a prose one, of which Zeno and Melissus are exemplars, and a poetic one, found in Empedocles' poetry and Gorgianic poetic prose. Such a technique would account for Empedocles being described as a founder of rhetoric as well as many of the features of Gorgias' reception.

Gorgias' own *Helen,* in fact, describes precisely such a model of a verbal technique applicable indifferently to persuasion concerning practical affairs and natural phenomena: "To understand . . . persuasion . . . one must study: first the words of the astronomers . . . make what is incredible and unclear seem true to the eyes of opinion; then, second, . . . debates in which a single speech . . . bends a great crowd . . . ; third, the verbal disputes of philosophers" (*Helen,* 13; Kennedy 1972, 53). Though the subject matters differ, the verbal technique applicable in all these three cases remains the same.

Conclusion

The testimonia suggest several things. First, that asking whether we should understand Gorgias as "a sophist," "a philosopher," or "a rhetorician" is simply a badly phrased question. He was a person who at various times in his life engaged in certain *activities,* some that would later be termed philosophic (studying with Empedocles, writing a treatise on metaphysics), some sophistic (display oratory, teaching), and others rhetorical (teaching, possibly—but not probably—compiling some sort of handbook), although, for Gorgias these seemingly disparate activities may have been part of a coherent and unified application of a type of verbal and conceptual agility practiced in Eleatic circles.[28] Next, a parodic reading of "On Non-Being," as a strong critique of Eleatic ontology, has no obvious support in the testimonia. Instead, taken en masse, the testimonia suggest that we should read "On Non-Being" seriously in its Eleatic context, functioning like the works of Melissus and Zeno to defend core Eleatic understandings of the world against pluralists, in the sense that it too rejects the changing world of phenomena as inherently illusory, positioning the sophist who discussed the phenomenal world, not as one who talks about things which are, but instead about things which are not, and in "On Non-Being" investigating non-being as other philosophers investigated being. Assuming a world of non-being as literally described by Gorgias, one could say of the relationship between his ontology of non-being and the world of his display orations, that:

> . . . as imagination bodies forth
> The forms of things unknown, the [sophist's] pen
> Turns them to shapes, and gives to airy nothing
> A local habitation and a name.[29]

Parmenides

Philosopher, Rhetorician, Skywalker

Thomas Rickert

Neither perception, Theaetetus, nor true opinion [*doxa alethes*], nor reason or explanation combined with true opinion could be knowledge.

Plato
Theaetetus

For the Greeks, O King, who make logical demonstrations, use words emptied of power, and this very activity is what constitutes their philosophy, a mere noise of words. But we [Egyptians] do not use words [*logoi*] but sounds [*phōnai*] which are full of effects.

Corpus Hermeticum

The deceiver [*apatesas*] is more just [*dikaioteros*] than the non-deceiver, and the deceived is wiser [*sopheteros*] than the non-deceived.

Gorgias

In 1962 archaeologists digging in a temple in Velia found a bust of Parmenides with the inscription "Parmenides son of Pyres *Ouliadēs physikos*" (Ustinova, 192; Kingsley 1999, 140).[1] Velia, formerly known as Elea, is on the eastern coast of Italy. As Herodotus relates, Elea was originally settled by the Phocaeans, who fled Caria, a region in Anatolia (Turkey), on account of the Persians (De Sélincourt, 162–67). The people of Elea maintained a conservative, traditionalist culture lasting hundreds of years. One of their traditions was that of the priest-healer, *iatromantris,* what we might call a "medical prophet" (Nutton, 46, 331n64). Previous busts of medical figures had already been found in the same temple. In 1958, a sculpture of a man was discovered bearing the inscription "Oulis son of Euxinus of Hyele [Elea], *iatros* [healer] *phōlarchos* in the 379th year" (Kingsley 1999, 56; Ustinova, 192). Inscriptions were also found for a *phōlarchos* in 280 B.C.E. and another in 446 B.C.E. (Kingsley 1999, 57), indicating that Elea maintained a thriving *phōlarchos* tradition for at least five hundred years. *Phōlarchos* means something akin to the "lord of the lair," referring to priestly practices of deep, divinely oriented meditation, sometimes lasting for days at a time (hence the reference to hibernation in the notion of a lair or animal den), that the Greeks called incubation. Dates were given for all the busts save the one of Parmenides. He seems to occupy a position akin to "year zero"—that is, a founder or figurehead, someone integral to the beginnings of the temple and its medical and theurgic practices.

Parmenides of Elea is known as the key figure in a school of philosophical thought known as the Eleatics, which also includes Empedocles and Zeno. One question that is only recently beginning to be explored—as the discovery of Parmenides' bust has largely gone unremarked in philosophical circles—is why someone known to be a philosopher, perhaps the most important one until Socrates and Plato, is presented as a key, perhaps founding figure in a temple for priest-healers who sought altered states via incubation for purposes of religious devotion and healing. This picture seems far removed from our sense of what a philosopher is, as well as complicating the picture of Parmenides as a key figure in the rising of Western rationality from a mythopoetic bed.[2] Further, it opens up a slew of questions about how this evidence fits with our basic understanding of his philosophical thought.

Parmenides' fellow Eleatic thinker Zeno is reputedly his friend, his student, or perhaps even his adopted son. Zeno is famous for coining numerous paradoxes on space and motion, such as Achilles and the tortoise. Zeno also led an active life, including political and military duties. These pursuits led to his death. Elea was allied with the Liparans, who resided on an island off the Italian coast and who were resisting an Athenian attempt at takeover. Zeno was aiding them by running arms. However, according to Diogenes Laertius, Zeno was caught, tortured by the tyrant Demylus (or Nearches as some sources have it) so that he would reveal his coconspirators, and slain (IX.5.25–26). Accounts vary of what happened under torture—some say that Zeno named Demylus' own friends, inducing Demylus to kill them; others that he bit off Demylus' nose; and another says that he bit off his own tongue so as not to speak.

However, Plutarch in the "Reply to Coletes" makes a curious remark about the event: Zeno "revealed when tried in the fire [of torture] that the teaching of Parmenides in his heart was like the purest gold and equal to the proof" (1126d; Einarson and de Lacy, 307). What teaching of Parmenides is referred to here? It seems far removed from our understanding of Parmenides as a thinker of cosmology and logic. Plutarch speaks to a deeper teaching, something akin to life training that provides strength and bravery in the face of hardship and death. It is difficult to reconcile Plutarch's picture of Parmenides with the one we have of him today. Nevertheless, as the Stoic author Cebes wrote in his *Tablet,* there certainly was something in antiquity known as the "Parmenidean way of life," indicating that Parmenides' teaching, as presented in the fragments we have of his poem "On Being" (*Peri Phuseōs*), was understood by some ancients to be more than just a "philosophical" argument (*Tablet* 2; Seddon, 2).

Currently, Parmenides is peripheral at best in rhetorical studies, but I claim that he merits a significant place in rhetorical history—or, better, prehistory, since he predates the group we call the sophists, and, further, it is likely that *rhētorikē* is a coinage of Plato's, and hence, not quite applicable to Parmenides.[3] I am also in agreement with Stephen Olbrys Gencarella's assertion that classical rhetoric defines the field too narrowly and needs to expand its range of material (253, 267). This assertion resonates with earlier and ongoing work in the field pursuing such expansion, including Vitanza, Kennedy, Lipson and Binkley, Ballif, and others.[4] Further, as Robin Reames argues in the introduction to this volume, it remains far from certain that basic conceptions underpinning rhetorical history—that *logōn technē* must be understood as growing self-consciousness about language use, that it must be conceived across a theory/practice split, and so on—can be maintained. Such assumptions constitute a fore structure, shaping in advance what is considered and thought, and insofar as they become part of the dominant definitions of rhetoric, they come to be self-fulfilling prophecies.

Challenging assumptions and categories, then, is tantamount to reexamining assumed theories of rhetoricity itself, and thereby reopens the question of rhetoric, going back to the Greeks. These ideas help frame the concrete reasons for examining Parmenides anew. First, presenting him as a philosopher proper delimits fuller understanding of his work and its relation to Greek thought and culture. The dominant picture of Parmenides as the father of Western rationality, embroiled in point-counterpoint with his rivals to present a monist theory of being, is inaccurate. Parmenides was also a performer, a healer, and a practitioner of theurgy. Second, he was rhetorically savvy and utilized rhetorical principles in his work, functionally as part of the poem's diction and wordplay, and thematically, such as when he invokes *pistis* (good faith, trust) and *peithō* (persuasion) directly in fragments 1 and 2; beyond this he treats persuasion and *mētis* in more subtle ways as inseparable from the poem's performance.[5]

While Parmenides does develop sophisticated logical techniques, these are sourced not just from reason but also from revelation, achieved via theurgic techniques (incubation) from a source named the goddess (most likely Persephone) in the poem. Indeed, given the need for recovering female figures of rhetorical interest in antiquity, it is noteworthy that the goddess has not been addressed, as compared to, say, Aspasia or Diotima (who may herself be fictional). Finally, the poem's purpose is protreptic in the widest sense; it is meant to transform how one lives. Parmenides, we shall see, is a *physikos*—someone interested in the inner continuity between the world's cosmology and life's betterment. The poem was intended for performance: its epic hexameter verse form; intricate, dense, and confounding wordplay; and rapid argumentative pace have transportive effects, inducing in particular altered states of mind that mirror

Parmenides' opening image of being carried away by the gods. These effects reinforce the Parmenidean theme that, while logic is important, ultimately there is no escape from persuasion and illusion—rationality alone can never suffice. Finally, this suggests that the role Parmenides plays in rhetorical theory and history, particularly as a foil for the sophist Gorgias, will need careful rethinking.

However, if Parmenides attended to the role of deception in everyday life, this already suggests that Gorgias was perhaps not so much opposing as continuing Parmenidean thought. Finally, a methodological note: historiography is overly reliant on received categories, such as "philosophy," "rhetoric," "sophist" and so on, which have unveiled themselves over time in particular ways; it is, however, frequently anachronistic to impose these categories on ancient figures, or use such terms to carve them up into groups. As Reames rightly argues, we thereby lose the evolutionary perspective on rhetoric's emergence, and thus insufficiently examine the larger ecology within which rhetoric emerges. Thus, I seek not only to make Parmenides a figure important to rhetoric's emergence, but to put Parmenidean themes back into rhetoric's ecology, and hence into the question of what philosophy, sophistry, or rhetoric is, or could be.

Parmenides: More or Other Than a Philosopher?

Parmenides, born around 520 B.C.E., is often hailed as the first true philosopher and logician on the basis of the surviving fragments of his philosophical poem, "On Being," consisting of a proem, a section on truth, and a section on opinion. Parmenides is particularly important, even for the ancient Greeks, as witnessed, for instance, by Plato calling Parmenides "Father" (the father that in turn must be "killed" for Plato's philosophy to thrive) (*Sophist* 241d).[6] While Plato and Aristotle are no longer considered entirely reliable reporters about Parmenides, still, philosophy's picture remains in line with their basic outlook: Parmenides was a proto-philosopher who despite his obscurity was among the first to attempt to explain the world via rationally derived first principles, to ground truth claims in reason, and to introduce logical techniques such as the law of noncontradiction.[7] W. K. C. Guthrie, for instance, famously claimed that Parmenides marked the before and after of Greek philosophy, when reason was first given priority and the path to science was opened (1965, vol. 2: 1). This is in keeping with the dominant narrative concerning the ancient Greeks: that they put the Western world on the road to rational thought and science.

Most contemporary scholarship extracts what is considered the philosophical content from Parmenides' poetic work, especially from the section on truth (*alētheia*), the more "logical" aspect of the poem. The fact that Parmenides wrote in dactylic hexameter, the same form as his epic forebears Homer and Hesiod, still presents problems for interpreters. If Aristotle complained of the need for clarity back then, today we have pronouncements by such critics as Jonathan Barnes that not only are Parmenides' meter and poetical style impenetrable but that Parmenides' poetry is unlightened by any "literary joy" (Barnes 1982, 155; cf. Aristotle, *Rhetoric* 185a7–12). In other words, it is not only obscure but bad.[8]

Such complaints about style help enforce a kind of no-fly zone for conducting other kinds of analysis, literary or otherwise. For instance, in her survey of new work on the pre-Socratics, Patricia Curd grants that increasing attention is being paid to other aspects of Parmenides' work, such as the oft-ignored introduction, known as the proem (19). But in the end, the scholarly focus through eight pages remains Parmenides' logical arguments on being, not being, and human apperception. Even if some attention to cultural context and poetic form now contour those interpretations, the only indication that Parmenides might be other than a philosopher proper and that aspects such as the proem and stylistics might be genuinely significant is presented in a footnote buried at the end of the essay (31n134).

Curd's essay well reflects the state of the study of Parmenides, which presents him as a proto-philosopher best approached through the logical analysis of what are taken to be arguments, with all else subsidiary.[9] John Palmer in turn outlines Parmenides' contemporary reception, issuing a sharp critique of Guthrie, but in the end his arguments do not significantly shift the basic interpretative schema, holding to the idea that Parmenides is special because he was the first to explore rationally the consequences of being, not being, and possible being.[10] When the rhetorical possibilities of Parmenides are considered, the Aristotelian framework separating rhetoric from philosophy conditions what is said. For instance, Mansfield details with tremendous erudition the rhetorical features of Parmenides' poem, noting its ties to the ancient poets, and demonstrates that Parmenides persuaded rhetorically. But he did not thematize rhetoric on this account, and so Parmenides remains a proto-philosopher, even if the categories between rhetoric and philosophy were unimportant then (11).

Rhetorical theory inherits the philosophical portrayal of Parmenides. This may be unfortunate, but it is in keeping with the perennial conflict between philosophy and rhetoric. While interest in Nietzsche may have helped to kindle rhetorical interest in Heraclitus, Parmenides has had no such renaissance. Parmenides appears in rhetoric as philosophy sees him: an imposing, and masculinist, figure of rationality advocating monism. So, for instance, Edward Schiappa presents Parmenides as a monist attacking an earlier age's mythopoetic mindset while still mired within it, which accounts for his obscurity and awkwardness (2003b, 121–22, 124). Schiappa's purpose is firstly to illuminate Protagoras, so his picture of Parmenides is understandably incomplete, but this sharpens the point: Parmenides is not considered to be of primary rhetorical interest because philosophy has claimed him and codified his thought. Robert Wardy plies a similar path, presenting Parmenides' arguments as a target for Gorgias' "On What Is Not" (9). Wardy fruitfully suggests that Parmenides presents a new model of persuasion, but that model is logical argument, an attempt to "fuse reality with persuasive truth by way of rational compulsion"

(12). Michelle Ballif, Susan Jarratt, Victor J. Vitanza, and Richard Enos all discuss Parmenides, but again, largely to consider him as a logician and philosophical precursor to Plato and often as a foil for more sophistic figures, such as Heraclitus or Gorgias.[11] These readings of Parmenides in rhetoric are unavoidable given the overwhelmingly philosophical understanding of Parmenides—even in antiquity, Parmenides inspired primarily philosophical engagement. Gorgias' "On What Is Not" is thus primarily read as a reversal of Parmenides' philosophy of being, both then and now.

It is only recently that a different picture of Parmenides has begun to emerge that allows us to see that he does not fit the narrow frame philosophy has created for him. To see this, it is necessary to take the introductory proem seriously. While the proem has frequently been dismissed as a literary device introducing the poem's philosophical core, a variety of evidence indicates that the proem frames all that follows, performing acts of initiation and revelation in line with other ritualistic practices in the ancient Greek world. Further, taking the proem seriously resonates with the above evidence concerning Zeno's death and Parmenides' bust. In short, Parmenides should now be understood as someone with wide-ranging interests, including teachings that involve not just cosmology but theurgy, healing, life-training, and rhetoric. Our understanding of Parmenides' use of reason should be thought within this broader scope. Instead of being a precursor to Plato's escape from the cave of ignorance to the light of reason, on the traditional philosophical read, Parmenides is engaged in *katabasis,* a descent into the cave, to receive knowledge.

Caves, *Katabasis*, and Incubation

Caves are everywhere in ancient Greek literature and practice. Plato's myth of the cave in the *Republic* is only the most famous example. Caves figure prominently in Greek religious, healing, and wisdom traditions. Caves were often considered to be gateways to Hades, and thus there are numerous tales of *katabasis,* or a descent into the underworld. Orpheus, Herakles, and Odysseus all made such journeys. One of the Seven Sages, Epimenides (ca. 600 B.C.E.), fell asleep as a young boy in a Cretan cave, arising bewildered fifty-seven years later, graced by gifts of wisdom and prophecy (Diogenes Laertius I.10.109–15). Minos reputedly received his laws as divine oracles from Zeus in a Cretan cave, perhaps the same one as Epimenides (Strabo 10.4.8); Plato began his dialogue *Laws* with a discussion of this event (624b). The Derveni papyrus, which adds material to the theogony of Orpheus, describes the scene of Zeus entering a sanctuary (*adyton,* meaning a sealed-off part of a temple) of Night for instructions on ruling (Burkert, 86). Pythagoras and the Pythagoreans are surrounded by stories of descents into the underworld alongside other rituals and mysteries (Rohde, 600–601).[12] Pythagoreans placed great emphasis on revealed wisdom, particularly that which came through dreams and incubation. Pythagoras would reportedly describe descending to the underworld to report back as a messenger from the gods (Kingsley 1999, 102; cf. Burkert, 112–13). But further emphasis should be placed on the sheer number of caves known to be religious sites. Yulia Ustinova surveys over forty caves, grottoes, and underground sanctuaries, many of them associated with oracles, including several established for Apollo, such as Delphi, Didyma, Claros, and Patara (53–54).

There are several surviving accounts of what transpired at sacred cave sites. One of the more fascinating comes from Strabo. In his *Geography,* he tells us that between Tralleis and Nysa in Anatolia (modern Turkey) lies

> the Plutonium, with a costly sacred precinct and a shrine of Pluto and Korē [Persephone], and also the Charonium, a cave [*antron*] that lies above the sacred precinct, by nature wonderful; for they say that those who are diseased and give heed to the cures prescribed by these gods resort thither and live in the village near the cave among experienced priests, who on their behalf sleep in the cave and through dreams prescribe the cures. These are also the men who invoke the healing power of the gods [*theōn iatreian*]. And they often bring the sick into the cave and leave them there, to remain in stillness [*hēsychia*], like animals in their lair [*phōleos*], without food for many days. And sometimes the sick give heed to dreams of their own, but still they use those other men, as priests, to initiate them into the mysteries and counsel them. To all others the place is forbidden and deadly. (Jones, 259)[13]

Strabo here describes an intermixture of divination, magic, healing, and something akin to meditation called incubation (Patton, 194–95).[14] Properly trained priests—quite often associated with Apollo, considered the god of incubation—would descend into the cave, achieving trancelike states lasting up to several days, and receive visions and messages from the gods. Masters of dreams, we might call them, so long as we understand that the mastery is in reception, as the dream was delivered by the gods.[15] People who were ill would come to the shrine to be helped by such priests and, given incentive and guidance, perhaps attempt incubation themselves. Incubation is here described with two unusual Greek terms: *hēsychia* and *phōleos. Phōleos* refers to a den, lair, or hole, usually underground, where animals reside (Ustinova, 197). *Hēsychia* is a particular form of quiet, peace, or stillness. The priests would lie down in the cave, like an animal in its lair, becoming receptive to dreamlike forms of cognition, which, to them, were disclosed as signs from the gods. *Hēsychia* referred to the "stillness" of this altered state of consciousness.

The word *phōlarchos* is the same one used by Strabo to describe the priests who incubate; that is, priests who lie down in a cave like an animal in its lair. The term *phōlarchos* and its derivatives, remarks Ustinova, "provided an excellent metaphor for the trance experienced by human suppliants in the subterranean oracular caves" (198). The bust that was found of Parmenides in the

Velian medical compound grants him the title of *physikos,* which indicates some difference between Parmenides and those who followed him—he is not simply *iatromantis.* "Physikos" is a curious term, being the root for both "physician" and "physicist," a person who heals and a person who investigates the nature of the universe, respectively. The term was often used to describe early proto-philosophers, suggesting that, beyond the search for the basic principles underlying physical reality (which is the way Aristotle understood them), there was a practical side that included healing. Thus, it is unsurprising that busts and inscriptions were discovered in a building with medical instruments, statues of Asclepius and other physicians, and other paraphernalia, as well as a *cryptoporticus,* an underground chamber used for incubation and other rites (Ustinova, 192). It may be that this notion of healing stretches our everyday conceptions of medical practice, but it seems to be an explicitly Parmenidean goal.

There is a further conclusion to be reached, however, beyond the fact that Parmenides served as a founder for a long-running *iatromantis* tradition. Parmenides himself practiced incubation. Plato is received as a philosopher because he left the dark cave of ignorance for the bright day of rationality. Parmenides' path was different. He would lie down in a cave, like Epimenides and Orpheus before him, and incubate, and with his visions came wisdom. But now we have to ask: What wisdom? And in what way does his poem deliver it?

Parmenides' Proem as *Katabasis*

Parmenides' poem begins with a great sense of rush (fr. 1). He tells us he is being led by mares, and the verses emphasize the movement as he is carried as far as *thymos*—often translated as desire but compellingly rendered by Peter Kingsley as longing, "the energy of life itself"—will take him (2003, 27).[16] The mares lead him to maidens, who we soon learn are divinities, daughters of Helios. Onward Parmenides is led to gates on the pathways of Night and Day, where Dikē (Justice) is cleverly persuaded (*peisan epiphradeōs*) by the maidens to open the grand gates wide, and on he flies through, led still by the mares and maidens. And there he meets the goddess (most likely Persephone). She takes him by the right hand, welcomes him, and prepares him for the lessons she will teach him about the unshaken heart (*atremes etor*) of persuasive truth (*aletheies eupeitheos*) and the opinions of mortals that cannot be trusted.[17] She then tells him of two roads, one that IS and one that IS NOT, and the one that IS is also the road of Persuasion (*peithous esti keleuthos*), since Persuasion is Truth's attendant (*Aletheiei gar opedei*) (fr. 2). The road that IS NOT, we learn, is closed. After this, the proem turns to the central portion, known as the "Aletheia," a series of obscure and densely argued theses on being and nonbeing (fr. 8).

Parmenides is not describing any traditional notion of ascent to truth. Instead, Parmenides is describing a *katabasis,* a descent into revelation, not an ascent into rational truth. There are both similarities and differences when compared to Plato's cave myth. In the *Republic,* Plato envisions prisoners who are living in a cave, chained in such a way that they are forced to look at a wall before them; behind the prisoners, and unbeknownst to them, people go to and fro bearing puppets, while a flame behind the puppeteers casts puppet shadows on the wall the prisoners face (514–19d). They take these shadows for reality. But occasionally, one escapes or is otherwise forced up and out, to be dazzled by the light of the sun; eventually he ascertains that this is true reality, that life in the cave is false, whereupon he heads back down to enlighten the other prisoners. The metaphor is obvious: we live in a world of illusions, but a truth-seeking philosopher can gain insight into the truth beyond appearance. Parmenides is traditionally read as initiating precisely this philosophical journey, as the mares carry him to the goddess who grants him the truth of the eternal oneness of being that rends the illusions we customarily live by. Even if, finally, Parmenides is obscure and frequently mistaken, it is argued, he leads to Plato because rational argumentation takes us out of the cave.

This picture is strikingly at odds with Parmenides' proem. Parmenides finds truth in the cave, not by escaping it; nor is the theme of deception so clearly delineated from truth, as in Plato. Plato's revelation is one of seeing—seeing the light of reason, cast as the sun, with the idea that the cosmos and the divine are themselves rational. Parmenides is led by mares, daughters of Helios, the goddess Dikē, and finally the goddess Persephone herself to a revelation of "well-persuasive truth." Interestingly, Parmenides is the lone male, an idea that ought to complicate his masculinist reception. All the others—the horses, the divinities—are female. As Kingsley points out, at the beginning of the poem this circumstance is veiled, although from the first line even simple words ("road" and "which") are in the feminine (2002, 370–71). This reverses certain conventions, most notably the predominance typically granted to men, as with Plato's cave escapee; but it also foreshadows a key theme, that things are not necessarily what they appear.[18] In this way, at least, Parmenides' poem resonates with Plato: appearances are not all. But in other respects, his poem is at odds with Plato, since his primary allusions are to the mythopoetic underworld descents of Epimenides and Orpheus (Burkert, 89). When the gates of Night and Day open, the poet is confronted not with light, not with brilliance, but rather with an empty yawning (*chasma achanes*), an abyss, reminiscent of the terrible chasm Hesiod tells us even the gods fear (*Theogony* 736–44).[19]

Plato's myth describes those who depart the cave to learn truth, and upon learning it, they return to the cave dwellers and enlighten them as to the truth. It is a journey from darkness to light, the classic representation of rationality. Parmenides' journey is the reverse, from light to darkness. He is not departing the cave but entering it—entering the underworld, Hades, which for the Greeks was located where Parmenides, as Hesiod before him, describes: just past the gates of Night and Day, near the mansions of Night and Tartarus. That is why the goddess who greets him is not the goddess of truth, as is often asserted (even by Heidegger [1998]), but most likely the goddess of the underworld,

Persephone. As Kingsley points out, it was common to refer to Persephone via epithets such as "the goddess" or "the maiden" (*korē*) (1999, 96).[20] This is perhaps unsurprising; like He Who Shall Not Be Named substituting for Lord Voldemort in the Harry Potter series, Persephone is best evoked euphemistically.

Parmenides is going where people die. This is why Persephone tells him it is "no evil fate" that sent him there—he is not dead. Rather, he is an initiate, a *kouros* as the goddess addresses him, and he has been led there by immortals (for he needed guides to get there) to learn the mysteries.[21] The truth he learns is not only given as revelation but delivered as an incantatory, riddling text. The proem tells us that what follows are not Parmenides' but the goddess's words.

Performing and Materializing Wisdom

Parmenides' great poem cannot be interpreted solely through its logical arguments because it is also a performative text. It not only *addresses* thinking and being—philosophy, rhetoric, and more—but it *enacts* conditions for understanding them. The two aspects merge with and reinforce each other, mirroring the importance of materiality to the prehistory of rhetoric. Parmenides' poem can be investigated not only in the most traditional way—that is, by extracting its received logical content—but also in a new way that reveals its materialist grounding and its embodied effects. This entails asking questions about the power of words and revelation, not simply as stories we tell but as material experience and phenomena.

The ancient world did not ignore such questions. For instance, Pliny the Elder asks whether formulas and incantations have any real power, admitting that some charms have been tested by experience, even if he is shy about quoting them (Versnel, 105–6). In the *Corpus Hermeticum,* an Egyptian author lambasts the Greek philosophers for forgetting the power of words: "For the Greeks, O King, who make logical demonstrations, use words emptied of power, and this very activity is what constitutes their philosophy, a mere noise of words. But we [Egyptians] do not use words [*logoi*] but sounds [*phōnai*] which are full of effects" (Festugiere, 232). Iamblichus is even more forthright about the ability of those who are divinely inspired, or possessed by the gods, to remain impervious to pain, to be unscathed by fire, and in general to display nonhuman qualities (3.4–5). Even contemporary science is beginning to demonstrate that "false" mental beliefs and environmental factors can produce material effects—placebos, for instance (Kaptchuk et al.).[22]

The transformative, even magical, power of words was a lived experience in the ancient world. It therefore makes sense that Parmenides' work would seek to evoke the revelatory experience it describes in its audience. This is not as unusual as it might seem; even in Plato, one of the most common motifs is how Socrates' interlocutors are stunned, disoriented, and transformed by his twists and turns of language. Even if Socratic language is primarily rational in its goal of perfecting souls, its performance produces additional effects. Parmenides is also performing; he performs as the *physikos,* aiming to heal both the body and mind as well as to provide an understanding of the world. He seeks to describe a transformative experience that parallels the poem's arguments while simultaneously preparing an audience to favorably receive those arguments.

Parmenides' use of dactylic hexameter, like Homer's and Hesiod's usage before him, is not simply a matter of his time period. In a study of Homeric poetic performance, Egbert Bakker argues rather that it has a performative purpose: the rhythm propels the consciousness of the singer forward, so that the words and their power are experienced as coming from somewhere other than the seat of consciousness, "an authority located beyond everyday experience and the source of immutable knowledge and authority" (136). Thus, the performance of the poem dislocates the speaker's consciousness.[23] Further, the content of the proem itself describes a mystical, transporting experience, so three levels of the poem reinforce a common point: truth and authority are given by a nonhuman other. A cave's material properties foster altered states conducive to revelation; the performance of epic poetry dislocates the speaker/singer's sense of originating source, creating the experience of revelation; and Parmenides himself speaks of a rushed journey to the underworld, where he is initiated into divinely revealed truths.

Again, what the poem describes bears similarities to shamanism. F. M. Cornford remarks that if the only thing that survived of Parmenides were the opening lines, he would be set aside as a magician (104). We might take the shamanistic connection more seriously. A shaman actively seeks altered states for purposes of divine inspiration and revelation in order to unite a community and provide guidance and healing.[24] Aspects of Parmenides' poem directly invoke shamanistic practices. In addition to the feeling of rush and the confrontation with the yawning abyss, there are other details as well: the sounds of piping (*syrinx*) from the spinning of the chariot's axles; the constant movement, as the maidens push back their veils, the wheels whirl, and the grand doors open with the turning of the alternating keys; and the sound of the doors on their hinges, which is also linked to pipes. Taken together, these images and sensations evoke the embodied sensation of incubation. Iamblichus describes the experience as including an encompassing sense of intangible spirit, a whistling or hissing sound (*roizos*) that diffuses itself in all directions, shining lights, a feeling of openness, a wholesome freeing of the body and soul, an alert wakefulness of the senses, and an awareness or consciousness about all that is happening in this state between being awake and asleep (3.2). The whistling and piping sounds are a leitmotif dotting the literature surrounding incubation and meditation, and thus it is perhaps not surprising that, once we acknowledge these shamanistic aspects of Parmenides, we also see them evoked in his poem.

These techniques resonate not just with shamanic traditions, but more directly—and historically—with ancient Egypt. Egyptian religion, as scholars such as Jan Assman have detailed, comprised an entire semantic universe where cultic practices sustained the world, and its practices were often initiatory, experiential, even in a sense monotheistic, and heavily invested in the power of language (404, 408). The many deities we associate with Egyptian polytheism are actually different manifestations of a single divine, the One, and language had a more direct signifying function, not simply representation as we understand it (Assman, 417). The goal of Egyptian religion is to sustain the world through ritual and practice, while preparing the soul for the afterlife. In the "Busiris" (11.28), Isocrates relates the importance of Egyptian thought for the Greeks, basically claiming that the Greeks, particularly Pythagoras, learned philosophy from them, for the purpose of preparing the soul to return to the divine, which itself entails investigating the nature of the world and cosmos (Norlin and Van Hook, 22, 24). Algis Uždavinys details how the Greeks reworked Egyptian thought into their own idioms, while nevertheless keeping alive the fundamental orientation of philosophy as a "rite of transformation and noetic rebirth" (ix). Thus, the rhetorical power of language in Parmenides—the quick turns of logic, intricate wordplay, riddles and puns, deep symbolism and association, and incantatory performance—casts light on language's sacred and transformative function, one with Egyptian roots. And the goal of such ritualistic, sacred speech is, finally, "one's transformation, awakening, and rebirth" (Uždavinys, vii).

Parmenides Skywalker: New Paths, New Questions

Parmenides is not well served in his current role as the standard bearer for rationality, the pre-Socratic who set us on the journey from night to day, myth to reason.[25] Parmenides was a practitioner of incubation and a founding figure for a long-running *iatromantis* tradition associated with Apollo, the god of incubation. There was even a common Greek phrase, "taken by Apollo," to refer to the experience; such priests were sometimes known as "skywalkers," as, for instance, the shaman-like figure Abaris Skywalker (*aithrobatēs*), who delivered an arrow to Pythagoras (Rohde, 327–28; Kingsley 1999, 112). The poem itself is a performative *katabasis,* meant to achieve what it says—it is not just words but sounds full of effects.

Attending to Parmenides as part of rhetorical prehistory suggests that rhetoricity cannot be bounded by its sophistic disclosure and resulting codification. What we end up doing is taking received categories and reading them back into the past. Certainly, then, in looking to Parmenides' rhetorical wordplay and performance, we can see that he utilizes rhetorical techniques as we typically understand them. What is more difficult to do is put the question of rhetoric back into play, and ask if Parmenides opens up other possibilities for what rhetoric is or could be, possibilities that are still latent within it today, those perhaps not so well understood or theorized. Further, in considering the power of caves, incantatory language, and what appears to be human beings' physiological predilection for altered states that include a sense of the oneness and the divine, we cannot simply disregard such trans-human experience as merely subjective. Specifying the powers of materiality and embodiment, including language, and placing them within an ecological and catalytic framework require us to rethink rationality's elevation to the status of most desirable good or sine qua non of human being, a narrative that underpins much philosophy still. Thus, the "logical" "Aletheia" section of "On Being" cannot only be a first example of philosophical argumentation. It develops the proem's proto-rhetorical thematics, including its incantatory and transformative aspects. To work toward a conclusion, then, I want to explore other rhetorical aspects of the poem—specifically, not only how its rhetorical work achieves its effects, but what it might say about what will later come to be called rhetoric. That is, persuasion is not simply present as a technique; Parmenides knits persuasion and deception into his philosophy, and, I argue, his ontology. In this sense, rhetoric takes new bearings from Parmenides; and, if these bearings are picked up and not opposed by those who follow him, including Zeno, Empedocles, and Empedocles' student Gorgias, then there is significant revision to be made to our rhetorical histories.

M. Laura Gemelli Marciano argues that one reason the "Aletheia" section has given the logicians fits is because the "logic" is often flawed: leaps and tautologies abound (42). Further, the arguments are rushed, mimicking the rush with which the proem begins. Persephone's arguments are a quick jumble of words and images (many of them repeated, particularly the verb *esti* ["is"]) that already resemble the continuous whole—the One—that Parmenides supposedly argues for (Gemelli Marciano, 38, 42–43).[26] This performance is spellbinding and traps Parmenides within its gambits. The words are not isolated bits to be analyzed but a rhythmic stream used to "enchain and paralyze the thoughts of the *kouros* [initiate] and guide him to the experience of eternity, immobility, and completeness" (44). This form of persuasion has already been foreshadowed in the proem, as when the maidens persuade Dikē with soft words and the goddess invokes persuasion as the attendant of truth.

There is good reason, too, for the evocation of persuasion, incubatory stillness (*hēsychia*), and oneness at the heart of reality—they constitute the spring for Parmenidean wisdom—and, as Uždavinys argues, the sense of oneness has Egyptian ties as well. Stillness, which Parmenides learned from his teacher Ameinias, puts him in touch with the divine, which is to say, nothing human per se (Kingsley 1999, 187). We need not share Parmenides' sense of divine revelation to understand the larger lesson about the incursion of the nonhuman into the human as a source for what IS. Put differently, Parmenides suggests both human limits, since wisdom requires help from beyond the human proper, and human capacities, since it is possible through concrete practices and techniques to obtain help and wisdom. In this sense, there is something ephemeral about Parmenides, for which he has been critiqued. But, as perhaps becomes even clearer in his student Empedocles and his emphasis on the four elements (earth, water, air, fire), there is no denying the sensory world. Rather, he offers a preview to the arts of life in such a way as to include the material and the ephemeral. This can illuminate how Parmenides is fully attuned to every aspect of a worldly situation, even as he remains aware of its deceptive nature in light of the truth of oneness. But how to navigate this conundrum? Here we see that the entire poem is an art of living predicated on an evocation of *mētis.*

These themes of deception and *mētis* manifest themselves particularly in his description of the plight of his fellow human beings. In fragment 6, the goddess tells him of mortals who know nothing, calling them two headed, undiscerning, and helpless. These terms are striking. "Two headed" (*dikranoi*), or "fork headed," refers to being of two minds, at loggerheads; "undiscerning" (*akrita phula*) has two possible meanings: it can refer to the masses one cannot distinguish among and to the inability to decide (Kingsley 2003, 95, 99). "Helpless" is a translation of *amēchania,* which might be better rendered as "without a ruse," which is to say, lacking in *mētis* (91). People are so overloaded by their senses and customs, by what in fragment 7 is described as "habit born of long experience," that they have no idea what to do, how to decide. They have no *mētis* to steer them through illusion, and it may be important to recall that *mētis* is a form of cunning, a decisive means of steering through what comes before us (Detienne and Vernant, 2, 3, 5, 11; Ballif 2001, 190–92). Governed neither by logic, nor rules, nor categories, *mētis* calls us to navigate the twists and turns within what is given as it evolves. It is a kind of cunning that stems from total attention to what is going on around us. And, as Hoffman argues in his essay in this volume, *mētis* has its own rationality, different, perhaps, from the principle-driven conception that emerges with Socrates and Plato, but nevertheless one that suggests complex balances at work in Parmenides' thought.

Reasoning, then, is certainly at work here, but it is combined with other faculties—affective, perceptive, rhetorical. Parmenides' oneness is the realization of a fundamental interconnectedness but not as a representation that takes oral or written form, that is, a metaphysical oneness. Rather, it is an enacted experience of incubatory oneness. It amounts to transduction, rather than representation, the goal being to shed accepted categories that bind and constrain.[27] Gemelli Marciano likens it to de-automatization, whereby the goddess is so effective in ensnaring Parmenides that he is deprogrammed, persuaded to shed his "habits born of long experience" (39–40; cf. Parmenides fr. 7). We thereby see that the poem is as much about healing and wisdom as it is about cosmology and rationality. Wisdom begins by understanding that the inability to cut through opinion is *amēchania,* lacking in *mētis*; the experience of stillness, and not the logical sorting of truth and falsehood, is the means to begin its cultivation. Parmenides does not espouse logic alone or metaphysical cosmology as being the keys to existence. Following such paths leads only to more fork-headedness, indecision. *Mētis,* if we are to find it, begins with accepting confusion as ontologically fundamental.

In his portrayal of being beguiled and bound by the goddess, Parmenides reinforces the inescapability of persuasion, including its traps. This is one of the ways that Parmenides belongs to rhetoric's prehistory. We do not need to take on or simply adapt to Parmenides' teaching, for what his poem enacts is less adaptation than *exaptation,* that is, the development of a new feature or trait from out of what has already evolved (Tattersall, 44, 68). *Mētis* includes logic as a limited, often deceptive faculty within a larger bundle that it uses not to adapt to but to evolve within circumstances. So too Parmenides' poem is a "crafting and exploration of human perception within the changing limits and affordances of [a] new creative ecology" (Malafouris, 193). Parmenides as skywalker is a crucial element in this creative ecology. It may or may not be mysticism. But that perhaps is not the issue, even if mystic experience cradles the "still heart of unshaken truth" the poem seeks to evoke. Truth includes nonrational sources for Parmenides, at least from our contemporary perspective; and his proto-rhetoric attunes us to persuasion's necessity amid the world's snares and illusions. *Mētis* finds its cunning in acceptance of these truths, in exapting within them, not escaping them, as Plato finally sought to do. And persuasion itself exceeds any simple notion of communication, rational or otherwise; that is, it is an attuning experience that transcends the individual, connecting one primordially to the world. While this is but an inkling of what might be learned from Parmenides, the example of Zeno suggests that such teaching can and did run deep.

What Parmenides suggests about rhetoric, then, is that truth must be accompanied by persuasion; but that truth itself is a fickle thing, possible perhaps to experience as an ineffable oneness but not so easily made concrete and communicated. There is no direct line to the divine. Deception, veiling, and the unknown are equally written into the world, snaring and confounding us. In this, I find a deep sympathy for human plight in Parmenides. And there is no simple escape into the comfort of owning the truth. Parmenides showcases his own need for help; and the goddess, Persephone, tricks him throughout, even telling him that she has her own deceptions, all of which are part of her teaching. The larger lesson is that rhetoric's necessity springs from this ontology, where deception and illusion are inseparable from life and world. Here we see that a later figure such as Gorgias may well be continuing Parmenides' thought, and not rejecting it, in that Gorgias continually thematizes deception, illusion, magic, and the power of words in his sophistic *logos.* Gorgias' famous statement that "the deceiver [*apatesas*] is more just [*dikaioteros*] than the non-deceiver, and the deceived is wiser [*sopheteros*] than the non-deceived," ostensibly about the theater, has as deep and wide an existential meaning as Shakespeare's line about our strutting and fretting our hour upon the stage (fr. 20). Still, I can only gesture at that possibility here, and much work, I think, remains to be done on this and other aspects of Parmenides' thought and its rhetorical legacy.

Still, it is not a new idea that reason has its snares and may be less sure or achievable than we have thought. Despite some dissonances between Parmenides and Plato, it worth remarking that, even in a rigorous dialogue such as the *Theaetetus,* the attempt to define knowledge comes, finally, to naught: Socrates concludes that "neither perception, Theaetetus, nor true opinion [*doxa alethes*], nor reason or explanation combined with true opinion could be knowledge" (210a), thereby also suggesting that there are limits to what the art of reason can achieve (210c). Even science itself is now challenging the idea that it can fully self-correct or completely remove falsifying human motivation from its work.[28] These remain questions, not answers, but thousands of years ago Parmenides already was suggesting that rationality might not, despite philosophy's hopes, finally save us from illusion, thereby inscribing a need for rhetoric into his ontology.

But there is something further to be added: life training. From a Parmenidean perspective, what remains at issue is *physikos*: a merging of cosmology, healing, and the everyday arts of life, a fundamental transformation of not just the representation of the world through communication but our way of being in the world. For Parmenides the real illusion is that rationality or human enterprise alone will grant us truth and deliver us from falsehood. Instead, we can but inculcate *mētis,* which acknowledges our inability to escape the cave of illusion and seeks ways of thriving within it, aided by logic but also by the appropriate forms of persuasion tempered by nonrational means and engagement with the nonhuman—including the divine, as he saw it. Parmenides offers rich, new sources for rhetorical theory, particularly concerning the powers and limitations of reason and the individual; the power of and need for transformation; and the development of wisdom and fortitude in the face of hardship. And he does so through a profound vision of persuasion's permeation of all that IS. In such proto-rhetorical fashion, then, Parmenides integrates what will later be narrowed as rhetoric proper into a conception of wisdom into the very arts of life itself.

Heraclitus' Doublespeak

The Paradoxical Origins of Rhetorical *Logos*

Robin Reames

Heraclitus has received little attention from rhetorical scholars due to a general presumption that the pre-Socratics instantiate proto-philosophy and proto-science, but not proto-rhetoric. Nevertheless, Edward Schiappa convincingly argued over a decade ago that the common understanding that rhetoric deals with the ability to argue convincingly on both sides of an issue—an idea attributed by multiple ancient sources to Protagoras—ultimately may be traced back to the Heraclitean ontology of flux and the so-called "unity of opposites." Schiappa identifies a natural coherence between this rhetorical commonplace of two sides, the Protagorean *dissoi logoi,* and Heraclitus' observations about the unity of opposites in the material world. Indeed, he finds that Protagorean *dissoi logoi* was an extension into language of the Heraclitean doctrines on the material world (2003b, 89–95). Protagoras' unique contribution to the thought revolution from mythopoeia to reason, Schiappa suggests, is that he identifies in language itself the same oppositional potentialities that Heraclitus identified in the world. Heraclitus, however, "does not address language itself as an object of inquiry" (97).

In contrast to this claim, the Heraclitean *logos* may be understood as an explicit (albeit riddling and paradoxical) theorization of language that is consistent with rhetorical *logos,* since both possess the dual possibility of arguing two sides of an issue. Consequently, a rhetorical understanding of Heraclitean *logos* may contribute to the ongoing debate over the *logos* in DK22b1.[1] For over a century, scholars have wrestled with the double-meaning of *logos* found in the opening lines of Heraclitus' book on nature and have struggled to interpret its secondary meaning without undue reliance on anachronistic metaphysical concepts of *logos* (as reason, as the Stoic divine mind, and so forth) that did not exist for Heraclitus. Current interpretations problematically simplify that paradoxical depth of *logos* by defining it as universal law or *nomos.* This moves readers of Heraclitus to neglect the basic concept of *logos* as speech, and through this neglect, *logos* ceases to function as a paradox or riddle, where deeper meanings are discovered by penetrating and playing with apparent ones. Ultimately, this alienates the *logos* from the style and content of Heraclitus' other paradoxes, hidden meanings, and thoughts on nature. My counter-interpretation would avoid these problems through a consideration of Martin Heidegger's analysis of the *logos* of DK22b50 originally published in 1951, and to a lesser extent, his earlier discussion of the first fragment in the 1935 lecture course, published in English as *Introduction to Metaphysics.*[2] This interpretation considers *logos* not as a law, measure, or rule, but in what Heidegger suggests was an earlier sense as a laying down and a gathering up. Understood as this physically oppositional activity, *logos* grows more consistent not only with the other Heraclitean paradoxes, but also with the "two sides" of rhetorical *logos.*

Preliminary Problems

According to Diogenes Laertius, Heraclitus flourished in the sixty-ninth Olympiad, or toward the end of the sixth century B.C.E. (*Lives* 9.1; Hicks, 409). The earliest surviving records of his thought and words come from references in Plato and Aristotle, followed by numerous sources in the doxographical tradition of late antiquity. As Charles Kahn has suggested (referring to Diels' scholarship on Heraclitus), the doxographers' text of Heraclitus came from Theophrastus' *phusikōn doxa,* which by the first century B.C.E. had been distilled, reduced, and redacted to a Stoic-influenced text that is now lost (20). In other words, Heraclitus' words travel to us in two kinds of leaky vessels: the early ones fired in the kilns of Plato and Aristotle, who Gadamer claims are our "sole philosophical access to an interpretation of the Presocratics" (10), and the late ones from the ovens of Stoicism. Neither vessel gives us direct access to Heraclitus or his philosophy.

In addition to these difficulties that necessarily haunt any scholarship on Heraclitus, rhetorical scholarship must deal with a further challenge in this field of investigation. Given the hypotheses of Thomas Cole—that rhetoric as a self-conscious discipline only arose after the literate revolution of the fourth century B.C.E. (1991, x)—and of Schiappa—that the term *rhētorikē* was coined by Plato in the fourth century (1999, 109)—rhetorical scholars are rightly hesitant to consider the relevance of Heraclitus to the formation of rhetorical discipline. Nevertheless, Carol Poster was the first to argue for the historical and theoretical relevance of Heraclitus in the discipline of rhetoric. Poster responds to the warnings of Cole and Schiappa by contending that Heraclitus merits the attention of rhetorical as well as philosophical scholarship not only because Heraclitus had such a profound influence on the thought and work of thinkers who would later become the ancient rhetorical canon, but also because Heraclitus' surviving compositions embody "the rhetorical and hermeneutic consequences of an ontology of flux within a tradition of religio-philosophical rhetoric" (2006, 2).

Poster's analysis of the wordplay and observations about the critique of language in DK22b48 model a mode of inquiry that may be applied as a challenge to the longstanding debate over the meaning of *logos* in Heraclitus' opening lines.[3] In her analysis of the bow fragment, Poster shows how Heraclitus' wordplay is not a simple matter of compounding a term's common sense with an uncommon sense. Rather, it is a subtle doubleness that elucidates the tension and strife in the material world through revealing the tension and strife hidden within a single term. Heraclitus' discourse aims to draw conscious attention, and therefore understanding, to this phenomenon not only as it manifests in the material world, but also as it manifests in language itself.

Through this analysis Poster observes that, according to Heraclitus, "one can learn something about the nature of things by examining the nonliteral senses of their names" (Poster 2006, 15)—in other words, one can learn about the material world by studying the hidden, unapparent depths of meaning that might be enclosed within a single *logos.* Furthermore, as Poster's analysis both enacts and describes, this examination is accomplished when one dwells in and tarries with the apparent meanings until unapparent meanings disclose themselves. These hidden, unapparent meanings are both a highly complicated form of wordplay—the signature Heraclitean wit—but they are also much more than a literary device. One learns about the hidden, paradoxical nature of the world through an analysis of language because language itself is "part of a radical instability of the world" (Poster 2006, 16).[4] Language in this case is not above or outside of the volatile flux of *phusis*—language, *logos,* is inextricable from and implicated in the very matter it describes.

Following Poster's recommendation that the first fragment should be interpreted "in light of less difficult material" (2006, 5), a similar analysis of the wordplay enclosed in the opening lines of Heraclitus' book can be applied in order to critique the metaphysical interpretations of *logos* in DK22b1.[5] In contrast to the method of seeking within a term the hidden meanings that inhere within that term itself (as Poster does in her analysis of DK22b48), the metaphysical views of the DK22b1 *logos* (*logos* as reason, divine mind, or eternal fire) seek hidden meanings through recourse to other terms in the Heraclitean fragments. This method of seeking a riddling rather than a denotative meaning for *logos* in DK22b1 leads away from the metaphysical view of *logos.*[6] Scholars who ascribe to the metaphysical *logos* (with exceptions, which I discuss) presume a definitional consistency between the "*logos* fragments" (DK22b1, 2, 45, 50, 72, and 115) and the "*nomos* fragments" (DK22b2 and 114) when the relationship between these fragments should be understood as analogical rather than identical. By constructing external (through reference to other terms) rather than internal (through reference to other senses of the single term) double-meanings for *logos,* these definitions lack altogether the clever, riddling wordplay and signature Heraclitean wit, making them inconsistent with the standard form of the Heraclitean paradoxes. This leads to a concept of *logos* that is exceptional to and not implicated in the radical flux of *phusis.*

The *Logos* Paradox

The analysis of the first *logos* fragment begins with Aristotle, the earliest writer to have recorded the opening lines of Heraclitus' book on nature, but whose commentary on Heraclitus has been too hastily dismissed by modern scholarship.[7] Aristotle's interest in the first fragment is motivated quite innocuously by the grammatical puzzle it affords and not by the religious or philosophical import of *logos*.[8] He uses it to exemplify the difficulty entailed by the double-modification accomplished by "always" [ἀεὶ]. Aristotle wrote: "To punctuate the writings of Heraclitus is a difficult task because it is unclear what goes with what follows or with what precedes. For example, in the beginning of his treatise he said, [τού δὲ λόγου τούδ ἐόντας ἀεὶ ἀξύνετοι γίγονται ἄνθρωποι] 'Of the *logos* that exists always ignorant are men.' It is unclear whether always goes with what proceeds [*sic*][or with what follows]" (*Rhet.* 1407b; Kennedy 1991, 117; Kahn, 28). In other words, it is unclear whether the "always" should modify "ignorant" ("Of the *logos* that exists, always ignorant are men") or whether it should modify "exists" ("Of the *logos* that exists always, ignorant are men"). Aristotle does not indicate what significance *logos* in the opening lines may have had; and yet, if we investigate its status *as* a puzzle, two observations strike us.

First, Aristotle's analysis of the modification of ἀεὶ (always) is made possible in the first place by the viability of more than one meaning of *logos*. The syntactic ambiguity—the possibility that the term could modify "is," "ignorant," or both—arises for Aristotle from this more fundamental semantic ambiguity that a *logos* that exists and a *logos* that exists always are equally possible. If one or the other of the two meanings of *logos* were illegitimate, then no puzzle could ensue regarding the proper modification of ἀεὶ or the punctuation of the sentence. Both a *logos* that is particular to Heraclitus' discourse, which hearers *always misunderstand*, and a *logos* that *exists always*, which particular hearers misunderstand when they encounter it, are equally viable interpretations for Aristotle. Aristotle's explanation of the grammatical ambiguity tacitly indicates that he, like contemporary readers, could read the *logos* of Heraclitus' opening lines in either of these two senses—as doublespeak, as it were. Second, however, and unlike most modern-day readers of Heraclitus,[9] Aristotle leaves this double *logos* alone and does not attempt to compress its meaning. If he were to resolve the double-meaning into a singular meaning, it would lose its value as an example of a squinting modifier for Aristotle.

Double, difficult meanings are a common feature of Heraclitus' observations about the nature of the material universe: "The straight and the crooked path of the fuller's comb is one and the same" (DK22b59; Burnet 1892, 137); "The path up and down is one and the same" (DK22b60; Barnes 1987, 103); "The sea is the purest and the impurest water" (DK22b61; Kahn 61); "Immortals are mortal, mortals immortal, living the other's death, dying the other's life" (DK22b62; Kahn 71).[10] These and other fragments illustrate the well-known Heraclitean insistence on the paradoxical harmony of opposites and the ubiquity of material flux, transformation, and change. Where Aristotle refers to Heraclitus' riddles, he leaves them unsettled in a way that is similar to his use of the above grammatical example.[11] By contrast, he explicitly challenges what he considers to be misreadings by Heraclitus' professed followers (*Met.* 1010a) who imagine (*Met.* 1005b) that Heraclitus offers in these paradoxes general principles that are formally true in all circumstances, such as the idea that all things are true (*Met.* 1012a), that no true statement can ever be made (*Met.* 1062a), or the principle that the same thing both is and is not (*Met.* 1005b). By explicitly claiming that these general, unambiguous, or, as Aristotle puts it, "one-sided and sweeping statements" (*Met.* 1012a; Barnes 1984, 1598) that are not bound to any discrete material expression are flawed understandings of Heraclitus' thought, Aristotle implies that readers misunderstand Heraclitus' *logos* insofar as they generalize the paradoxes and create out of them noncontradictory, non-paradoxical principles.[12] Aristotle implies that readers routinely mistook his *logos* about material paradoxes for a non-paradoxical principle that was somehow separate and distinct from the matter it described.

Like Aristotle, Heraclitean scholars of the last hundred years have acknowledged the grammatical ambiguity of the first fragment. Although a minority of scholars deny any significant doubleness to the term,[13] most agree that the "syntactic ambiguities by which [*logos*] is surrounded" (Kahn 97) indicate a secondary, nonobvious meaning of *logos*. Unlike Aristotle, however, contemporary scholars have tended to disambiguate the modification of ἀεὶ through recourse to other Heraclitean fragments in an attempt to construct this definition of the secondary, nonobvious *logos*. By attempting to disambiguate the *logos* that *always is* (ἀεὶ ἐόντας), most interpreters are led inexorably away from matter and toward a metaphysical sense of *logos* (that is, the so-called "the Doctrine of the Logos") as a divine law or cosmic principle, defying our common understanding that Heraclitus' thought could not have extricated itself from matter.

Despite the brevity of Aristotle's analysis of Heraclitus' opening lines, the above observations indicate a dissonance between the former and the bulk of modern interpretations of Heraclitean *logos*. If we were to allow Aristotle's interpretation to guide our own, we are led to three preliminary observations. One, we recognize that Aristotle's brief example indicates that there is (at the very least) a double-meaning for the term, and that double-meaning is hidden, unapparent, complex, and paradoxical. Two, paradoxes do not ask to be resolved; to do so would disable the paradox *qua* paradox. Three, the proper reading and interpretation of *logos*, then, is not to disambiguate, simplify, and constrict its meaning. Rather, since *logos* is a paradox, our task is quite the opposite—to plumb the hidden depths of potential meanings and expand as much as possible the riddling potentialities of *logos*.

Poster's analysis is a model of this expansive interpretation. As demonstrated in her analysis of DK22b48, the immediately apparent meaning for *toxon* is *bow,* but upon further investigation of the language itself, we encounter *bios*—the synonym for *bow* and homonym for *life.* The bow itself, as a physical object, functions harmoniously through the tension of opposite forces—between the limbs and the string, the nocking point and the arrow rest. But there is also a conceptual tension in the physical object, given that the bow assures the life of the hunter only through the death of the prey. The bow, along with the river, the lyre, fire, war, and many other examples, illustrates the general principle that for Heraclitus "what differs agrees with itself. It is an attunement of opposite tension" (DK22b51; Barnes 1987, 102).[14] Thus the tension of opposites that inheres in the very architecture of the physical bow also inheres in the word itself. As Poster explains, we discover this unapparent doubleness through pondering the terms themselves. This linguistic self-consciousness is, Poster claims, the heart of Heraclitus' critique of the epic tradition. Similarly, to inaugurate a consideration of the potential *logoi* that lay beneath the surface of *logos* in DK22b1, I follow a similar method. I begin by considering first the simplest, most immediate sense of *logos,* whereby the claim in the opening line is simply and unambiguously human discourse or speech.

The most obvious, primary meaning of Heraclitus' *logos* is discourse or speech. The term's appearance at the beginning of a book was a standard practice within contemporaneous proems, of which Heraclitus' opening lines would have been a species. As Kahn noted, "we know that when Heraclitus begins his proem with a reference to his own *logos* he is following a literary tradition well established among early prose authors" (97). Moreover, we know from Aristotle that such proems followed a predictable sequence of standard content: they (1) appeal directly to the audience, asking them (2) to listen to the discourse in order (3) to dispel false beliefs and misunderstandings for which (4) their true discourse was supposed to serve as a remedy (*Rhet.* 1415a).[15] It is obvious from the first fragment that Heraclitus' opening lines are true to proem form—he begins by assuring his audience of the reliability and correctness of his *logos* and contrasts it to the ignorance of those who hear it and do not understand it, who behave as though asleep. The longer record of the beginning of Heraclitus' book, found in Sextus Empiricus' *Against the Mathematicians* (7.132; Bury, 72), indicates even more clearly to what extent the opening lines conform to proem conventions. The longer fragment is as follows:

> τοῦ δὲ λόγου τοῦδ' ἐόντος ἀεὶ ἀξύνετοι γίγνονται ἄνθρωποι, καὶ πρόσθεν ἢ ἀκοῦσαι, καὶ ἀκούσαντες τὸ πρῶτον. γινομένων γὰρ πάντων] κατὰ τὸν λόγον τόνδε ἄπειροισιν ἐοίκασι πειρώμενοι καὶ ἐπέων καὶ ἔργων τοιούτων ὁκοίων ἐγω διηγεῦμαι, κατὰ φύσιν διαιρέων ἕκαστον καὶ φράζων ὅκως ἔχει. τοὺς δὲ ἄλλους ἀνθρώπους λανθάνει ὁκόσα ἐγερθέντες ποιοῦσιν, ὅκωσπερ ὁκόσα εὕδοντες ἐπιλανθάνονται.

> Though this *logos* is always uncomprehending are men, both before they have heard it and when they have heard it for the first time. For although all things happen according to this *logos,* men are like people of no experience, even when they experience such words and deeds as I explain, when I distinguish each thing according to its nature and declare how it is; but the rest of men fail to notice what they do after they wake up just as they forget what they do when they are asleep. (DK22b1; Kirk 1962, 33).[16]

In this way, the common proem themes of speech, listening, and hearing are the most obvious indicators that Heraclitus is at the very least drawing the most basic understanding of *logos* as speech.

Beyond the obvious significance of this primary meaning of *logos,* however, lies profound interpretive flux. While most contemporary authors opened their discourse with a self-reflexive commentary on the discourse itself, none of them did so with such riddling ambiguity and doubleness of meaning. Before returning to the question of what unapparent meanings may lie hidden beneath the apparent meaning of *logos* as speech or discourse, we will first consider the dominant view in contemporary scholarship of Heraclitus' double-meaning. Because of the hermeneutical vulnerability of texts that rely too heavily on anachronistic interpretations of Heraclitus in order to develop a metaphysical sense of *logos* as reason or divine mind,[17] we will deal primarily with the more influential approach that seeks a broader definition for *logos* through reference to other Heraclitean fragments, and consequently defines the *logos* of DK22b1 as a divine law or cosmic principle that, in some cases, takes the material form of fire.

*Logos—Nomos—*Fire: The Interpretations

In Aristotle's references to Heraclitus' paradoxes there is a set of suspended interpretations that, in their suspension, deepen or develop more complicated understandings, which, as Poster's analysis demonstrates, are ultimately produced through a more expansive appreciation of Heraclitus' use of wordplay and wit to add complexity to the apparent meaning of words. The bulk of contemporary Heraclitean scholarship stands in contrast, seeking to decode and demystify the riddling *logos.* One of the best developments of a contemporary view of Heraclitus' secondary meaning in the first fragment is provided by Charles Kahn, who wrote: "For Heraclitus, at least, the thing which made things behave as they did was some kind of κόσμοι or order, an aspect of the Logos or formula which underlay the working of the sum of things. . . . Yet it was not, one may suppose, from the examination of the constitution of individual things that Heraclitus arrived at the idea of a common formula of behavior: rather an *a priori* demand for an underlying unity in the world, together with a consideration of the regularity of large-scale natural changes, led him to 'distinguish each thing according to its constitution', and to find the universal formula operating in the behavior of even the smallest objects" (43).

According to Kahn and most other proponents of this view, as a "universal formula," the larger *logos* dictates the behavior of things that live, move, and have their being in the material world, but it is not an element in that material world. It is a law that manifests in and through materiality, but it is not materiality itself. Likewise, it may be illuminated through Heraclitus' speech, but it is not speech as such.

In order to establish this connection between *logos* of the first fragment and a universal formula, measure, principle, or law, scholars routinely apply a consonance between the *logos* fragments and the *nomos* fragments. A justification for this consonance may be found in the lexical coherence between DK22b114 and DK22b2, which share the term *xunos* (common). In the former case (DK22b114), it occurs in an analogical discussion of both speech and laws: ξὺν νόῳ λέγοντας ἰσχυρίζεσθαι χρὴ τῷ ξυνῷ πάντων, ὅκωσπερ νόμῳ πόλις καὶ πολὺ ἰσχυροτέρω· τρέφονται γὰρ πάντες οἱ ἀνθρώπειοι νόμοι ὑπὸ ἑνὸς τοῦ θείου. "Those who speak [*legontas*] with sense are made strong by what is common [*xunon*] to all in the same way as a city [is made strong by] its law, and with much greater strength, for all the laws of men are fortified by one law, the divine law" (Kirk 1962, 48).[18] In the latter case (DK22b2), however, *xunos* (common) modifies or describes *logos:* "Therefore we are bound to follow the common [*koinos*]. But although the *logos* is common [*xunon*] the many live as if they had a private understanding" (Kirk 1962, 57).[19] On the basis of this terminological similarity, many scholars read the "divine law" of DK22b114 as though it defines *logos* and therefore decodes the *logos* fragments as a whole. This moves Kirk, Raven, and Schofield, for example, to conclude: "Human laws are nourished by the divine universal law; they accord with the *Logos,* the formulaic constituent of the cosmos" (212). Similarly, Barnes concludes that "Everything happens in accordance with Heraclitus' account: the account is 'common to everything' (B 114 = 23 M; cf. B 80 = 28 M); and it is analogous to, or identical with, the single divine law which 'nourishes' all human laws (B 114)" (1982, 48). Kahn concurs: "the characteristic achievement of Heraclitus lies in articulating a view within which the opposites can be seen together as a unity. . . . Men may live as if they had a private world of thinking and planning, but the *logos* of the world order, like the law of the city, is common to all (III, D. 2 with XXX, D. 114)" (14). Guthrie agrees that Heraclitus' *logos* is "responsible for the government of the whole world (1962, 432). And Thomas Robinson describes the *nomos* 114 as a law of nature that "applies to all people and all things, and does so at all times (see fragment 1)" (156).[20]

This interpretation, however, is problematic because it flattens very important differences between the contexts for these terms. Even though *logos* appears in DK22b2 and DK22b114, it is used in two very different senses, ultimately suggesting that *nomos* does not define the content of *logos* but relates to it by analogy. In DK22b2, Heraclitus suggests that *logos* itself is common—a definition, it may be noted, that does not necessarily refer to anything other than the most basic concept of speech, which must be common among interlocutors for it to function as speech. In DK22b114, however, Heraclitus does not suggest that the *nomos* is common to all, or that *logos* is a kind of *nomos.* Rather, he suggests that those who speak are strengthened by what is common *in the same way that the polis* is strengthened by its laws. The term Heraclitus uses here to construct this comparison (ὅκωσπερ, how, just as, in the same way as) is a conjunction clearly denoting an analogical comparison between two things. In this case, the *polis* and its laws supply a *phoros* for the theme of *logos* and its commonality. By collapsing the distance between *phoros* and theme in this analogy, these authors transform the statement that "a city must rely on its law [which is] strengthened by one law, the divine law" (DK22b114) from an analogy to an example or illustration of *logos* at work.[21] As an analogy, its purpose is to emphasize the necessary reliance of *logos* or speech on that which is common to all. As an example, however, it no longer emphasizes the reliance of one on the other, but defines *logos* in terms of *nomos.*

The analogy in B 114 takes the following form: The *logos* (A) is to the common (B) as the city (C) is to its laws (D); A is to B as C is to D. The relationship between terms of the analogy (A and B, C and D) is established by the similar way in which the latter strengthens the former (A is strengthened by B just as C is strengthened by D). But in the dominant interpretation of contemporary scholarship, this relation of reliance is obscured. These interpretations suggest that laws "accord with the *logos*" (Kirk, Raven, and Schofield, 212; Barnes 1982, 48) and that the *logos* is analogous *or identical* with *nomos* (Barnes 1982, 48), although the analogy links *logos* not to the law but to the city. These interpretations manifestly supplant the relationship of analogy with a relationship of identity.[22] More careful attention to the structure of the analogy, however, demonstrates that the *polis,* not the law, is the analogue for *logos;* the equation between *logos* and *nomos* is, consequently, ruptured. In other words, *logos* may rely on that which is common or "universal," but it is not identical to that which is common, universal, or divine, no more than the city is identical to its laws. For this reason, the *logos* of the first fragment cannot be defined through its identity with the divine law of DK22b114.

This interpretation which construes *logos* as a "divine law" invokes an implicit sense that the unapparent meaning of *logos* in the first fragment is a distinctly metaphysical, nonmaterial concept when, it is widely acknowledged by contemporary scholarship, in the early fifth century, this separation of material and nonmaterial beings or of a material content from its nonmaterial form was not yet theorized.[23] Again, Aristotle's citations reinforce the understanding that Heraclitus' thought was in fact material. His uncritical reception of Heraclitus' paradoxical descriptions of the material world accords with Aristotle's general understanding of Heraclitus as a material philosopher. In the *Metaphysics,* Aristotle groups Heraclitus with those "first philosophers" who "thought the principles which were of the nature of matter were the only principles of all things; that of which all things that are consist, and from which they first come to be, and into which they are finally resolved" (*Met.* 983b6; Barnes 1984, 1555–56).[24] Here Aristotle not only groups Heraclitus with the material philosophers, he also suggests that the early philosophers prior to Socrates never attained any notion of a cause that was nonmaterial.[25]

One way of handling this problem is found in a subset of the *logos*-as-*nomos* hypothesis advanced by Kirk and Guthrie, according to whom the *logos* of Heraclitus is a universal law, principle, or measure that is itself material. Because Heraclitus' thought would have been bound to matter, and the doxographers contended that Heraclitus' first material principle was fire, Guthrie concludes, "It cannot be wrong to identify it with the Logos, and agree with the Stoics and Hippolytus when they say that the fire of Heraclitus is 'rational' and, responsible for the government of the whole world" (1962, 432)—in other words, that *logos* is *nomos,* and that the *nomos* is made of fire. And Kirk concludes similarly, "This Logos, in its material aspect, must be a kind of fire" (1954, 248). This view is unsatisfactory for the simple reason that, insofar as this view approaches a material concept of *logos,* it does so without extricating itself from the *logos*-as-*nomos* hypothesis, which relies on a problematic equation of the *logos* and *nomos* fragments. Moreover, the material explanation of *logos*-as-fire is flawed in two additional ways. One, as Hoffman suggests, no fragments exist in which Heraclitus equates *logos* with fire (2006, 10). Two, the equation of logos with fire is problematically reminiscent of the divine fire of Stoic doxography (Guthrie 1962, 432).[26]

Another problem ensues when *logos* is defined in terms of either *nomos* or fire. These interpretations also inexorably draw *logos* away from its primary meaning as speech, despite the fact that speech and discourse figure so prominently as a vital theme in Heraclitus' book. Consequently, as a double-meaning for *logos,* both *nomos* and fire fail to provide us with a rich paradox or riddle.

The likelihood that verbal expression or speech—the foundation of *logos*—was essential to the second meaning of *logos* in DK22b1 is made apparent when we consider that no explicit attention to these secondary meanings for *logos* that deviate from its most basic sense emerged until the Stoics took up Heraclitus as their prophet and prototype. Despite Aristotle's indication of the squinting modifier in DK22b1, neither he nor Plato calls explicit attention to Heraclitus' use of the term *logos.*[27] Indeed, since none of the early commentators found it necessary to deliberate over the seemingly exotic use of the term, it seems likely that they took any double-meaning to be common, and therefore rooted in verbal expression.[28]

The importance of discourse and speech for Heraclitus' work as a whole is even more apparent when his text is compared to contemporaneous and earlier texts. In the fragments of Xenophanes, Parmenides, Anaxagoras, and Empedocles, the standard *topoi* of proems (speaking, hearing, listening, and understanding) appear in a relatively small number of fragments. Despite significant variations in length, proem *topoi* appear in an average of three to four fragments, a reasonable length for introductory remarks.[29] Heraclitus, on the other hand, employs standard proem *topoi* in *over thirty* fragments—roughly one-quarter of the extant fragments as a whole. About twenty-seven fragments refer to misunderstandings or foolishness that must be remedied, and roughly five appeal to the hearer and reference speaking or hearing.[30] This seems to indicate not that Heraclitus' proem was inordinately long, but that for Heraclitus, unlike other thinkers who used similar compositional methods during the same and preceding century, the meta-discourse about his own composition and its reception by hearers does not occur as an isolated remark that is separate and distinct from the more central *prothesis* of the discourse on nature. The uncommon prevalence of these *topoi* throughout the collected fragments as a whole seems to indicate that the first fragment is a standard *proem,* and at the same time, that discourse itself is a recurrent theme within Heraclitus' discourse on the natural world.[31] *Logos*-as-*nomos* hides this emphasis.

By overlaying secondary meanings extrinsic to the primary meaning of *logos* as speech, the external *logos*-as-*nomos* interpretation also stylistically alienates the wordplay in the first fragment from that which marks the rest of Heraclitus' book. The semantic estrangement of *logos* from *nomos* (on the one hand, speech or verbal expression, and on the other hand, law or principle) entails that, as a double-meaning, it lacks the signature wit and riddling wordplay of other Heraclitean double-meanings. This style can be seen more clearly in other fragments that were of less interest to the Stoic and Christian doxographical traditions, where Heraclitus' wordplay proceeds not through adding second meanings that are unrelated to the primary ones, but by finding a hidden second meaning in and through the primary meaning. The contemporary interpretation that renders the double-meaning of *logos* as cosmic or universal *nomos* grows shallow when considered alongside the wordplay of DK22b48—in the latter case, Heraclitus not only deploys a double-meaning, but he does so in the form of a riddle that hides both harmony and opposition.

The latter point indicates a possibility that, with few exceptions, is incompletely theorized in Heraclitean scholarship. In Heraclitus' discussion of *logos,* including his discussion of speech and discourse, hearing and listening, he considered *logos* to be part and parcel of the selfsame material universe that the greater part of his inquiry was devoted to investigating.[32] *Logos* is not a word or principle that exists above or beneath matter as a cosmic law or universal measure, but it is concomitant with the matter itself, and as such, is marked by the same strife, tensions, and flux that mark the river, the sea, the bow, and the lyre. Moreover, to uncover the tension of opposites that inhere within Heraclitean *logos* is to enter into the riddle and play that is constructed within the paradox of the first fragment. While the *nomos* interpretation is partially supported by the text, it is troubling in its anachronism and nonmateriality. Although the fire interpretation is material, it lacks wit and wordplay and is not supported by the text. In short, we have yet to define a *logos* that does not either flatten Heraclitus' paradoxical wordplay and doubleness of meaning or anachronistically apply nonmaterial senses of the term. Most interpretations do both.

The *Logos* of Laying and Gathering

My critique offers a set of criteria to guide our inquiry into the *logos* of the first fragment, a concept that antedates the development of *logos* as rhetorical *technē.* These criteria are as follows. One, any attempt to explore the riddling, paradoxical *logos* of the first fragment should proceed through its primary and obvious meaning as speech or discourse. Two, meanings that exceed this basic sense ought to constitute an unapparent, riddling wordplay, in keeping with the style of other Heraclitean fragments that contain unapparent paradoxes, such as DK22b48. Three, the layers of meaning for *logos* should be understood as participating in the paradoxical tension and strife that mark the rest of the material universe. I propose an alternate view of Heraclitus' double-meaning for *logos* that conforms to these criteria and suggests how this meaning may be relevant to our understanding of the development of rhetorical *logos.*

Burnet was correct when over a century ago he claimed that the term referred to nothing more than "speech,"[33] but he was wrong insofar as he assumed that speech meant the same thing to an early Greek audience that it means to us today. As Heidegger observes, in reading Heraclitus, "Most question-worthy is what is most self-evident, namely, our presupposition that whatever Heraclitus says ought to become immediately obvious to our contemporary everyday understanding" (1984, 59–60). To solve the riddle of the *logos,* we must therefore set aside our modern supposition that the activity of speaking, of verbal expression, is the utterance of sounds, signifying meaning, established by use. Our task is to imagine verbal expression as a concept deeply rooted in the raw experience of human materiality as it would have been for the early Greeks, and to identify the doubleness that inheres in that raw experience.

According to the verbal root of *logos,* the term contains double, even contradictory meanings, and these meanings are not only the primary senses of the term, but, as Martin Heidegger suggests, these contradictory meanings would have resonated in the ear of every early Greek listener, whether they were conscious of the resonance or not. The verbal noun *logos* is inextricable from its root verb *legein,* which, Heidegger claims, has two more primary definitions hiding behind its meaning as to say or to speak—these are (1) to lay and (2) to gather. A clear example of this layered meaning of *legein* may be found toward the end of the introduction to the *Rhetoric.* This example is merely a transitional remark, segueing Aristotle's opening observations about rhetoric's relation to dialectic with his closer discussion of *pistis.* This example is offered not to establish a relation between Heraclitus' *logos* and Aristotelian rhetorical *logos,* but because, even in translation, this example illuminates the equal viability of *logos* as speech, laying, and gathering to contemporary readers.

At the end of the first chapter of *Rhetoric* (1355b), Aristotle wrote, ἤδη τῆς μεθόδου πειρώμεθα λέγειν, which could be translated as (1) Let us speak of the method itself; (2) Let us lay out the method itself; (3) Let us gather/take up the method itself. In this example, all three translations are equally viable, and the differences between them make little difference in how the phrase is understood. This example illustrates in translation how all three meanings may be present in the same term in a way that approximates the simultaneity of meanings for the Greek ear. It is this double, oppositional meaning of laying and gathering, a meaning always at play in the use of the term λόγος, that should define our understanding of the wordplay in Heraclitus' opening line.

In his essay on the *logos* of DK22b50, "Listening not to me but to the *logos* it is wise to agree that all things are one" (Kirk 1962, 65), Heidegger explains how laying down and gathering up, which seem to be opposite activities, are in fact inverse but nevertheless wedded gestures, and how these harmoniously opposed activities constitute the essence of human speech.[34] He describes how the term was used in communal activities where gathering up, choosing, and picking were also at one and the same time a laying out, storing, and sheltering:

> The gleaning at harvest time gathers fruit from the soil. The gathering of the vintage involves picking grapes from the vine. Picking and gleaning are followed by the bringing together of the fruit .... But gathering is more than mere amassing. To gathering belongs a collecting which brings under shelter.... If we are blind to everything but the sequence of steps, then the collecting follows the picking and gleaning, the bringing under shelter follows the collecting, until finally everything is accommodated in bins and storage rooms. This gives rise to the illusion that preservation and safekeeping have nothing to do with gathering. Yet what would become of a vintage [*eine Lese*] which has not been gathered with an eye to the fundamental matter of its being sheltered? The sheltering [*Bergen*] comes first in the essential formation of the vintage. (1984, 61)

In this description of the harvest, which is much more than an illustration since it was the literal context for ancient uses of the term in question, Heidegger indicates that the vintage harvested becomes precisely what it is, not by any one discrete function in the sequence of activities, nor by its essence as ripe fruit, ready for harvest. Rather, he suggests, the collective and not the individual tasks of choosing, picking, gathering, laying, and sheltering are interpenetrating aspects of the same activity, defined collectively as *logos,* or the laying that gathers/the gathering that lays. These layered meanings of *legein,* which came to also mean speech, do not simply exist alongside one another in the way that *logos* as speech and *logos* as universal *nomos* might. "Rather," Heidegger wrote, "gathering is already included in laying. Every gathering is already a laying. Every laying is of itself gathering" (62) and, we infer, every speech is simultaneously also a laying and a gathering.

Legein was used to indicate this process of picking out, gathering together, laying down in contexts that concerned the harvest, the building of walls, marshaling of troops and, as we know, speaking. Heidegger indicates that, through these common uses of the term *legein*, speech is linked to these other activities because, "like the letting-lie-before that gathers, saying receives its essential form from the unconcealment of that which lies together before us" (64). In this way, the *legein* of Heraclitus is always a double, oppositional gesture that is itself redoubled by further oppositional gestures—it gathers and lays, and likewise, discloses what is concealed, and conceals what is disclosed. As Heidegger wrote: "disclosure is [by definition] ἀλήθεια[35] . . . Λέγειν lets ἀλήθεια, unconcealed as such, lie before us (cf. B112). All disclosure releases what is present from concealment. Disclosure needs concealment. . . . Λόγος is *in itself and at the same time* a revealing and a concealing. . . . [It] lets lie together before us in one presencing things which are usually separated from, and opposed to, one another, such as day and night, winter and summer, peace and war, waking and sleeping, Dionysus and Hades" (71). Elsewhere, Heidegger insists that it is this sense of gathering that is foremost and primary in the uses of this term in the first fragment, outstripping even its sense as discourse or speech, since "genuine hearkening [to *logos*, to speech] has nothing to do with the ear and the glib tongue, but instead means obediently following what *logos* is: *the gatheredness of beings themselves*" (2000, 137).

In slightly simpler terms, *logos*, speech, selects and gathers from the world various things that, like the vintage not yet harvested, lie at distance and in separation or opposition from one another. As it gathers up and lays out these things—the bow, the lyre, the way up, the way down, the sea, the fuller's comb, fire, the river, war—*logos* brings them out of obscurity and into unity with each other, and in so doing, shows them that they might be seen. This showing, at the same time, conceals their obscurity, their dispersal, their distance, and as such, showing is also hiding. The hidden harmony and unity of opposites is not only the *prothesis* of Heraclitus' discourse; it is the function of discourse—*logos*—as such. Heidegger's exegesis of Heraclitus' *logos* suggests that, when we strip down speech to the "the primordial, essential determination of language" (1984, 64), we find that the tension of opposites present in the world is present also in the phenomenon of human speech. Listening, not to Heraclitus, but to his *logos*, to what takes shape in its very timbre and vibration of its utterance, we see what it gathers to and lays before our attention. In so doing, his *logos*, by definition, shows. But in laying words in this way and not in another, in gathering certain things and not others, *logos* obscures and hides those very things that are not gathered to and laid before our attention. In other words, *logos*, speech, unites the opposing physical forces of gathering up and laying out. In so doing, it shows what has been gathered up and laid out to its hearer so that it might be seen. But against this unity of the opposition between laying and gathering there is yet a further opposition, since what is shown necessarily hides what is not shown.

Heraclitus' *logos* in DK22b1 refers not only to speech, established through the convention in contemporaneous prose of referring to one's own discourse; it also refers to the function of *logos* that is always—*logos* as such always functions both a laying down and a gathering up. By following the Ionic prose conventions of self-reflexive proems, Heraclitus is employing the "the new scientific language" (Kahn, 97), which contrasts with epic poetry primarily in its "general tendency . . . toward directness and clarity of expression" (97). By invoking the double-meaning, however, of what *logos,* by definition, *always is,* Heraclitus draws attention to, calls into question, and subtly critiques the possibilities of the very prose conventions he employs. At the same time that he uses a prose convention that values clarity and directness—a proem that states unequivocally what the *logos* will be about—the discourse itself, at once both a laying and a gathering, conceals what is not apparent: the tension of opposites that inheres in the material world.

By turning a critical eye to this shared quality of world and word, Heraclitus, in effect, composes our first understanding of the rhetorical effects of language. Speech has the particular capacity to gather and to lay, and in so doing it shows, but it also hides. For those who are heedful to what *logos* both gathers and lays, both shows and hides, it will lead to wisdom. But those who are inattentive to the full range of the activity of *logos,* both to what discourse reveals and what it conceals, will be as ignorant as they were before the discourse gathered and laid it in the first place.

Directions

By this reading, Heraclitus is a thinker who explicitly pointed out the two-sidedness of *logos*—an early systematization of the double-function of *logos,* later more robustly theorized in rhetorical texts like Aristotle's. It is likely that in the opening remarks of his book Heraclitus was not only making the standard reference to the discourse that was to follow. Rather, through the doublespeak of his proem, he was subtly demonstrating that the same tension of opposites, a power of two opposing forces, that inheres in things also inheres in *logos* itself. The contribution to rhetorical theory Schiappa credits to Protagoras' *dissoi logoi,* in this case, has a more definite and explicit antecedent in the thought of Heraclitus than has been commonly recognized. The physical opposition within Heraclitus' *logos,* by this interpretation, is an explicit theorization of language that lays the template for Protagorean *dissoi logoi* and rhetorical two-sides. In this way, the *dissoi logoi* Schiappa identifies in Protagoras and which he suggests is the explicit (and non-paradoxical) precursor to the disciplinary truism that rhetoric is concerned with being able to argue opposite sides of a question, eventually codified in Aristotle's rhetorical theory,[36] is found to have an even older genealogy. In other words, the materially oppositional sensibilities that accompany the contextual range of uses for *logos* in Heraclitus are a precursor for the logically oppositional sensibilities later developed in Protagoras and fourth-century rhetorical theory. While this does not suggest evidence of an explicit rhetorical theory prior to the fourth century, non-explicitness does not preclude the presence of rhetorical theory in riddling, paradoxical form—in doublespeak, as it were.

Rhetoric and Royalty

Odysseus' Presentation of the Female Shades in Hades

Marina McCoy

The birth of rhetoric as a formal discipline is often associated with Plato, who may well have coined the term, as Schiappa has argued (1990). While the use of the term *rhētorikē* is widespread by the fourth century, not only by Plato but also by thinkers such as Alcidamas, there is no earlier extant use.[1] Schiappa argues that the use of the new term also implies a new self-understanding among the Greeks about the nature of rhetoric itself, displaying a clear shift from the mere use of persuasive speeches to the first ideas of meta-rhetoric. However, the nature of *rhētorikē* is disputed even in the earliest texts that use the word. For example, while Plato at times indicates that rhetoric is a systematic set of rules or principles in the *Phaedrus*, Alcidamas in "On Those Who Write Written Speeches" uses *rhētorikē* quite differently, to indicate the skillful use of flexible, extemporaneous speech to affect and influence one's audience (McCoy). Even once the term is introduced, its relation to other terms such as *philosophia* is by no means shared among all thinkers. Kennedy (1957) and Cole (1991) have also cautioned against the careless use of the term "rhetoric" in reference to Homer, also on the basis of a more strictly formal understanding of rhetoric as systematic.[2]

Still, while rhetoric as a formal system began with the advent of philosophical texts about the deliberate use of rhetoric, one finds the use of rhetorical techniques much earlier than Plato or Aristotle. In the *Odyssey*'s "catalogue of women," we see Odysseus use techniques that demonstrate a concern with persuasion in speech. While Homer himself did not formally systematize an art of rhetoric, we see in Odysseus' catalogue the use of strategies later conceptually described by writers reflecting on the nature of rhetoric. Three that are especially prominent in Odysseus' speech are creating a favorable view of himself in the eyes of his audience (*ethopoiēsis*); techniques that influence his audience's disposition (*diathesis*); and attention to *kairos*, using his capacity to attend to the "right moment" and even to shift the orientation of speech in accordance with changes in one's audience. While these concepts would not have been explicitly named until much later, Odysseus' practice anticipates concepts outlined in later discussions of rhetoric. As Rachel Knudson has recently argued, a wide variety of ancient sources from Plato to Philodemus to Cicero understand Homeric heroes to be practicing rhetoric or proto-rhetoric. For example, in Plato's *Phaedrus,* Socrates describes Nestor, Odysseus, and Palamedes as practicing *technai peri logon,* a term commonly used to denote the ideas in handbooks of rhetoric (*Phaedrus* 261b).[3]

In offering any discussion of the use of rhetoric by a speaker, we might distinguish three degrees to which theory forms a part of rhetorical practice. The most sophisticated sort would be rhetoricians who can both speak persuasively and also can offer an explicit account of the theory of rhetoric, as found in Aristotle's *Rhetoric.* They possess a *technē* of rhetoric and can offer a rational account or metatheory about that *technē.* At the other extreme would be speakers who simply have a "knack" for public speaking, through a kind of empirical or experiential knowledge, but who are incapable of giving any account of their practice, or speakers whose persuasive speech is understood to be inspired or a gift from the gods, or some kind of chance event.[4] However, we also find speakers who use rhetorical techniques, that is, who exhibit certain rational patterns of rhetoric that can be named and described, without also offering a meta-rhetorical theory about their own speeches. It is within this last category that I locate Odysseus' speeches to Arete and Alkinoos in the *Odyssey,* as a form of rhetoric that I term "proto-technical."

In some ways, this middle sort of use of rhetoric is easy to defend, since no one doubts that one can use a rhetorical technique without at the same time discussing it. But in another way such use is difficult to defend, since the evidence that a person is using a technique, without his ever referring to his own practice abstractly, must rely on indirect evidence. One kind of indirect evidence is a speaker's patterns of action—rather than an action that is a one-time occurrence—especially patterns of speech that are flexible and change in response to new situations. Where we see patterns of practice and adaptability to new circumstances, it is more likely that there is some kind of technical skill at work. Such skill need not be expressly articulated in a theory, however (not even privately in the mind of the speaker). My contention is that Odysseus in his speech to the Phaiakians is engaged in this in-between kind of rhetoric—one neither grounded in a fully developed metatheory nor practicing a mere empirical "knack," but one that shares certain characteristics with the possession of a *technē.* I name this kind of rhetorical knowledge "proto-technical," as it shares some features of a *technē* but without rising to the level of an art accompanied by *epistēmē* (scientific knowledge).[5]

Proto-*Technē:* Between *Empeiria* and *Epistēmē*

Many ancient philosophical accounts of *technē* insist that the person who practices one must also have an accompanying *epistēmē* (scientific knowledge). Socrates in the *Gorgias* distinguishes a *technē* from a mere *empeiria* insofar as the person with the *technē* must be able to give an account of the nature of its subject matter (*Gorgias* 465a). Similarly, Aristotle contrasts the person who has a masterful *technē* or *epistēmē* from the person who has mere experience; the true craftsman can give an account of causes, such as *why* a certain remedy lowers the fever, and not only *that* a remedy lowers fever (*Metaphysics* 981a–b).

If all techniques had to be grounded in a theoretical *epistēmē,* then it would seem that no ancient author who lacks a theoretical account of rhetoric could be practicing rhetoric strictly speaking. However, there is a kind of technical proficiency that is not verbally expressed in theories about the techniques in question, but that nonetheless shows a kind of expertise. In his speech to the Phaiakians, Odysseus' use of rhetoric rises above that of a mere "knack" or "inspiration," insofar as Odysseus uses rhetorical strategies that follow rational, nameable patterns; demonstrate some understanding of cause and effect; and are flexible in response to new situations (for example, knowing that changing his speech in a certain way for a new audience should produce a certain kind of outcome). However, he does not offer an account of the practice that he undertakes. His rhetorical knowledge shares some characteristics of *empeiria* and some of *technē.*

We know that such kinds of "proto-technical" knowledge exist in other domains of expertise. For example, a performing musician might know how to play C, G, and A chords and that they sound harmonious, but may not know that the movement from G to C is a V→I dominant tonic progression. In this case, the musician does possess technical knowledge of the chords, and likely has learned their structure and how to play them as a result of being taught by another expert musician. However, he or she may lack the higher theoretical account of chord progressions. Or a person might know how to fix a problem with a bicycle without having the expertise to write a manual on bicycle repair. One might not know the names for the tools, or for the method used to fix it and might not even be very good at explaining it to others verbally. For this reason, he or she lacks an explicit theoretical account of the practice. However, if one's knowledge of fixing the bicycle is not only based on understanding that arises from experience, but also shows some understanding of cause and effect and flexibility in new situations, then that knowledge moves beyond *empeiria* and shares at least *some* characteristics of a *technē.* Yet it is not yet the sort of more extensive ability to speak about bicycle repair that would be required to write a manual, which would require more extensive theoretical knowledge.

In other words, there exists a kind of technical knowledge that is not always accompanied by the capacity to verbalize one's knowledge in precise terms but that exceeds mere empirical knowledge that "this works." Many technically proficient musicians lack such a capacity to give a full verbal account of what they are doing, but may still be distinguished from beginning musicians who lack technical skill, or a self-taught musician who picks up a guitar and finds that he or she has a "knack" for playing but cannot read music or name a chord.

Experiential knowledge can progress from mere knowledge of particulars into knowledge of universals but not yet be articulated as such. Odysseus' practice indicates the possession of something more than mere empirical knowledge, moving toward *technē.*

Indeed, Aristotle's own theory would seem to be open to the notion of a transitional phase of knowledge in between a person who has merely empirical knowledge and one who can make universal, theoretical judgments. In the *Metaphysics,* he emphasizes that the arts come about as the result of extensive experiences and memories of those experiences (980b28–981a7). Noticing how fever responds to various remedies in Callias, Socrates, and other individual cases is part of the evidence that leads to universal judgments of how fever may be reduced in general, and what the underlying cause of fever is. Aristotle's idea that universals arise from the experience of many particular experiences suggests that those who are developing an art, such as medicine, will go through a time in which they are not yet in possession of a fully developed *technē,* but are on the way to having one. Incidentally, Aristotle makes no suggestion that the possession of a theory is better for the sake of *practice* in any particular case; a person who can reduce Callias' fever is just as helpful to Callias as one who knows the causes and remedies for fevers more generally (*Met.* 981a13–24). A person with purely theoretical knowledge but no experience often fails to cure. However, those with knowledge of the causes are wiser and can teach.

In the *Sophistical Refutations,* too, Aristotle indicates that, in the development of rhetoric as an art, his contemporaries are "the heirs (so to speak) of a long succession of men who have advanced them bit by bit, and so have developed them to their present form" (183b29–36, 185a9–185b2; Barnes 1984, 314), in contrast to arguments by syllogism, whose development is entirely recent and based on experimental researches. Aristotle noted that such programs are still not complete, again suggesting that an art can be incomplete or in progress. There is even a kind of prudential knowing that is undemonstrated but that "sees" what is the case accurately, he noted in the *Nicomachean Ethics.* Intellect in matters of action concerns itself with particulars: "For these ultimate particulars are the principles [or starting points] of that for the sake of which one acts; the universals arise from the particulars. Of these, then, one must have a perception (*aisthesis*), and that perception is intellect (*nous*)" (*Nic. Eth.* VI.1143b4–6; Bartlett and Collins, 130). He goes on to add that such intellectual perception is developed in the course of a lifetime through experience: "As a result, one ought to pay attention to the undemonstrated assertions and opinions of experienced (*empeirōn*) and older people, or of the prudent (*phronimōn*), no less than to demonstrations, for they have an experienced eye (*ek tēs empeirias omma*), they see correctly" (*Nic. Eth.* VI.1143b11–14, Bartlett and Collins, 130). Aristotle said there is a kind of seeing what the right thing is to do that is not exhibited in discursive demonstrations but is genuinely wise. *Empeiria* develops an intellectual capacity to see correctly.

Rhetoric, too, is concerned with action, and knowing what to say in order to persuade seems to be a kind of knowing that either may be expressed in terms of precise universals (as in Aristotle's *Rhetoric*) or in a more developed experiential knowledge without explicit universals or demonstrations. Indeed, Aristotle opens his own *Rhetoric* by saying that previous works of rhetoric have focused too much on forensics to the exclusion of political oratory, and ignored the enthymeme, and so have not fully developed an art of rhetoric (I.1354a11–21, 1354b23–28). This does not mean, however, that no steps were taken in the development of such an art, or that everyone who practices rhetoric without such an art lacks knowledge altogether.

Odysseus is a speaker whose rhetorical practices strongly imply the existence of knowledge that is "on the way" to becoming a *technē* and already beyond a mere empirical experience of particulars, but not yet a fully developed art of rhetoric. Terms from Aristotle's *Rhetoric* can be used to describe some of the rhetorical techniques that Odysseus uses, but only with a caution that neither Homer nor Odysseus needs to have named or understood these techniques as universals, or if they formulated universals, these principles may not have been formulated in the precise way that Aristotle phrases them. Nonetheless, these terms are useful to show that Odysseus has some knowledge of technique that goes beyond familiarity with particulars and is "on the way" to becoming knowledge of universals.

Odysseus' capacity to apply the same kind of strategy across multiple instances, and even to two different audiences (Arete and Alkinoos) suggests knowledge that can apply across kinds of cases and can respond to novel situations. If a person is persuasive once, it may simply be a chance occurrence, or one that repeats something that one has seen before (like the non-doctor who knows how to lower a fever from watching a doctor do it). But Odysseus is far more skillful, and displays knowledge of how to influence his listener's disposition (*diathesis*) and to create a favorable view of his character in the eyes of his audience (*ethopoiēsis*) in multiple ways. He displays knowledge of how one can create mildness in the face of anger and suspicion, and to two different people with different (and sometimes opposed) sets of concerns. It is uncertain whether Odysseus would be able to verbalize what he is doing and the principles that he is following. However, a kind of proto-technical knowledge of rhetoric grounds Odysseus' speech to Arete in the catalogue of women and the second speech to Alkinoos that follows.

There are several textual reasons outside the descriptions of the shades that support the idea that Odysseus' description of the Hades episode is rhetorical and displays a self-awareness of some techniques of persuasion. First, we have an abundance of evidence elsewhere in the *Odyssey* that Odysseus is a crafty storyteller concerned with securing his own advantage: for example, he deliberately deceives Athena while she is still in disguise and unknown to him upon his arrival in Ithaka (XIII.256–86) and soon afterwards deceives

Eumaios at their first reunion with the cloak story (XIV.199–359). Second, the Hades story alone among his stories to the Phaiakians contains an interlude in which Odysseus breaks off his narrative and his audience speaks a while, thereby drawing our attention to their presence. There, Arete for the first time expresses support for Odysseus' petition, and the story continues only because Alkinoos insists that Odysseus go on (XI.363–74). Odysseus' audience and their concerns not only implicitly but also explicitly drive his narrative forward. In addition, the techniques that help Odysseus to change his audience's disposition toward him require some understanding between cause and effect—for example, that to praise persons' ancestors will make them feel more amiable toward the one who offers the praise, while speaking ill of another's family will make them feel less well disposed to the speaker. Odysseus' change in approach when he shifts to speaking to Alkinoos will later show that the origin of his ability to persuade is not chance, inspiration, or empirical "knack," since he displays his capacity to make his audience feel mild and well disposed toward him across different circumstances. We witness in Odysseus a person with rhetorical skill across different scenarios, with a flexibility that points back to some sort of technique that grounds his capacity to persuade.

Odysseus' Proto-Technē:
Ethopoiēsis, *Diathesis*, and *Kairos* in the Catalogue of the Shades

In the *Odyssey,* Odysseus reports his encounter in Hades with a number of female shades to the Phaiakians. The section appears to be a descriptive list of well-known women in mythology, along with a few elements of their stories; thus, the term "catalogue of women" is often used as its description. Few interpretations focus on Odyssean rhetoric in this section of the text, although commentaries on the connections between the catalogue form and oral poetry abound.[6] The catalogue, for example, can be understood as a device for composition and as a form that is particularly adaptable to the needs of the oral performer of epic according to the needs of the present audience.[7] My examination attends to the rhetorical practices of the character, Odysseus, and his use of what will later be named techniques of rhetoric. While Odysseus offers what appears only to be a description of the women in Hades, the manner in which he adjusts that description to the different concerns of Arete and Alkinoos shows a concern with persuading his audience.

There are a number of textual reasons to consider the rhetorical value of the catalogue of women in the *Odyssey.* Odysseus neither speaks with nor has any personal connection to the female shades. Moreover, while it would seem natural for Odysseus' conversation to begin with the male shades, his former companions, Odysseus speaks with the women first. In neither case does Odysseus ask to speak with the shades; Persephone sends both sets to him, but without explanation for why these women are sent. However, if we understand

Odysseus' aims in describing this episode to the Phaiakians to be rhetorical, then the inclusion of the passage makes more sense of his character's interest in describing them so extensively. Odysseus reports his encounters with the female shades in order to win the approval of Queen Arete and so to gain wealth and a safe conveyance home to Ithaka. He praises those mortals associated with Poseidon, to whom Arete is related, and also offers a picture of marital fidelity morally consonant with both his own past liaisons with goddesses and his desire for a swift return home to Penelope.

Odysseus relies upon three general identifiable principles of rhetoric in order to persuade his audience. First, he displays awareness that a speaker should know the characteristics of his audience and be responsive to its particular disposition (*diathesis*). Second, he seeks to present himself in such a way that the "self" that he constructs for Arete is harmonious with her concerns about him and about her own status in the kingdom (*ethopoiēsis*). Third, Odysseus displays attentiveness to *kairos* in his ability to shift his speech to the concerns of the king, Alkinoos, when he realizes that his attention to Arete has backfired. When King Alkinoos interrupts his speech, Odysseus shifts his course to cater to more masculine concerns, even reversing some of his previous praise of women. This shift in his approach with the advent of a new audience and situation reveals that Odysseus has the flexibility to apply the same kinds of techniques differently in novel situations. While a formalized system of rhetoric is lacking in Homer, we find in the character of Odysseus the use of techniques that later, more systematic accounts will name as central to the practice of good rhetoric.

Odysseus' care for *diathesis* is shown in his attention to praising women who are closely associated with Poseidon and in his reflections on their marital fidelity. The rationale for Odysseus' praise of Poseidon and his descendants is fairly clear. Both Alkinoos and Arete are descendants of the god, as Odysseus finds out from the disguised Athena just before entering the king's mansion (VII.54–77). Alkinoos is the son of Nausithoos, who is the son of Poseidon and Periboia. Arete is the daughter of Alkinoos' brother Rhexenor—that is, she is her husband's niece. To praise Poseidon's liaisons with mortals and their offspring, then, is also to praise Alkinoos and Arete. While Odysseus also reveals his enmity with Poseidon to the Phaiakians, his attribution of it to a conflict with a Cyclops is to his advantage, for the Phaiakians themselves were driven from their previous homeland as a result of conflicts with the Cyclops (VI.2–10). The praise of the descendants of Poseidon helps to offset further any hostility the Phaiakians might feel towards Odysseus as a result of his disfavor in the god's eyes. Later, Aristotle in his discussion of epideictic rhetoric will say, "we ought to speak about whatever is esteemed among the particular audience, whether Skythians, Lacdemonians, or philosophers, as actually existing there" (*Rhet.* 1367b30).[8] Here, Odysseus praises his audience's ancestors as noble in order to gain their favor.

Odysseus' presentation of the issue of fidelity is rhetorically more complex. Odysseus presents a picture of marital fidelity and infidelity in which an affair is base and terrible if with another human being, yet not only acceptable but praiseworthy if with a god. Here we see attention both to his audience's state (*diathesis*) and to the careful construction of his own character (*ethopoiesis*). Odysseus has good rhetorical reason to claim that affairs with the gods are different in kind from those with other human beings, and do not constitute a betrayal. On the one hand, he seeks to return home to his wife, Penelope, with the hopes that she has remained faithful to him. On the other hand, Odysseus was found on the seashore by Nausikaa, the maiden princess who encourages him to come to the castle with her, and his motives with her are in question. Odysseus is wearing some of the clothing that Nausikaa and her maids were washing after he found himself naked on the shore after the shipwreck. These adventures might seem to lead Alkinoos and Arete to question whether he acted temperately with Nausikaa. Odysseus needs to demonstrate to the king and queen that he has acted honorably with Nausikaa despite being dressed in clothes that she has provided, and to provide an explanation for his presence on the island with her. Further, he has just spent seven years engaged in an affair with Kalypso, and a number of months going with Kirke to her "surpassingly beautiful bed" (X.480; Lattimore 1967, 164).[9]

Odysseus needs to demonstrate that his main desire is to return home to wife and kingdom, in order to assure himself both a safe passage home and one appropriately endowed with wealth befitting his station. Through linking liaisons with the divine to the cultivation of noble family, while emphasizing the importance of fidelity in human marriage, Odysseus links his own narrative to a genealogical narrative about Arete's family. Here, Odysseus reconstructs his own character, shifting away from the possibility of being seen as an intemperate philanderer, to one whose own story resonates positively with those of the descendants of Poseidon standing before him. Aristotle argues that examples, including fables about the past, can function like witnesses, when the example serves the end of being like a logical proof (*Rhet.* 1394b13–18). Here Odysseus implies that, if his audience's ancestors were praiseworthy for their couplings with the gods, then his own relationships with Kirke and Kalypso are also not to be condemned. It is not necessary that Odysseus be capable of articulating the usefulness of this strategy in terms of a logical proof, as Aristotle does. However, his praise of his audience's ancestors in ways that resonate with his own story indicates some knowledge that such comparisons are effective in creating a positive disposition in one's audience.

Initially, Odysseus has reason to believe that Arete's approval is of greater importance than that of Alkinoos, or so he believes from what Nausikaa tells him. She advises him to pass by her father and instead to throw himself before her mother, if he wishes to return home again (VI.327–34). We see in Nausikaa's suggestion that decorum, or attention to what is fitting, *to prepon,* is best fulfilled by seeking her mother's approval. Nausikaa's honor is also in danger with Odysseus' arrival in their home, and she makes a judgment as to the most tactful way to address this potentially morally compromising situation. Odysseus does as Nausikaa recommends and sits in the ashes near the fire, until Ekheneos insists that Alkinoos give Odysseus a place of honor at the table. Alkinoos complies, although apparently mostly with thought to whether Odysseus is a god in disguise (VII.201–21). Arete's feelings about Odysseus remain unknown, however, for she makes no direct comment upon his petition to return home that night or *anytime* until after the Hades story.

However, Arete also seems wary of Odysseus as a potential sexual threat to her daughter. She inquires about his identity and clothing with some suspicion, since he is wearing a cloak and tunic made by her own servants; these items were among the clothes which Nausikaa was washing, unaccompanied except by her maids. Any wariness as to whether Odysseus and Nausikaa may already have interest in a relationship is not entirely unwarranted, for Nausikaa is at an age where she anticipates marriage fairly soon (VI.66–68), and her attraction to Odysseus is apparent later when she gazes at him in wonder after his bath (VIII.458).[10] Odysseus explains that he has come from the island of the goddess Kalypso, who loved and cared for him (VII.256) and that Nausikaa merely offered him food, wine, a bath, and clothing when he awoke on the island.

Of course, Odysseus' story of surviving shipwreck and being in need of clothes as a result of the accident are not the only interpretation to be found in his bearing clothes from Nausikaa. Perhaps suspecting that Odysseus acted sexually with the princess, the king offers Odysseus two alternatives: either to have Nausikaa in marriage if he chooses to remain, or to be taken home on Phaiakian ships. Although Alkinoos' offer appears generous, it is quite possibly also a test to see whether Odysseus would prefer to marry, and to find out whether his daughter's honor has been violated. At minimum, we might anticipate some wariness on Odysseus' part of a sudden offer of marriage to the daughter of a king whom he has hardly met. Nausikaa herself comments on the possible jealousy of the Phaiakians towards outsiders (VI.282–84), suggesting that Alkinoos does not intend an offer of marriage so much as a hope to discern Odysseus' relationship to his daughter. When Odysseus refuses the offer, he not only responds to the king's concerns about what might happen in the future; his reiteration of a desire for his wife, but not the princess, also helps to allay fears about what might have happened in the past.

Queen Arete's attitude towards Odysseus is equally unclear. She suggests that his gifts be "well lashed" for the trip home, suggesting that he already has enough gifts without the addition of any others (Dimock 154) and that his Phaiakian shipmates may not be as hospitable toward him as he might hope (VIII.443–45)![11] In light of his ambiguous standing, Odysseus must persuade the queen and king that he is no threat either to their daughter's honor or to their kingdom, and that he is worthy to be taken home to Ithaka.

As Doherty (1992) has argued, Odysseus breaks many rules of the bard when he addresses a woman as his intended audience. While the more usual audience of an epic performance of the sort that Odysseus gives is a meal hosted by a king, in which men are the central audience, both Odysseus' supplication and his poetic presentation are oriented toward Queen Arete. A typical response to such storytelling would be reward by a king with the authority to confer gifts (see, for example, Odysseus' own rewarding of Demodocus in book 8; Doherty 1992, 165). However, Odysseus assumes that Arete is the person who holds such sway in her household, not Alkinoos. As it turns out, Odysseus miscalculates, although he is able to recover with his skillful account of the male shades in Hades. Nonetheless, his willingness to orient the content and manner of his speech to a woman already suggests Odyssean skill at shifting the manner of his speech to the right audience at the right time—that is, care for *kairos*, or what this moment demands.

Further evidence for Odysseus' rhetorical concerns is found in the remarkable brevity of his account of his affairs with the goddess Kalypso. While the audience of the *Odyssey* hears a detailed description of his time with Kalypso in book 5, the Phaiakians hear very little indeed. Odysseus' description of Kalypso is brief; while he says that she "loved me excessively and cared for me, and she promised to make me an immortal and all my days to be ageless," he immediately adds that he perpetually wept, never being persuaded by her to want anything other than to return home (VII.255–57; Lattimore 1967, 117). Here we find parallels to Aristotle's observation that angry people will feel more mildly if they are made to feel pity for those at whom they were angry (*Rhet.* 1380a), and that benevolence is encouraged when one can show great need (*Rhet.* 1385a). Later, Odysseus reiterates his lack of consent with Kalypso and Kirke, both of whom he says detained him (IX.29–32). Odysseus has a continued concern with *diathesis* as he seeks to create mildness and sympathy for his plight in being detained by these goddesses and for his suffering now in being separated from Penelope, in place of suspicion about his character (thus also undertaking a reconstruction of the perception of his character, or *ethopoiēsis*).

Odysseus ends his larger story with another mention of Kalypso, but again speaks remarkably briefly. His entire account is seven lines long:

> From there I was carried along nine days, and on the tenth night
> the gods brought me to the island Ogygia, home of Kalypso
> with the lovely hair, a dreaded goddess who talks with mortals.
> She befriended me and took care of me. Why tell the rest of
> this story again, since yesterday in your house I told it
> to you and your majestic wife? It is hateful to me
> to tell a story over again, when it has been well told.
> (XII.447–53; Lattimore, 196–97).

The length of this description to the Phaiakians contrasts sharply with the one in book 5, and so ought to provoke our attention.[12] Odysseus avoids a lengthy description of his time with Kalypso and emphasizes his lack of consent in order to avoid drawing attention to his apparent infidelity. Indeed, when Odysseus tells Kalypso that he must return to Penelope, even though his wife's beauty and status do not come close to that of the goddess, the poet describes Odysseus as *polumetis*, or resourceful, which may in part alludes to his skill with words. To this extent, Homer presents part of persuasion as including a willingness to reshape or even to suppress elements of the truth in order to persuade one's audience.[13]

The content of the catalogue of women also seems designed to cultivate Arete's favor, thus displaying care for his audience's *diathesis*. Sammons has argued that the catalogue form is often used to offer paradigms that contribute further to the speaker's overarching narrative. For example, Agamemnon and Athena speak to Diomedes about Tydeus, his father, as a paradigm with the aim of getting Diomedes to fight (20). Here Odysseus uses the examples of women as paradigms of a sort, but not in order to persuade Arete to be a different type of woman! Rather, through praising examples of women who had intercourse with gods, Odysseus attempts to realign his own past history with that of Arete's family, and so reconstruct his character in her eyes. All of the women he describes are noble, and many are also offspring of the gods. Arete, too, is both a noble and a descendant of the gods. The emphasis on female-divine liaisons in particular seems most helpful to Odysseus' rhetorical purposes; were Odysseus only to cite mythological examples of men with goddesses, he would not yet overcome the otherwise plausible accusation of a "double standard" in evaluating his own and Penelope's behavior, which is the *precise* problem he wishes to avoid.[14]

Odysseus' list of shades includes fourteen women (aside from his mother). Two (Tyro and Iphimedeia) are Poseidon's lovers, and one is married to one of Poseidon's offspring from such a divine-human coupling (that is, Khloris, married to Neleus, Tyros' son by Poseidon). Both Poseidon and his lovers are presented not only favorably but also with detailed illustration. Poseidon disguised himself as the river god Epineus, whom Tyro loved, in order to make love to Tyro. Poseidon's deceit is described as a lovely scene of seduction:

> . . . taking his [Enipeus'] likeness, the god who circles
> the earth and shakes it
> lay with her where the swirling water finds its outlet,
> and a sea-blue wave curved into a hill of water reared up
> about the two, to hide the god and the mortal woman;
> and he broke her virgin zone and drifted a sleep upon her.
> But when the god had finished with the act of lovemaking,
> he took her by the hand and spoke to her and named her, saying:

"Be happy, lady, in this love, and when the year passes
you will bear glorious children, for the couplings of the immortals
are not without issue. You must look after them, and raise them.
Go home now and hold your peace and tell nobody
my name, but I tell it to you; I am the Earthshaker Poseidon."
(XI.248–52; Lattimore 1967, 174)

Poseidon is a gentle and tender, albeit deceitful, lover in this story, and Pelias and Neleus are Tyro's rewards for the encounter. Significantly, Odysseus lets his audience know that Tyro also bears children to her husband, Kretheus (who, as in the case of Alkinoos, is his wife's uncle).[15] Not only does Odysseus *not* suggest that Tyro's liaison with Poseidon is an instance of marital infidelity; he also implicitly presents her mothering of both Kretheus' and Poseidon's children as compatible enterprises, honoring her as "queen among women" (XI.258; Lattimore 1967, 174). Additionally, Poseidon's own use of deception to persuade is presented as praiseworthy, on account of his divinity. Odysseus, too, takes care to present the gods only in a favorable light. Perhaps his concern is not only for his human, but also divine, audience.

Iphimedeia is Poseidon's other lover among the shades. Iphimedeia bore sons to Poseidon, Otos, and Ephialtes, who attempted to overthrow the gods at Olympos, but Apollo shot them down. Otos and Ephialtes are presented rather sympathetically for potential overthrowers of the Olympian gods (some of whom favor Odysseus). Odysseus says that these men are "handsomest by far, after famous Orion" (XI.310; Lattimore 1967, 176) and that they were merely unbearded boys when shot down, who might have been successful had they been fully grown (XI.317). But Odysseus also describes Iphimedeia as the wife of Aloeus (XI.305), again with admiration only of the offspring of the divine-human encounter. This story seems especially designed to praise Arete, for Athena has already told Odysseus that Periboia, Arete's grandmother, was the daughter of Eurymedon, commander of the giants (VII.58–59). Here Odysseus seems to take on the voice and perspective of Iphimedeia in his description, thus practicing a form of *prosopopoeia*.[16] Odysseus' somewhat wistful praise of the young giants is in stark contrast to Athena's attitude when she tells how Eurymedon "lost his recklessly daring people and himself perished" (VII.60; Lattimore 1967, 112), suggesting that Odysseus takes on the Iphimedeian perspective out of concern for his audience's familial commitments.

Other divine and human liaisons are extolled, though none quite so highly as those involving Poseidon. Antiope is Zeus' lover and mother of the founders of Thebes, Amphion and Zeus (XI.260–65). Odysseus describes Alkmene as both as the mother of Herakles, conceived "after lying in love in the embraces of great Zeus" (XI.267; Lattimore 1967, 175) and as "Amphitryon's wife" (XI.266; Lattimore 1967, 175). Immediately after describing Alkmene, Odysseus mentions Megare, Kreon's daughter and wife of Amphitryon's "weariless" son (XI.270;

Lattimore 1967, 175). In subsequent mythology, Megare is Herakles' wife.[17] Odysseus has described Herakles as the offspring of *both* Zeus and Amphitryon; he thereby suggests that Zeus' liaison with Alkmene was not an instance of infidelity, but more like a "divine contribution" to the family. Moreover, since Zeus took Amphitryon's form, Alkmene could hardly be responsible for her actions, again suggesting that one cannot help oneself with the gods.[18]

The one instance of a divine-human coupling left unpraised is Maira, who is only mentioned but not described here (XI.326). In the *Scholia* she is a devotee of Artemis, deceived by Zeus into becoming his lover. Unlike in the other accounts of affairs with gods described above, Maira betrays a goddess, not a human being, and there is no mention of a human marriage to which she returns.[19] When she bears the child Lokris and no longer comes to the hunt, Artemis shoots and kills her. While infidelity to another human for the sake of a god is acceptable, the betrayal of another god by breaking vows of chastity is not.

An even more striking rhetorical maneuver on Odysseus' part is his description of Leda, whom he calls wife of Tyndareus, by whom she is mother to Kastor and Polydeuces (XI.298–301). Odysseus remarkably makes no mention whatsoever of Helen, Clytemnestra, or any liaison with Zeus. His omission is especially striking given the centrality of both women to the narrative of the *Odyssey* itself.[20] Later, Odysseus will speak of Helen as the cause of the deaths of many men (XI.438), Penelope describes Helen as the daughter of Zeus (XXIII.219), and Agamemnon calls Tyndareus the father of Clytemnestra (XXIV.199).[21] But here Odysseus deliberately omits Leda's links to Helen and Clytemnestra; doing otherwise would only represent Leda's link to unfaithful women, and Odysseus is concerned to present positive images of women and their offspring where the gods are concerned, again showing concern for his audience's disposition (*diathesis*).

The remainder of the figures whom Odysseus says he encountered in Hades are not mentioned for their links to the gods but to other important men, and accordingly Odysseus' praise is either moderated or absent. Their inclusion helps to resolve the second half of Odysseus' rhetorical problem, which is to show his audience the urgency of his need to return home before his wife marries another man, as another aspect of his concern with the *diathesis* of those who listen. Odysseus strikes a delicate balance between, on the one hand, displaying the genuine betrayal involved in infidelities of women and, on the other hand, presenting these women carefully, lest he present women too unsympathetically for Arete's taste.[22] The women are Epikaste, the daughters of Minos (Phaedra, Prokris, and Ariadne), Clymene, and Eriphyle. All except Epikaste are mentioned in the very last eight lines of the description of the female shades; his brevity thus underscores his rhetorical aims.

Odysseus describes Epikaste as the mother and wife of Oedipus, and although he presents her situation as monstrous, still Epikaste comes across a bit more sympathetically than Oedipus. Epikaste's marriage to her son is described as performed in ignorance (XI.273–74), and the description of her suicide reflects her horror at her own deed. Phaedra, Prokris, and Ariadne are mentioned in a single breath. Although Odysseus makes no comment upon Phaedra's and Prokris' identities, in subsequent mythology they are the daughters of Minos; here, Ariadne alone is identified as his daughter (XI.373). In many versions of Ariadne's story, Ariadne aids Theseus in his defeat of the Minotaur in exchange for a promise of marriage. In one typical account, she is abandoned by Theseus on an island, and then married to Dionysus.[23] In this account, however, Theseus "got no joy" of her (XI. 324; Lattimore 1967, 176). Rather than rescuing her from the island, Artemis kills Ariadne due to the "witness" of Dionysus. Again, Odysseus presents an account of a woman who betrays a man—this time her father—and is punished for it.

The last of the female shades is Eriphyle. Odysseus only hints at her story before concluding his own story, but his evaluation is clear from what little he does say. He describes her as "Eriphyle the hateful, who accepted precious gold for life of her own dear husband" (XI.326–27; Lattimore 1967, 176). Later sources say she was married to Amphiaraus, and later in the *Odyssey* Amphiaraus' death at Thebes is linked to gifts given to a woman (XV.246–47). In these accounts, Polynices bribes Eriphyle to persuade Amphiaraus to go on the expedition to Thebes (an expedition which Amphiaraus opposes), and as a result he dies in battle.[24] Odysseus' strong words of criticism for a woman who deliberately betrays her husband for money are a sudden shift in tone; it is his sole description of infidelity untempered by pity. Through these mentions of women who betray their husbands, Odysseus alludes to the urgency of his own need to return home, to prevent his wife from betraying him out of ignorance (as with Epikaste), for love (as with Ariadne), or for money (as with Eriphyle). On the one hand, Odysseus praises women who have had affairs with the gods and then returned home to their husbands but, on the other hand, he is carefully critical of human-human betrayals. He thus makes clear both his need and moral justification for a safe return home in a manner befitting his status. Odysseus apparently planned to conclude the story of his travels with the list of female shades, for he reports the encounters with Tiresias, Odysseus' mother, and the other women, and then adds, "It is time now for my sleep, either joining my companions on board the fast ship, or here; but you, and the gods, will see to my homeward journey," before falling silent (XI.330–32; Lattimore 1967, 176). Thus the story of the male shades and the tales that follow the account of the women in Hades seem to be an addition that Odysseus originally did not intend to tell.[25]

Odysseus' account includes careful attention to his audience's character and family history, displaying a care for the cultivation of their *diathesis*. He attends to Arete's femininity and her stature as a woman of power with influence in her own political community through describing like women with praise. Odysseus draws attention to other women in mythology who have asserted their own power; often they do so through their connection to the gods or their connection to important male figures. Here we see something akin to Aristotle's observation that "we like those who show good feeling toward us, for example, admire us, show us respect, who take pleasure in our company, and especially those who are well disposed to us with respect to matters in which we most desire to be admired or thought worthy or pleasing" (*Rhet.* 1381b). Odysseus praises implicitly Arete's power and her being worthy of admiration, which may be goods that she especially values, if Nausikaa is correct that it is best to approach Arete for assistance. Here, Odysseus creates a narrative for Arete that also helps to reconstruct his own character and history in light of her own familial history: *ethopoiēsis* and concern for audience *diathesis* mutually inform one another.

Odysseus also presents his own character favorably insofar as his praise of women as mothers reinforces his image both as a husband who genuinely desires to return home to his wife, and perhaps more favorably disposes Arete regarding the question of whether he has treated Arete's daughter, Nausikaa, honorably. In order to construct his character as a man whose only concern is to return home to wife and kingdom, Odysseus exercises care in what details he includes and omits by abbreviating his description of his own affair with Kalypso, emphasizing his lack of full consent in that relationship, and omitting references to Helen's infidelity in his account of Leda. Odysseus' omission of significant information mirrors that of his protector Athena, who, for example, refuses to reveal much to Telemachus about his father's whereabouts so that Telemachus can grow through his journey in search of his father (XIII.416–17), and even Penelope herself, who deceives her suitors by failing to mention that the shroud she weaves each day is also being unwoven each night (II.90–110).[26]

The speech has the intended effect on Arete, who is the first to speak in response to Odysseus. She immediately suggests that the Phaiakians offer him gifts before they send him home (XI.339–41). However, while the soldiers acknowledge that they are willing, Ekheneos adds that they will first wait upon the word and deed of Alkinoos (XI.346). The king commands that Odysseus be given many gifts, after another day's rest, and adds, "for mine is the power (*kratos*) in this district" (XI.353; Lattimore 1967, 177). Alkinoos seems to resent the perception that Arete holds power, and he explicitly asserts his own authority to determine the best course of action concerning Odysseus.

Alkinoos insisted that Odysseus continue with the story and report whether he saw any of his companions from Troy, perhaps to test him as to whether he has first-hand familiarity with these men. For although Alkinoos claims that he believes Odysseus to be telling the truth, he may be obliquely alluding to his *distrust* of Odysseus when he said: ". . . we as we look upon you do not imagine that you are a deceptive or thievish man, the sort that the black earth breeds in great numbers, people who wander widely, making up lying stories (*pseudeia*), from which no one could learn anything. But come now, tell me this and give me an accurate answer: Did you see any of your godlike companions, who once with you went to Ilion and there met their destiny? Here is a night that is very long, it is endless. It is not time yet to sleep in the palace" (XI.363–66, 370–74; Lattimore 1967, 177).

Alkinoos suggests that Odysseus' story is well crafted but does not clearly prove the truth of his claims. Alkinoos is not yet content that Odysseus is not an imposter. Indeed, his words may well be heard with an undertone of suspicion or even anger. Nausikaa's advice turns out to have been at least incomplete, if not misguided: not only Arete but also Alkinoos must be won over, although Alkinoos had seemed easy to please at first. Indeed, Odysseus' emphasis on feminine power seems to backfire with the king. Alkinoos is eager to assert his male authority over Arete's power, and expresses some anger in his insistence that he holds the real power in the region. Although Odysseus has succeeded in gaining Arete's favor, he has miscalculated in orienting his speech primarily to her, and is forced to continue the Hades story. Odysseus now must face the suspicion and anger of the king, which seems to have been aroused by Odysseus' attention to and praise for women in addressing Arete. The shift in Odysseus' subsequent story indicates a self-conscious awareness of his rhetorical concerns with audience and the reconstruction of his own ethical concerns in light of his changed audience.[27]

Odysseus shifts his rhetorical aim towards pleasing Alkinoos, even risking the displeasure of Arete. If the themes of presentation of the female shades are fidelity and love, then the themes of the presentation of the male shades are betrayal and war springing from betrayed love.[28] As Sammons argues, with the catalogue of heroic men, a new emphasis on "crime and punishment, virtue and reward" (98) becomes prominent. Odysseus' presentation is a complete reversal of his previous praise of women. Agamemnon is the first to speak to Odysseus, and Agamemnon's description of Clytemnestra's betrayal more than compensates for Odysseus' ill-planned praise of women only moments earlier: "She with thoughts surpassingly grisly splashed the shame on herself and the rest of her sex, on women still to come, even on the one whose acts are virtuous. . . . So by this, do not be too easy even with your wife, nor give her an entire account of all you are sure of. Tell her part of it, but let the rest be hidden in silence" (XI.432–34, 441–443; Lattimore 1967, 179).

Odysseus suggests that women are not to be trusted; even those who *appear* to be virtuous should at best be allowed limited information and power. He thus implies that Alkinoos' impulse to resist his wife's influence and to decide the matter for himself is not only commendable, but prudential. Thus Odysseus quickly recovers from his exclusive focus on Arete as holding the power in the kingdom, moving towards Alkinoos as the true bearer of power, in opposition to the idea that women often bear the true power as mothers and bearers of the children of the gods that he had outlined only moments earlier. Later authors will reflect on the attentiveness to *kairos*, or speaking in the right manner at the right moment, as a key feature of good rhetoric. Alcidamas, for example, argues in "On those who write written speeches" that a good speech is one that is "ensouled" and that such speeches can, like a living creature, respond to changes in the surrounding environment (in a way that written texts cannot). To be able to exercise a care for *kairos* in the changing circumstances of one's audience is a mark of not only good rhetoric, but also true *philosophia* (§ 28; Muir, 33).[29] Odysseus also shifts the presentation of his own ethical concerns, from a more hopeful stance about the nobility of women (one that can be separated somewhat from the sole question of fidelity, at least in the case of divine-human couplings) to a stance more suspicious of women.[30] He thus redirects any anger that Alkinoos feels toward him toward women who inappropriately wield power. Here we see parallels to Aristotle's recommendation that men become mild at a person when they spend their anger on other persons instead (*Rhet.* 1380b). Again, Odysseus need not have held this principle abstractly, but he shows awareness of the causes at work in knowing how to respond to Alkinoos' anger by redirecting anger to another object. Odysseus influences the *diathesis* of his new audience of the king through displacing Alkinoos' anger.

The male shade who next appears to Odysseus is Achilles. Achilles' well-known speech teaches Odysseus of the limitations of even a glorious and heroic death: living the hard life of a common man is preferable to ruling Hades. From Achilles, Odysseus himself learns that a return to home is desirable. But Odysseus also links his and others' deaths at Troy to erotic desire for women. He says that he told Agamemnon's shade: "Many of us died for the sake of Helen, and when you were far, Clytemnestra plotted treason against you" (XI.438–39; Lattimore 1967, 179). A woman caused the war, which then contributed to another woman's misdeeds; in effect, not one but *two* women are responsible for Agamemnon's betrayal.

The contrast to the first half of the speech to Arete, in which Clytemnestra was entirely omitted from the catalogue of women, is striking. Again, Odysseus underscores the losses that men have suffered on account of women, and the necessity of male control, in order to please Alkinoos. Of equal importance is Odysseus' insistence that the mistake that Achilles made, to choose a life of fame over a return home as king, is not one that Odysseus wishes to make. Odysseus thus reinforces the overarching theme of his account of Hades that his sole desire is to return home to his own wife and child, and not to marry Nausikaa or otherwise interfere in the lives of the Phaiakians.[31] He also deflects any anger toward himself back at women, thus encouraging Alkinoos' mildness with respect to Odysseus.

Conclusion

After Odysseus reports the remainder of his adventures, Alkinoos reiterates that Odysseus will be sent home on Phaiakian ships, and orders that each man is to give to Odysseus "a great tripod and a cauldron" (XIII.13–14; Lattimore 1967, 198), although it will be so costly that the king will have to levy a tax on the people to pay for the expense. Odysseus is sent home, endowed with wealth, at last. To this extent, Homer presents Odysseus' rhetoric as efficacious in allowing him to achieve his goal of returning home. Odysseus through the use of *ethopoesis,* care for *diathesis* (especially turning anger to mildness), and attention to *kairos* manages to transform himself from a naked man, covered with seaweed and salt, without men, ship, or wealth, into a king sent back with wealth and honors from another king's friendship. As in his account of the women of Hades, addressed to Arete, Odysseus uses these same techniques of praising his audience's character, his own character, and speaking in a way that turns anger and suspicion into mildness and goodwill. But with Alkinoos, the emphasis is on the king's manly authority, the men's rule over their wives, and Odysseus' own return home (lest Penelope commit an infidelity before his return). Odysseus deliberately reverses the priority of feminine and masculine power that he has previously set out before Arete, now that he is mindful of Alkinoos' power.

For a time, Odysseus' voice and the voice of the bard are nearly indistinguishable; Alkinoos himself compares Odysseus to a bard (XI.367–69). Yet Odysseus' choices in speech are not only poetic but also rhetorical, in his practice of techniques that seem designed primarily to win over the goodwill of his audience so that they might act in a way that supports his own ends. To this extent, the catalogue of women, though not a political speech, shares elements of not only *epideixis* but also deliberative rhetoric, to borrow from Aristotle's categories. Odysseus does more than show a capacity to speak beautifully about his encounters with the dead in Hades. He skillfully uses the description of that encounter also to persuade the king and queen to undertake action. Odysseus does not engage in meta-discourse about his own rhetoric. However, he nonetheless practices what later authors will name as *ethopoiēsis, prosopopoeia,* concern for *diathesis,* and careful attention to changing one's speech in accordance with the present moment (*kairos*).

Last, Odysseus uses his speech to reunify his audience of king and queen, and so also to bring political harmony back to this political and domestic sphere. While Odysseus' speech about Hades points out the tensions between the male and female, divine and human, his final words to Alkinoos are a wish for unity and reconciliation between the sexes: "May you in turn, remaining here, bring comfort and cheer to your wedded wives and your children, and may the gods grant success in every endeavor, and no unhappiness be found in your people" (XIII.43–46; Lattimore 1967, 199). Similarly, his final words to Arete are for a blessed life, death in old age, and the united felicity of queen, king, children, and countrymen (XIII.73–78). What Odysseus wishes for the Phaiakians is also what Tiresias prophesies will come true for Odysseus (XI.111–52). Thus, although the Hades episode speaks of conflict between husband and wife, gods and human beings, from the beginning such conflicts are set against a larger standard of harmony and peace, an elusive goal, but one achieved in part through the use of rhetoric by Odysseus by the end of his odyssey.[32]

Mētis, Themis, and the Practice of Epic Speech

David C. Hoffman

In framing the intellectual history of ancient Greece, it was common at one time to posit a transition from a "mythopoetic" worldview that was supposed to have prevailed in archaic Greece, to a more rational outlook governed by *logos* that emerged in the sixth century B.C.E. This narrative had its origins in George Grote's *History of Greece,* which told of how "scientific" thinkers came to reject "mythic" thought, and was carried on by John Burnet (1892) and Eric R. Dodds, and in Eric Havelock's (1963) account of the transition from oral to literate culture.[1]

The "myth to reason" framework has been questioned within the field of classics for many years now. Francis Cornford showed that the early Ionian "physics" has as much in common with myth as it does with modern physics. Jean-Pierre Vernant (1983 and 1988), along with other French structuralist classicists, promoted a structuralist approach to Greek mythology, based on the work of Claude Lévi-Strauss, that finds a kind of deep rationality in these stories. Richard Buxton's *From Myth to Reason* summarized the critique of the myth/reason framework up to the point of its publication in 1999.

Despite these developments in classics, the "myth to reason" framework remains powerful in histories of rhetoric. Many treatments of the emergence of rhetoric accept the idea of a transition from orality and myth to literate reason and align the thought of the sophists, and the beginnings of the "rhetorical tradition," with literate rationality. As Edward Schiappa has it, "The *logos* of the Sophists challenged the traditions of poetic discourse both in substance and style. . . . For example, when Protagoras attempted to set aside the issue of the existence of gods, he was both challenging the traditional status granted to *muthos* and preparing the way for what now would be called an anthropological approach to theology. This is called *arguing* rather than *telling.* The substantive challenges to traditional ways of thinking brought a new humanistic rationalism to *logos*" (2003b, 56). Elsewhere, he wrote, "The *logos* of sixth-century and fifth-century thinkers is best understood as the rationalistic rival to traditional *muthos*" (1999, 77). In his alignment of the sophists with a new spirit of rational thought made possible, at least in part, by the advance of literacy, Schiappa's account is in general agreement with the work of Thomas Cole (1991), who sees the emergence of rhetoric closely tied to the rise of literacy, and Christopher Johnstone, who shows the connection of sophistical conceptions of *logos* and *sophia* (wisdom) and the Ionian beginnings of physical science.

In the "standard narrative" of the progression from the mythopoeic worldview to a rational one, "reason" and "rationality" are aligned with the modern scientific quest to articulate a set of context-independent laws that govern the functioning of the whole of the cosmos, and remain constant regardless of time or place. In contrast, the "mythopoetic mind" was supposed to have seen the universe as governed by gods who "do not act according to stable ordinances" (Johnstone, 23). The rise of the concept of *logos,* in this view, was understood to represent the first step toward the discovery of such a set of abstract, governing laws. The sophists and their "craft of *logos*" (*logōn technē*) are figured as participating in this bold step forward.

This view that the *logōn technē* of the sophists, and the art of rhetoric that emerged in its wake, represents a break from the mythopoetic worldview has been challenged by a number of scholars. Susan Jarrett argued that a certain rationality does in fact exist within the "mythic condition." Jeffery Walker argues that "the art of rhetoric" originates from "an expansion of the poetic/epideictic realm" (18) rather than a break with mythopoesis.[2]

A particular kind of "strategic" rationality bridges the supposed gap between the mythopoetic worldview and the rational worldview. This is a sort of rationality that does not partake in the quest for field-independent standards of argument or universal laws of nature, but rather excels in the application of contingent rules to shape the ever-changing flow of life's events. But is this strategic rationality any less rational because it deals only with the context-bound and the "field dependent"? This species of rationality can be demonstrated to have existed in the mythopoetic world of Homer's epics and to have echoes in the views about pedagogy and citizenship expressed in Isocrates' discourses. A focus on this context-bound form of rationality should advance the understanding of the relationship between the "proto-rhetoric" of the mythopoetic world of epic poetry and the rhetoric of the "rational" world of the fifth century B.C.E.

This epoch-spanning form of rationality is governed by the influence of the two goddesses who are in Hesiod's account the first wives of Zeus.

> Now Zeus, king of the gods, made Metis his wife first, and she was wisest among gods and mortal men. But when she was about to bring forth the goddess bright-eyed Athene, Zeus craftily deceived her with cunning words and put her in his own belly, as Earth and starry Heaven advised. For they advised him so, to the end that no other should hold royal sway over the eternal gods in place of Zeus; for very wise children were destined to be born of her, first

> the maiden bright-eyed Tritogeneia, equal to her father in strength and in wise understanding; but afterwards she was to bear a son of overbearing spirit, king of gods and men. But Zeus put her into his own belly first, that the goddess might devise for him both good and evil (ll. 901–906). Next he married bright Themis who bare the Horae (Hours), and Eunomia (Order), Dike (Justice), and blooming Eirene (Peace), who mind the works of mortal Hesiod, The Homeric Hymns, and Homerica men, and the Moerae (Fates) to whom wise Zeus gave the greatest honour, Clotho, and Lachesis, and Atropos who give mortal men evil and good to have. (*Th.* 886–906; Evelyn-White 87–88)

Although this account of *Mētis* (Μῆτις) and *Themis* (Θέμις) comes some nine hundred lines into Hesiod's poem *Theogony,* the importance of these two goddesses should not be underplayed: as structuralist classicists Marcel Detienne and Jean-Pierre Vernant assert, these early wives embody two essential principles of Zeus' Olympian hegemony. *Mētis* is the goddess of "cunning intelligence," of hidden plans realized at the right moment. *Themis* is the mother of the *horai* or seasons, the goddess of all things regular and returning, of the order that brings peace and justice. Zeus, the model *basileus* or king, needed both of these goddesses close by in order to rule. The trick to exercising will and retaining authority often lay in being able to recall the right *themis* (law, custom, or precedent) at the right time. Detienne and Vernant explain, "The combination of these two marriages ensures the supremacy of the new king of the gods, for the two goddesses correspond to each other, forming a pair of powers that are both complementary and opposed" (107).[3]

Ultimately, the two principles embodied by *Mētis* and *Themis,* which form the foundation of Zeus' rule, correspond to *kairos* and *philosophia* (in the Isocratean sense) in classical rhetorical theory, and have connections to both the practice of speech in epic poetry, and to Pierre Bourdieu and Michel de Certeau's contemporary "theories of practice." Together, they comprise the basis for a kind of strategic rationality that bridges the gap between "mythopoesis" and the "new humanistic rationalism" of the sophists.

Themis and *Mētis*

Themis, a word which is in some places translated as "law," was often something more like a "living tradition" in epic poetry, a way of life embedded in story and song, that was both past and perpetually returning, being performed anew by the *aoidoi* (poet singers) and invoked in the judgments and exhortations of the *basileus.* Kings are given "scepter and *themis*" by the gods as a sort of inheritance.[4] *Themis* is present at the place where a community gathers, the *agora* (Hom. *Il.* 11.807),and those who are without *agora* and *themis* are less than human, like the Cyclops (Hom. *Od.* 9.105, 9.112, 9.215). But the *agora* seems only to be the place where *themis* is "given" in the sense of being made manifest to the people. Clearly it is something that is always present, guiding life, and that is brought into play in a special way in the *agora.* Agamemnon is prepared to swear that he did not lie with Briseis, "as is the *themis* of mankind," (ἣ θέμις ἀνθρώπων, Hom. *Il.* 9.134, 9.276; Lattimore 1951, 201, 205). Here *themis* is something like universal custom, as is also the case when "*themis* to strangers," that is, hospitality, is invoked.[5] The clearest proof that *themis* is a body of tradition can be found in the *Iliad* at 9.156, repeated at 9.298, when Achilles is promised rich lands by Agamemnon where the inhabitants "under his scepter shall enact his rich *themis*" (οἱ ὑπὸ σκήπτρῳ λιπαρὰς τελέουσι θέμιστας; Lattimore 1951, 202, 206). A good king has been given a good body of tradition by the gods, a body of tradition that his subjects must enact and thus perpetuate.

Themis stands in close relation to *dikē* (δίκη), justice, but is not the same thing. When taken together, the lines that refer to *themis* and *dikē* give the impression that *themis* exists above the level of particular decisions, and that *dikē* is a *quality of* judges or decisions.[6] *Dikē* is the quality that allows the perpetuation of *themis.* This claim receives its strongest confirmation in Hesiod. In *Theogony* he said, of the heaven-nourished *basileus,* "All the people look to him discerning (*diakrinonta*) laws (*themistes*) by means of straight justice (*itheia dikē*)" (Hes. *Th.* 84–86: "οἱ δέ τε λαοὶ πάντες ἐς αὐτὸν ὁρῶσι διακρίνοντα θέμιστας ἰθείῃσι δίκῃσιν"; Wender, 25).[7] The verb *diakrinō,* often used to refer to the activity of judges, means to divide or distinguish. What is being distinguished here are *themistes,* the plural applications of *themis.* When we ask ourselves what the judge is in fact doing, the most sensible answer seems to be that he is distinguishing between precedents, *themistes,* in order to decide which one should apply to the present case. But further, the judge distinguishes by means of straight justice (*itheia dikē* in the dative). *Itheia dikē,* here, is not the judgment itself, but the quality that brings about a good discernment of precedents. The opposite of *itheia dikē* in both Homer and Hesiod is "crooked justice," *skolia dikē.* This is the quality of judges that employ *themis* in a suspect way. Hesiod rails against them in *Works and Days,* where the quality of *Dikē* is personified and those with the quality of "crooked justice" are represented as not dealing straightly with her. Even the crooked judges "give *themistes,*" but slanted rather than straight ones (Hes. *WD.* 217–24).

Themis is also a precedent for just distribution. The quality of "straight justice" is deeply connected with the whole notion of "due portion," which the Greeks called *moira* and is often translated as "fate." Indeed, the goddess *Themis,* in addition to being mother of the seasons, is the mother of the *Moirai,* the fates (Hes. *Th.* 904–6). The central disputes in epic poetry concern the distribution of things—land, prizes, honors—with surprising regularity. The central conflict of the *Iliad* is about distribution of prizes of battle: Achilles is outraged that Agamemnon reclaimed Briseis. In its own way, the *Odyssey* also concerns the wrongful consumption of a man's store, a theme which is closely related to distribution. The theme of distribution plays throughout Hesiod as well, sometimes in specific connection to the theme of justice. Similarly, *Works and Days* is written as a sort of complaint to the author's brother, Perseus, who got the better part of the inheritance through suspect justice. And the idea of distribution runs right through the Prometheus myth. To do justice, then, is both to discern the proper precedent and to distribute fairly in light of that precedent. Straight justice would distribute to each in proportion to the honor which was due that person.

Although *themis* was vital to the art of speech in archaic Greece, mastery of the oral tradition was not sufficient for Zeus, or any *basileus* in epic poetry, to sustain leadership. *Mētis,* the polymorphous goddess of cunning and guile, had perhaps an equal place in the sponsorship of political persuasion as *themis,* because it was she who taught the speaker to recall the right *themis* at the right time.

Mētis, according to Detienne and Vernant, "knows how to wait patiently for the calculated moment to arrive. . . . *Mētis* is swift, as prompt as the opportunity it must seize on the wing, not allowing it to pass. But it does not act lightly (*leptē*). With all the weight of acquired experience that it carries, it involves thought that is dense, rich and compressed (*pukinē*)" (15).[8] In the words of Nestor in the *Iliad,* "The woodcutter is far better for *mētis* than he is for brute strength. / It is by *mētis* that the sea captain holds his rapid ship / On its course, though torn by winds, over the wine-blue water" (Hom. *Il.* 23.315–17; Lattimore 1951, 458).

Mētis involves seizing opportunities as they arise in a way that is deeply informed by experience. It involves both the art of concealment and that of dramatic revelation at the right moment. One of the choice epithets of Odysseus is *poly-mētis,*he of much *mētis.* Odysseus' *mētis* was at work when he concealed himself in rags, waiting for the right moment to slay the suitors; when concealing himself in the horse, waiting to leap out and take Troy; or when concealing his name from the Cyclops by calling himself No One (*outis*).[9] In initiation rituals, which mirror to some extent the journey of Odysseus, Greek youth were typically relegated to the wild realm beyond the boundaries of the *polis,* there to develop a cunning which they will bring back to the center of the city when they become citizens (Vidal-Naquet 1998, 106–28). Thus *mētis* lives in both the heart of Zeus and the heart of the *polis.*

The Practice of Speech in Homeric Epic

In Homeric epic *mētis* and *themis* defined the conceptual boundaries of a species of competitive and strategic rationality. The good *basileus* needed to "see (*leussō* or *noein*) the past and the present."[10] When the *basileus* did this, he "present-ed" the past—brought it into contact with the present.[11] This operation involved not only the recall of *themistes,* but enough *mētis* to recall the right *themis* at the right time. Marina McCoy's essay in this volume on Odysseus' presentation of the female shades he met in Hades to the queen and king of Phaiakia can be viewed as an example of a speaker exercising *mētis* in selecting the right parts of the past for the present situation. In some cases, such as Phoenix's attempts to persuade Achilles to rejoin the battle at Troy (Hom. *Il.* 9.527–605), particular examples from the past are recalled at strategic moments in the context of a series of significant exchanges of prizes. In other cases, such as Telemachus' and Mentor's deliberations with the other citizens of Ithaca (Hom. *Od.* 2.25–259), epic debates are dueling invocations of *themis* that serve competing purposes. Two examples illustrate how the cunning of *mētis* informed the recall of *themistes* by various speakers in Greek epic.

Strategies of Exchange and Timing in the Embassy to Achilles

George A. Kennedy calls the speeches made by Odysseus, Phoenix, and Ajax to Achilles in the ninth book of the *Iliad* "the finest set of speeches in the poem," and makes the case that "Some of the techniques employed anticipate the categories of classical rhetoric" (1980, 11).[12] He goes on to dissect the structure of the three speeches and to comment on the role of ethos and pathos in the arguments of the speakers. Such proto-Aristotelian elements are certainly there to be found, and Homer's speeches are also marvels of linguistic characterization, as Hanna Roisman has shown: their phrasing, structure, and diction reveal much about the characters who utter them. More recently, Rachel Ahern Knudsen has produced a detailed account of the instances of arguments using enthymeme, *diathesis*, *ēthos*, *gnōmē*, *paradigma*, and topics in the *Iliad.* Clearly Aristotle drew on a deep tradition of rhetorical argumentation in his *Rhetoric.* But seemingly closer to the consciousnesses of the speakers in Homeric epics than these occurrences of rhetorical figures that later writers would classify is the verbal battle over the proper distribution of the prizes of war, an activity that lies within the domain of *Themis,* fought out with the sort of cunning of which *Mētis* is the patroness.[13] These battles involve invoking the right customs and precedents at the right time, and as such are just as deeply, if less formally, rhetorical as uses of enthymeme and paradigm.

The dramatic context of these speeches is that Achilles, the most powerful warrior on the Greek side at Troy, has withdrawn from the fight and is sulking in his tent. This was a result of a series of events that began with a Greek raid on a nearby town in which two women were taken captive, Chryseis and Briseis. As the booty was divided up, Agamemnon, the leader of the Greek forces, had kept Chryseis for himself and bestowed Briseis upon Achilles, his most skillful warrior. However, as it turned out, Chryseis' father, Chryses, was a priest of Apollo who called down a curse on the Greeks after they had refused his offer of a rich ransom for the return of his daughter. Faced with destruction through this curse, Achilles and the other warriors prevailed upon Agamemnon to return Chryseis to her father. Agamemnon did this, but only on condition that he could repossess Briseis from Achilles. Unjustly deprived of the most prized gift that had been bestowed upon him, Achilles flew into a rage and withdrew from the fighting.

After Achilles' departure, the battle turned against the Greeks, and the Trojans moved into a position to threaten their ships. Agamemnon came to recognize his mistake and sent three of Achilles' closest comrades—Odysseus, Phoenix, and Ajax—to persuade him to return. They are the "embassy to Achilles."

The whole series of speeches that begins with the debate between Achilles and Agamemnon about the return of Chryseis and runs through the embassy to Achilles is concerned with the topics of prizes (γέρᾶ; δώρων) and honor (τίμη). As Moses Finley, James Redfield, Walter Donlan, and others have shown, social status among the archaic Greeks was maintained by means of practices of "gift exchange."[14] Custom demanded that gifts be exchanged on occasions like marriages and long-distance visits to political allies. It also demanded that all prizes taken in battle be given to the leaders of the army to be redistributed to the warriors on the basis of their status and valor. As Donlan explains, "In Homer . . . the spoils of war and raid are distributed evenly, sometimes by lot, to all the warriors. However, those of highest rank, the leaders, are awarded an extra, or choice portion, as their due" (1980, 19). Chryseis and Briseis are both prizes of war, and it was the role of Agamemnon, as leader of the Greeks at Troy, to bestow them upon one of those he chose to honor. As such, "Wealth was a byproduct of prowess, a sign of success" (23). So closely are the prizes associated with status, that to be deprived of a prize is to be deprived of status, and is cause for deep resentment. As Kalchas the seer explains, Agamemnon dishonored Chryses by refusing the ransom he had offered for Chryseis' return, and in turn earned the enmity of Apollo (Hom. *Il.* 1.94–5). Agamemnon himself felt dishonored when he was compelled to return Chryseis, and Achilles' honor was deeply wounded when Agamemnon took Briseis to make good his own loss, especially since Agamemnon takes pains to make it clear that the action is intended to shame him: "I shall take the fair-cheeked Briseis, your prize (γέρας), I myself go to your shelter, that you may learn how much greater I am than you, and another man may shrink back from likening himself to me and contending against me" (Hom. *Il.* 1.184–87; Lattimore 1951, 64). The whole incident represents a reversal of the usual status-reinforcing circulation of gifts. Under normal circumstances, the leader, Agamemnon, is honored by being presented with all the prizes taken in battle, and he in turn recognizes the efforts and rank of the warriors by redistributing those prizes. But here things have gone horribly wrong. The disfavor of Apollo compels the warriors, led by Achilles, to demand that Agamemnon return his own prize of war, causing him to suffer a diminution of status. Agamemnon must in turn reduce the status of the leader of those who had risen up against him.

When Odysseus later offers recompense to Achilles on behalf of Agamemnon, he is at pains to emphasize how the gifts are not only material compensation, but are also meant to redress the injury done to his honor. The compensation is rich, including gold, horses, an honored place in Agamemnon's house, and the return of Briseis together with seven other women. But the richness of the gifts is important only as a sign of the honor in which Achilles is held. These are "worthy gifts" ("ἄξια δῶρα" Hom. *Il.* 9.261; Lattimore 1951, 205), and they include an offer to become Agamemnon's son-in-law. "He will compensate you even as Orestes" (Hom. *Il.* 9.284; Lattimore 1951, 205), Odysseus assures him. And if Achilles' wrath proves to be so great that he could never be reconciled to Agamemnon, he should take pity on the other Greeks who "shall repay you like a god" (Hom. *Il.* 9.301–02; Lattimore 1951, 206). In both of these cases, Achilles is promised that he will be compensated at a rate that signifies his high status, comparable to Agamemnon's own son, or a god.

Achilles' reply is also governed by the topics of honors and prizes. He is incensed by the lack of gratitude (χάρις) Agamemnon and the other Greeks have shown him, and complains that the "Portion (μοῖρα) is the same for the man who holds back, and the one who fights hard / All are held in the same honor (τιμῇ), both the coward and the brave" (Hom. *Il.* 9.316–19; Lattimore 1951, 206) The gifts are not enough to make up for the public insult that Agamemnon dealt to Achilles: "Not if he gave gifts as numerous as the sand and dust, not even so would Agamemnon persuade (πείθω) my soul until he has paid the price for all this heartrending insolence" (Hom. *Il.* 9.386–87; Lattimore 1951, 208).

The next speaker to try to persuade Achilles is Phoenix, who was Achilles' teacher in youth. He recalls the story of Meleagros, who, because of his anger at his mother, withdrew from the defense of his city of Kalydon against the Kouretes, even though the battle had gone well for as long as he was in it. Although the elders of the city offered him splendid gifts, he refused to return to the battle until the Kouretes were setting fire to the city walls and his wife, Cleopatra, beseeched him for protection. But because he had waited so long to drive off the Kouretes, the gifts he had been offered were no longer his to claim. Phoenix calls upon Achilles not to repeat the mistake of Meleagros: "Let not the spirit within you turn you that way, dear friend. It would be worse to defend the ships after they are burning. No, with gifts (δώρων) promised go forth. The Acheans [Greeks] will compensate you as an immortal. But if without gifts (δώρων) you go into the fighting where men perish, your honor (τιμῆς) will no longer be as great, though you drive back the battle" (Hom. *Il.* 9.600–05; Lattimore 1951, 214).

Finally, Ajax, in a departing salvo, asserts that Achilles has exceeded the bounds of what is proper and just in refusing so rich an offer. Odysseus, in his speech, had recalled that Achilles' father, Peleus, had observed that his son was prone to anger because of his proud heart, and advised Achilles to "hold back from ill-plotting strife, and all the more will the Argives [Greeks] honor you, both the young men and the old" (Hom. *Il.* 9.257–56; Lattimore 1951, 205). "So the old man advised," says Odysseus, "but you have forgotten" (Hom. *Il.* 9.259; Lattimore 1951, 205). Now, Ajax returns to this point, and comments to Odysseus: "Achilles has made savage the proud-hearted spirit within his body. He is hard, and does not remember that friends' affection wherein we honored him by the ships, far beyond all others. Pitiless. And yet a man takes from his brother's slayer the blood-price, or the price for a child who was killed, and the guilty one, when he had largely repaid, stays still in the country, and the injured man's heart is curbed. . . . but the gods put in your breast a bad spirit not to be placated, for the sake of a single girl" (Hom. *Il.* 9.629–38; Lattimore 1951, 215). Here Ajax makes out Achilles' refusal of the gifts that Agamemnon has offered in recompense to be an act that exceeds the bounds of *themis:* if a father should accept the blood-price for a slain child and let the matter go, how can Achilles justify the refusal of a greater compensation for a smaller offense? Achilles is exhibiting that proud-heartedness that his father warned about, and carrying it beyond all normal limits.

So, at one level, the speeches are about whether a series of exchanges have been conducted within the bounds of *themis.* Agamemnon must return Chryseis because Apollo was angered by his dishonorable refusal of her ransom, but Agamemnon's honor demands that he, in turn, be compensated for his loss, and so he takes Briseis, and thus provokes the wrath of Achilles who feels himself dishonored. Recompense is offered for this slight, but Achilles chooses to display the depth of his wrath by refusing to be placated by the gifts, an act which Ajax judges to exceed the bounds of what is proper. Tradition, the body of *themis,* is mined for examples to support or challenge the actions of the players in this drama of exchange. The words of Peleus, the story of Meleagros, and the wrongheadedness of rewarding the most skillful and the most inept warriors with the same portion, comparison of Achilles recompense and the blood-price of a slain child—these are all brought into play.

The element of cunning or *mētis* in this series of exchanges is manifest in the timing and escalation of the offers and accusations. Agamemnon justifies his original seizure of Briseis as a defense of his status, "that you may learn how much greater I am than you, and another man may shrink back from likening himself to me and contending against me" (Hom. *Il.* 1.186–87; Lattimore 1951, 64). He is craftily availing himself of an opportunity to create a precedent.

Achilles' actions are more directly informed by *mētis.* He at first thinks to take up arms against Agamemnon when Briseis is taken from him, but his hand is stayed by Athena, the daughter of *Mētis.* She promises, "Some day three times over such shining gifts shall be given to you by reason of this outrage" (Hom. *Il.* 1.213; Lattimore 1951, 64). In other words, Achilles can gain more by delaying his response, by waiting for the right moment. But when that moment comes, Achilles takes the opportunity not to reap the rewards of his patience, but to make an even stronger statement of his hatred for Agamemnon by refusing a recompense that is overwhelmingly generous. The *Iliad* is mainly about the wrath of Achilles, after all, and that wrath is nowhere more effectively displayed than in Achilles' refusal of these gifts.

A species of *mētis* is also present in the carrot-and-stick strategy employed by the embassy to Achilles. Odysseus, Phoenix, and Ajax work together to make the case that Achilles' honor would be well served by accepting the gifts they offer and returning to battle, and would be diminished by any further holding out. This is accomplished by representing Agamemnon's gifts as a worthy recompense for the slight he had suffered, on the one hand, and, on the other, by representing Achilles' failure to accept them as a violation of *themis* by means of the words of Peleus, the story of Meleagros, and the example of the blood-price. Thus a cunning trap is laid for Achilles, who is seemingly painted into a corner where he must either accept the gifts with great honor or refuse them and further damage his honor. The consistency with which all three speakers work to play out this underlying strategy is an example of *mētis. Themis* is evoked in the right way at the right time to attempt to constrain the choice of Achilles. Only too late is it realized that this was a wrong-headed strategy. As Diomedes remarks to Agamemnon, "I wish you had not supplicated the blameless son of Peleus with innumerable gifts offered. He is a proud man without this, and now you have driven him far deeper into his pride" (Hom. *Il.* 9.698–700; Lattimore 1951, 216).

The Contrary Demands of Custom at the Ithacan Assembly

The play of *themis* and *mētis* can be seen developing along different lines in the debate between Telemachus, Mentor, and the men of Ithaca in book two of the *Odyssey.* Here the underlying subject of dispute is not the division of the spoils of war amongst warriors, but rather which set of *themistes* should be followed by Penelope and her suitors.

The scene for the debate is set when Odysseus' son Telemachus summons the men of Ithaca to public assembly at the prompting of Mentor, a kindly advisor who is Athena in disguise. The topic of discussion is that the eligible men of Ithaca have taken up residence at the house of Odysseus, who is long overdue to return from Troy, and is thought by many to be dead. The men seek the hand of Odysseus' wife, Penelope, who still clings to the hope that her husband will return. Because of the custom that dictates hospitality toward guests, and because of the number and strength of the suitors, neither Penelope nor young Telemachus can credibly insist that they leave. So they remain, feasting away the wealth of the house.

In addressing the men of Ithaca, Telemachus evokes the goddess Themis herself as he insists that the suitors are acting shamefully: "Upon my mother suitors have fastened against her will, own sons of those men who are here the noblest. They shrink from going to the house of her father, Icarius, that he may himself see to his daughter's bride-gifts. . . . instead, thronging our house day after day, they slay our oxen and sheep and fat goats, and keep revel, and drink the sparkling wine recklessly; the larger part of our substance is already gone. . . . Be ashamed of yourselves, and feel shame before your neighbors who dwell round about, and fear the wrath of the gods, lest it happen that they turn against you in anger at evil deeds. I pray you by Olympian Zeus and by

Themis who dissolves and gathers the assemblies of men, stop this" (Hom. *Od.* 2.50–70; Murray and Dimock 51–52). Where custom would dictate, according to Telemachus, that the suitors present themselves to Penelope's father if they wish to seek her hand, they have shamefully descended upon her house. This abuse of custom is an offense that would anger not only Zeus, but also Themis, according to Telemachus.

The following speeches circle around the topic of whether Penelope should remain in the house of Laertes and Odysseus or return to her father's house. In answer to Telemachus' speech, Antinous, a leading suitor, tells Telemachus that he should send his mother back to her father's house (Hom. *Od.* 2.113). Telemachus replies that he can neither force his own mother to leave *his* father's house, nor could he afford to return her dowry to *her* father, as custom would require, if he were to do so (Hom. *Od.* 2.133–37).He again called upon Zeus to bring about "deeds of requital" ("παλίντιτα ἔργα"; Hom. *Od.* 2.144; Murray and Dimock, 56–57). As soon as he uttered these words, two eagles flew overhead, engaged in deadly combat, a sign which is interpreted to mean that Odysseus is on his way home to take vengeance on the suitors. Eurymachus dismisses this prophesy and again bids Telemachus to send his mother back to her father's house (Hom. *Od.* 2.195). After Telemachus asks for a ship that will take him on a voyage to seek tidings of his father, Mentor again chastises the assembly for its inaction.

The underlying situation is one in which custom is being played against custom. The suitors are right to say that Penelope should return to her father's house if Odysseus were dead, but this would have meant leaving the young Telemachus and the elderly Laertes to fend for themselves, a situation which could prove disastrous in the rough and tumble world of archaic Greece. By remaining in the house of Odysseus, Penelope implies that her husband still lives. But as long as she remains, custom dictates that hospitality must be extended to guests from the dwindling resources of the house. There appears to be strategy, then, in both Penelope's tarrying, and in the suitor's feasting. Penelope must buy time for her child to grow, counting on the suitors to prevent each other from harming her child or father-in-law. The suitors, for their part, know that sooner or later they will literally feast Penelope out of house and home, forcing her to remarry. In the assembly, then, Telemachus calls upon Zeus and Themis to witness the injustice done to him by the suitors, but the suitors are equally able to call upon custom to justify their behavior. In these speeches, one custom is played against another in a way that displays a certain amount of *mētis* on both sides.

Finley had the following general assessment of the public discourse that takes place in Homeric epic: "never in either the *Iliad* or the *Odyssey* is there a rational discussion, a sustained, disciplined consideration of circumstances and their implications, of possible courses of action, their advantages and disadvantages. There are lengthy arguments, as between Achilles and Agamemnon, or between Telemachus and the suitors, but they are quarrels, not discussions, in which each side seeks to overpower the other by threats and to win over the assembled multitude by emotional appeal, by harangue, and by warning" (122). To be sure, Finley does not have a very high estimation of the role played by *logos* in Homeric epic. But if the public "debates" of Homer fall short of the highest standards of deliberative logic, they are not without a certain logic of their own: one that involves the *strategic* use of custom and precedent. This is a legitimate form of rationality that can be found not only in the speeches preserved in Homeric epic, but also in at least parts of later rhetorical theory and practice. It is a context-bound rationality, innocent of any effort to stand above time and place. We can learn more about this kind of rationality from contemporary "theories of practice."

Themis, *Mētis* and Theories of Practice

The artfulness of these speeches lies in the cunning evocation of *themistes,* the ability of the speakers to recall the right custom at the right time. This species of artfulness can be thought about in terms of the logic of the "complementary and opposed" powers of *themis* and *mētis,* conceptions that were available within archaic Greek culture. It can also be understood through the lens of contemporary "theories of practice" articulated by Bourdieu and Certeau, whose time-and-place-bound logic differs from that of the "scientific" quest for context-independent laws that has been set up as the antithesis of the mythopoetic mind.

In *Outline of the Theory of Practice,* originating in fieldwork he had conducted in Kabylia, Bourdieu argues that anthropologists and other social scientists need to move from the study of "detemporalized" rules to the study of strategies that exist in time. He wrote: "To substitute *strategy* for *rule* is to reintroduce the element of time, with its rhythm, its orientation, and its irreversibility" (9). While the rules of social exchange dictate that a gift obliges a counter-gift, and an insult calls for a retort, the true meaning of such acts can only be discovered at the level of strategy, for it resides in the timing: "The skilled strategist can turn a capital of provocations received or conflicts suspended, with the potential ripostes, vengeances, or conflicts it contains, into an instrument of power, by reserving the capacity to reopen or cease hostilities in his own good time" (15). Thus Bourdieu argues that the anthropologist should study not only structures, in the mode of Claude Lévi-Strauss, or rules of exchange, in the mode of Marcel Mauss, but must also examine the practice of exchange, which puts into play elements of timing and nonequivalence that create the enduring relations of obligation and/or justifiable antagonism from which social structure emerges.

In *The Practice of Everyday Life,* Michel de Certeau organizes the advances of Bourdieu, Foucault, and others into a more general theory of practice.

Certeau is generally interested in what he calls "ways of operating" (xi) or ways of acting within structures which, often unwittingly, reproduce that structure. They consist primarily of ways of doing rather than ways of thinking. They include not only Bourdieu's "strategies," but also the "procedures" described by Foucault in such works as *Discipline and Punish.* These "procedures" enable the exercise of power through displaying, categorizing, and ranking individual bodies, and subjecting them to interventions deemed to be medically, morally, or socially corrective. They include "tactics" which are distinguished from strategies as having no "proper" place in a larger scheme or structure, and they include operations that make use of space as well as those that make use of time. Among the practices considered by Certeau are walking in the city, train travel, storytelling, and reading.

Within this larger inquiry into the practices of everyday life, Certeau treats the "art of speaking" or narration in terms explicitly derived from Detienne and Vernant's book on *mētis:* "Narration does indeed have a content, but it also belongs to the art of making a coup: it is a detour by way of the past ('the other day,' 'in the olden days') or by way of a quotation (a 'saying,' a proverb) made in order to take advantage of an occasion and to modify an equilibrium by taking it by surprise" (Certeau, 79). Certeau calls the sort of intelligence that guides such practices of narrative intervention *mētis.* The operation of *mētis* involves "the world of the memory" intervening at "the right moment" (84), an operation that is explicitly linked to the ancient conception of *kairos.*

We have come full circle, then, from Detienne and Vernant's identification of *themis* and *mētis* as "complementary and opposed" powers crucial to the hegemony to Zeus, through a reading of how certain passages in the *Iliad* and *Odyssey* can be understood in terms of the cunning use of custom, to suggestively related modern theories of practice, and right back to the concept of *mētis.* From the perspective of the theories of practice outlined by Bourdieu and Certeau, it is apparent that Achilles in the *Iliad* and Telemachus in the *Odyssey* are involved in a sort of gamesmanship, a "way of operating" that involves recalling the right part of the past at the right time. Achilles tries to maintain, and even augment, his prestige by nursing the injury Agamemnon had done him, and rejecting a generous offer of recompense as insufficient. What is Achilles doing other than, in Bourdieu's words (15), turning "a capital of provocations received . . . into an instrument of power"? Odysseus, Phoenix, and Ajax try to dissuade him from this strategy by taking a "detour by way of the past" and recalling the story of Meleagros, and Peleus' comment that his son was prone to the anger because of his proud heart. Telemachus and the suitors each try to advance their own interests by contending that customs dictate different courses of action with regard to Penelope. In both of these cases, the forces of *themis* and *mētis* are at play in a way that suggestively reflects contemporary theories of practice.

From *Themis* and *Mētis* to *Philosophia* and *Kairos*

The appearance of the *themis/mētis* framework in "Isocratean rhetoric" represents a strained continuity between the practice of speech in Homer and the classical *paidea.* Isocrates ran one of the foremost schools in Athens from about 392 to 338 B.C.E. Although Plato's rival Academy has more importance in contemporary perspectives of fourth-century Athens, Isocrates was remembered as the more prominent figure by scholars in later antiquity and the Renaissance.[15] Isocrates left no technical treatises dealing with the art he taught, but only a series of letters and speeches. However, because a number of the speeches have a strong didactic component, scholars have been able to reconstruct a fair picture of the Isocratean approach to the arts of speech.[16]

Rather than teaching his students a "bag of tricks"—a collection of techniques like proof from *eikos* or the use of *sēmeia* and *tekmēria*—Isocrates believed that his students were best served by being immersed in what might be called the lore of the *polis.* He was consistently critical of the writers of technical manuals on speech.[17] In the words of the French historian of classic education Henri-Irénée Marrou, "Isocrates adapted to literature the fundamental ideals of Homeric education: 'example' and 'imitation'—παράδειγμα and μίμησις" (84). Johnstone provides a thumbnail summary of the Isocratean program: "For Isocrates . . . proper civil education aims at cultivating a wisdom that permits the individual to see where true advantage lies, both in personal affairs and in public policy. . . . wisdom is nurtured in the soul through the study of politics (that is, through examination of great political discourses), ethics (primarily traditional Greek ethics, based on poetry and custom), and history (through examining the teachings of the poets and the works of Herodotus and Thucydides)" (158). Isocrates' educational program, in other words, was one that immersed his students in the words and deeds of the past in the hope that such immersion would bring wisdom and deliberative excellence. He apparently hoped that his students would mine the stores of tradition for nuggets of wisdom applicable to any dilemma that might arise in the present. It was this commitment to a broad study of political oratory, civic history, and popular culture that earned Isocrates the title "the father of humanism" in some quarters.[18]

Although his ultimate aim was to produce students with the ability to speak well on matters of civic importance, Isocrates spoke of himself not as a teacher of rhetoric, but as a teacher of what he referred to as *philosophia.*[19] This pursuit certainly involved a love of wisdom, but it was not the speculative pursuit of knowledge that would be practiced by Plato and Aristotle. Rather, it was the practically oriented study of oratory, history, and culture: this is what was meant by *philosophia* in the Isocratean sense. Ekaterina Haskins comments, "In calling this educational program *philosophia* and aligning it with the poetic tradition, he [Isocrates] challenges Plato's Academy" (2004, 31).

Isocrates' idea of *philosophia* has a certain relationship with the *themis* that the Homeric *basileus* needed to master in order to rule. It is a broader concept to be sure, encompassing not only the songs and stories that the archaic *basileus* might have heard from an *aoidos,* but also written history and oratory. However, it does, as Haskins asserts, retain a connection with the poetic tradition, and this expanded body of knowledge was intended by Isocrates to be used in a way similar to the way Homeric speakers used their knowledge of *themis:* with the sort of cunning that manifests itself in good timing, what Isocrates calls *kairos* rather than *mētis.* A term that has defied systematic theorization, *kairos*—translated variously as "the right time," "due season" and "opportunity"—perhaps stands in closer relationship to *mētis* than does *themis* to *philosophia.*[20]

The idea that the Isocratean orator should have the knack for making kairotic use of the past for the benefit of the present is articulated in any number of places. In the opening passages of the *Panegyricus,* for instance, a speech written as an address to a Panhellenic festival that counsels war against the barbarians, Isocrates stated: "What happened in the past is available to all of us, but it is the mark of a wise person to use these events at an appropriate time (*kairos*), conceive fitting arguments about each of them, and set them out in good style" (*Panath.* 9; Papillon 2004, 172). The same general advice is given in a number of other places: "When deliberating, make past events models (*paradigma*) for the future, for the unseen is most quickly comprehended from the seen" (*Ad Dem.* 34; Mirhady 2000, 26); "Consider current events and their consequences for both private citizens and kings. If you recall the past, you will plan better for the future" (*Ad Nic.*, 35; Too 2000, 164). In *Antidosis* 277, Isocrates does not directly comment on appropriating a piece of the past to reveal at a kairotic moment, but still describes how the superior orator must select materials that will be appropriate and effective from all the things that might be said about his topic. This presupposes that the speaker has a vast store of materials to choose from, gleaned from years of immersion in *philosophia,* and a well-honed sense of the moment.

Conclusion

There is in these speeches in Homer a kind a rationality that bridges the supposed divide between oral mythopoeic culture and literate rational culture. It is nothing very mysterious. It is simply the practice of carrying on an argument by (a) being familiar with a body of "lore" consisting of customs (later laws), examples, maxims, and anecdotes, and (b) having the knack for evoking the right bit of lore at the right time. The lore may be variously called *themis* or *philosophia* or *historia,* and the knack for invoking it may be called *mētis* or *kairos.* Although the rules of this sort of game are simple enough at this most abstract level, there is great complexity in the actual play, as is demonstrated both by our ancient examples from the *Iliad* and the *Odyssey* and by contemporary "theorists of practice." Inasmuch as this species of rationality demands the command of a core of cultural knowledge, and flows from its beginnings in archaic Greece to inform the output of Isocrates, the "father of humanism," it resides near the fountainhead of humanistic education.

None of the foregoing is intended to disparage the scientific quest for laws that stand above time and place. Neither do I wish to dispute that Greek thinkers of the sixth and fifth centuries B.C.E. were among those who took the first steps toward the goal of a scientific view of the cosmos. I merely wish to point out that the time-and-place-bound operations of the "mythopoetic mind" are not unworthy of the designation of "rationality," and that there is a strong thread of continuity that runs from the *basileus'* practice of bringing that past into meaningful contact with the present, through the Isocratean approach to rhetoric, right up to our own lived experience in the contemporary world.

It Takes an Empire to Raise a Sophist

An Athens-Centered Analysis of the Oikonomia of Pre-Platonic Rhetoric

Michael Svoboda

Many attempts have been made to explain the sudden emergence of that special group of "transnational" actors in the ancient world, the sophists. Each explanation has highlighted different factors. The emergence of democracy, especially in Athens, is thought by most to have created a market for intellectual goods of the sort trafficked by these figures. And the emergence of literacy is thought, by some, to have helped enable the sophists to create the intellectual goods they marketed.[1] Economic factors, however, have typically been addressed only in the most general terms. Less attention still has been given to the legal structures and accounting mechanisms that facilitated the economic developments of this period. As a result, the full set of preconditions for the emergence of the sophists has not been recognized, and the critical transformation of their emerging art(s) of speech through the responses of fourth-century Athenians has been misunderstood. Once these factors are examined more closely, two correlations among the variables can be observed.

First, the careers of the fifth-century sophists depended on the material wealth and operational norms created by the Athenian empire; it took not just democracy but an empire to raise the sophists. The transnational (multi-*poleis*) operations of these sophists were possible only because the Athenian empire pacified and stabilized international relations among the city-states that bordered and dotted the Aegean and Ionian seas, facilitated the creation of wealth (especially in Athens), and rationalized and routinized the spending of that wealth. Second, although the sophists reflected on broader issues that we might now call political or philosophical, their expertise was primarily economical; that is, it was aimed at the profitable management of the affairs of households, *oikoi,* especially the extended and often transnational households of landed families. For prominent Athenian households, the transnational sophists offered expertise on how to manage transnational affairs. Rhetoric before Plato was a subset of economics; the practices taught by the sophists were more useful for advancing the interests of the household (*oikos*) than the democratic process (*demokratikos*) or the state (*polis*). But with Athens' defeat in the Peloponnesian War, the conditions under which these households operated changed dramatically. With their wealth substantially diminished by the loss of their overseas holdings and by the damage done to their Attic estates, these households now had to compete in the market economy within Athens. Having observed the progression from empire to war to destruction, fourth-century Athenian thinkers slowly transformed the sophists' *oikonomia* into *technai* for politics. Among these was *rhētorikē*.[2]

My argument involves five steps. First, recent histories of rhetoric, including James Fredal's anthropo-economic explanation for fourth-century denunciations of the sophists, offer accounts of the conditions that led to the emergence of the first sophists.[3] In reviewing that portion of what Schiappa has dubbed "the standard account of rhetoric's beginnings" (1999, 3), the problem of the biased and refractory character of the available sources are also reexamined. Second, a set of markers by which to identify a "dual-economy" society is derived from David W. Tandy's anthropological account of the emergence of the market economy in eighth-century Greece. Third, texts from and about the first sophistic are searched for these markers in order to determine whether fifth-century Athens (and the city-states affiliated or entangled with its empire) can be described as a "dual-economy society," as a society in which elements of reciprocal exchange persist within an increasingly dominant market economy. Fourth, an alternative explanation is offered for Fredal's account of the hostility expressed by Isocrates, Plato, and other fourth-century figures toward the lesser and largely anonymous sophists still in Athens: with the defeat of the Athenian empire, a new economy emerged in which reciprocal and market exchanges were more thoroughly intermixed. I conclude, fifth, with an examination of the ways in which the different material conditions of the fifth-century sophists and their fourth-century Athenian critics might be reflected in their different perceptions of rhetoric and politics.

The dual economic system described by Tandy persisted beyond the eighth century, conditioning the norms for social and commercial interactions even in the fifth-century Athenian empire. The first sophists thrived because, within the empire, these norms both created a market for their goods and services and constrained competition. After the collapse of the empire, these norms were called into question, both practically and theoretically. The fourth-century arts of rhetoric were the results of political reflections on these new socio-economic conditions.

The "Standard Account" of the Sophists

In a wide-ranging reflection on nearly a century of "recent" scholarship on ancient rhetoric, Edward Schiappa challenged "The Standard Account of Rhetoric's Beginnings," the new consensus that was slowly built after George Grote overturned the largely negative account of the Platonists. Although scholars are right to question Plato's ethical objections to rhetoric, Schiappa argued, they need to recognize that the clearly focused "knack" to which he objected was in several respects his own fourth-century invention. In short, researchers were reading too much "discipline" back into rhetoric's predisciplinary roots. Largely in accord with Schiappa's assessment, I seek to "save the appearances" of the elder sophists, without invoking a fully formed *rhētorikē*, by identifying the material conditions of their practices.[4]

One version of these conditions can be drawn from the earliest stories of "the standard account," the stories about the invention of rhetoric by Corax and Tisias. Schiappa rightly questions their provenance (1999, 34–45), but the historical account of the land disputes that arose after the tyrants were deposed in Sicily and the humorous anecdote about the alleged countersuits lodged by Corax and Tisias both illustrate practical points that should be reconsidered in speculating about the conditions under which new practices of speech might have been marketed in ancient Greece.

The historical account appears in Cicero's *Brutus*, where it is attributed to a now lost book of Aristotle. Several works from the corpus of "the standard account" refer to this story, including histories by Marrou (53), Kennedy (1963), Cole (1991, 22–27), and Vickers (6).[5] Cicero's account is as follows: "Upon peace and tranquility eloquence attends as their ally, it is, one may say, the offspring of a well-established civic order. Thus Aristotle said that in Sicily, after the expulsion of tyrants, when after a long interval restitution of private property was sought by legal means, Corax and Tisias the Sicilians, with the acuteness and controversial habit of their people, first put together some theoretical precepts; that before them, while many had taken pains to speak with care and with orderly arrangement, no one had followed a definite method or art" (*Brutus* XII.45–46; Hendrickson, 49). Even if, as Schiappa argues, serious doubts may be raised about this account, it still offers a helpful explanation for the emergence of a new craft, the different elements of which merit closer examination. To be successful, this story suggests, anyone marketing a new craft must be able to sell it as a solution to a problem one's clients recognize. Here a clear and compelling problem can reasonably be inferred: a significant portion of the populace must challenge or defend claims to native lands.[6] Because many suits of the same type must be filed and argued, a successful formula, once devised, might be used again and again. And as winning or losing is vital and potentially life-defining for the claimants, many should be willing to pay for expertise that might provide them with an edge. In fact, there might be so much demand for this expertise that it could be worthwhile for the principal to train an associate to assist with the work. In other words, under the conditions suggested in Cicero's account of the origins of rhetoric in Sicily, an enterprising individual could sell not merely his services but his craft.

The humorous anecdote prompts other reflections about early efforts to market arts of speech. According to Rebhorn, the earliest extant version of this story comes from Sopater's *Commentary on the Rhetoric of Hermogenes.* At its heart are the paradoxically competing arguments of a teacher, Corax, and his student, Tisias. Each claims that, if he wins the case, the judgment should go to him. But if he loses the case, each also argues, that verdict would constitute evidence for the truth of his claim: that a winning practice of speech was successfully taught, should the student prevail over the teacher; that a winning practice of speech was not actually delivered, should the teacher prevail over the student.

We should note, first, that these opposing arguments create a kind of puzzle. Puzzles are intellectual products that can function within their own frame of reference. Such puzzles can be carried from place to place. But, second, once opposed, puzzles of the sort depicted in this anecdote cancel each other out: the case is returned to its beginning. These sorts of conceptual conundrums, which include arguments from probability, spread rapidly in the late fifth century. Clients may have felt the need to use them if only to neutralize their expected use by their opponents. Effectively, then, anyone who could create such puzzles could create a market for them by ensuring their widespread availability. Note, finally, that in some versions of the anecdote the case is argued before a judge, not a jury. This should serve to remind us that legal cases are not confined to democracies. Thus the emergence of democracy alone cannot explain the emergence, or failure to emerge, of a proto-art of rhetoric.

Even if apocryphal, then, these stories—the historical account from Aristotle via Cicero and the anecdote from Hermogenes via Sopater—set out some likely conditions for a marketable practice of speech.[7] These are the conditions:

Situations of sufficient similarity must recur with sufficient regularity as to constitute a recognized risk, problem, or opportunity.

The practitioner must be perceived as having a solution to this risk, problem, or opportunity.

The client must have reasons and means to pay the practitioner for his solution.

These elements are all present in Cicero's account of the origin of rhetoric and, indirectly, in the anecdote about the dueling lawsuits of Corax and Tisias. As the mode of rhetoric in both stories is forensic rather than deliberative, we might also infer that expert advice on how to win in court might be easier to sell than expert advice on how to succeed in politics. Further, expert advice presented in a clearly distinguishable form such as a fixed order for the parts of a speech or the patterned construction of probabilities might be easier to sell—quickly and in many different places—than a process of careful situational analysis. In sum, these accounts of Corax and Tisias offer a checklist of elements and observations to consider in assessing explanations for the subsequent success of the great sophists.

Five of the seventeen separate claims Schiappa isolates in "the standard account of rhetoric's origins" concern the sophists (1999, 6–9 and 48–82). Schiappa challenges this standard account by first noting that even in the restricted use intended here—some version of the "older" or "great" sophists—the label has been applied inconsistently, both by the ancients and by the moderns. The claim that they all share an interest in rhetoric or, more broadly, in public speaking, is also not consistently borne out by the evidence. The same holds for claims about the morality, relativism, or political focus of the sophists. But, while Schiappa succeeds in questioning other accounts, he does not explain the success of the sophists, such as Gorgias and Protagoras, who appear on virtually all lists for this group. Why was there a market for the goods and services they sold, however we describe these goods or services?

The answer most frequently offered is that provided in the story of Corax and Tisias—but without the sudden rush of lawsuits over land titles. Here is Jarrett's version: "The emergence of democracy in Fifth Century BC Athens, demanding broader participation in government and legal affairs, created the need for a kind of secondary education designed to prepare young men for public life in the *polis*" (xv).[8] In this view, the emergence of democracy sufficed to create a market—sufficiently similar problems recognizably recurring with sufficient regularity—for the intellectual goods and services the sophists sold. But are the deliberative situations of ancient Greek cities, even the democratic Greek city-states, really so similar that the same advice could be sold, by outsiders, to their citizens?

Some scholars provide a partial answer to this question by emphasizing Athens' extraordinary wealth and exceptional openness. Athens was a particularly important and accessible market for the sophists; the great wealth held by many of its citizens lowered the threshold for the instrumental value of their goods. In other words, because they had the wherewithal, Athenians were prepared to purchase goods or services at prices that might have been perceived as too dear in other ancient cities. Thus, according to these scholars, because Athens was one of the largest, wealthiest, and most open, democratic, and cosmopolitan of the Greek city-states, it provided a ready market for the sophists.[9]

Others go further, tying the emergence of the sophists to the social and economic conditions created by the formation of the Athenian empire. Most contemporary historians of fifth- and fourth-century Greece link the first sophistic with the age of Pericles. In this they follow the lead of Grote, who discussed the sophists as part of a broader reflection on "The Drama—Rhetoric and Dialectics—The Sophists" that he inserted in his *History of Greece,* between the final chapter on the Peloponnesian war and the start of the first narrative chapter on the fourth century (349–64). Hammond (1986) follows suit, inserting his chapter on "The Cultural Crisis of the Peloponnesian War" between "The Surrender of Athens" and "The Hegemony of Sparta" (420–36). Taking a slightly different approach, Fine discusses the sophists, chiefly by way of explaining their influence on Thucydides, at the beginning of his long chapter on the Peloponnesian War (442–525).[10] In these and in many other works, the careers of the great sophists are tied not simply to the emergence of democracy in the ancient Greek world but to a particular period in the history of Athens' imperial democracy. And that particular period began some decades after democracy had already been established at Athens.

Two classicists, Jacqueline de Romilly and G. B. Kerferd, articulate what they see as the intrinsic connections between the rise of the Athenian empire and the flowering of the first sophistic. Romilly expresses that connection in complementary terms: "[Athens] was thus simultaneously discovering and trying to resolve all kinds of problems to do with institutions, wages, warfare, and strategy. . . . A greater understanding of human nature was thus evolving with passionate haste. Meanwhile, greater understanding of human nature was also what the Sophists' teaching, starting with their rhetoric, was offering and establishing. What the Sophists had to offer was exactly what the Athenians were ardently seeking. Each side provided stimulus for the other" (1992, 25). The Athenian side of this relationship, however, was not confined to Athens. When sophists traveled across mainland Greece or sailed to islands in the Aegean or Ionian seas, they were still operating within the Athenian sphere of influence, often within city-states that were formally part of its empire. In other words, Athens set the terms of engagement for the sophists and their clients in many places besides Athens. Athens guaranteed the freedom of the seas across which they traveled. It established consistent rules of trade. And it specified the places and procedures for resolving conflicts and disputes: "In all kinds of litigations, the island inhabitants had to seek justice before Athenian courts" (19).[11]

G. B. Kerferd takes this a step further: "Athens for some sixty years in the second half of the fifth century B.C. was the real centre of the sophistic movement. So much so indeed that it would seem probable that without Athens the movement would hardly have come into existence at all" (15). But this was not merely a matter of the empire achieving and managing the necessary wealth and power. In Kerferd's view, the first sophistic was also the result of historical accident: "[The sophists] owed much to individual patronage, and above all to the patronage of one man, Pericles" (15). The emergence of the sophists, Kerferd concludes in his chapter "The Sophists as a Social Phenomenon," was "a development internal to the history of Athens" (22).

These accounts begin to approximate the conditions present in the stories about Corax and Tisias. As a result of Athens' promotion and regulation of intercity trade within and between the Aegean and Ionian seas, similar situations requiring similar sorts of solutions regularly arose throughout the empire. Familiarity with the rules governing these situations—and perhaps broader knowledge of Athenian customs and imperial procedures—might have been marketable to the many Greeks who could have expected to find themselves in one or more of these situations. In theory, a similar case might be made for expertise in political matters—at the height of the Athenian empire more democracies were linked together in more intricate ways—but the relevance of and rewards for expertise in legal matters seem more immediate. Finally, it is clear that the Athenians, at least, had the means to purchase this expertise. Non-Athenians may actually have had better reasons to purchase expertise about Athens' rules and procedures, but here we encounter another limitation of our sources.

The paying of fees for intellectual goods, however, was not merely a matter of means. Such fees conveyed (or incurred) important social meanings. As Guthrie noted in his account of the sophists in his *History of Greek Philosophy,* the charging of fees, often very high fees, was a defining characteristic of the great sophists (1971, 35–39).[12] And charging fees for knowledge of and proficiency in the culture and customs of a city, rather than offering them in exchange for a commodity or for a service rendered through manual or craft labor, marked a break with Greek custom, whereby such knowledge was passed on to young men by their elders. For the well-bred, or for those who aspired to that status, there were also customary barriers against selling one's labor in the marketplace. One managed one's own estate and affairs; one did not sell one's services to others.[13] Hence the for-fee teaching of the sophists was doubly controversial.[14] To successfully market their goods and services, then, sophists had to have clients who possessed both the necessary means and a rationale for surmounting the cultural barriers against using those means in this fashion.

James Fredal has addressed the social implications of the sophists' fees at length. To explain the disdain with which fourth-century Athenian critics repeatedly cited the fees sophists charged for their lessons, Fredal points to social changes underway in Athens at the time, which he describes as a transformation from a reciprocal-obligation gift culture to a transactional mercantile economy (149). The sophists simply seized this moment and, perhaps earlier than others were ready to accept, began charging fees for a good, knowledge, that had previously been governed by complex and often ritualized exchanges that sustained social hierarchies of interfamily, intergenerational, and other intra-communal relationships (158–62).[15] The disparagement of this practice by Isocrates, Plato, Xenophon, and others simply reflected the divide between a conservative and aristocratic elite who sought political stability in a return to the social forms of the past and a more ambitious, democratic, and forward-looking generation that enjoyed freedom from these constraining social norms (152–56). In a cosmopolitan city like Athens, where almost anything from anywhere could be purchased, it was inevitable that knowledge itself would be commodified (150).[16] The sophists were simply the first educators to recognize that this change had occurred, and thus they profited from it—handsomely. Fredal explains, "In this case, then, we should see sophistic fees not in terms of an opposition between the acquisitive sophists who charged for their wisdom and the benevolent philosophers who dispensed it freely, but between two different forms of exchange: one through the weighing of minted silver and the other through the winning of loyal followers" (158).

As an example of gift exchange based on won loyalty, Fredal relays the story of Criton and Archedemus from Xenophon's *Memorabilia.* Rather than hiring him outright to countersue his enemies, Criton draws Archedemus into his circle, periodically sharing profits from his enterprises—as small gifts. In time, Archedemus finds an opportunity to reciprocate, forcing one of his own opponents to withdraw his suit against Criton as part of their settlement (163–64).

Fredal's innovation here is to suggest that the antagonism between the sophists and their post-Socratic critics is in part due to the coexistence of two economic frameworks. The sophists were part of the vanguard of a democratic political economy; Xenophon, Plato, Isocrates, and others sided with the rearguard of the landed Athenian aristocracy. By so highlighting these different but coexisting frameworks for exchange, Fredal links both the sophists and their critics to socioeconomic developments within Athens. But missing from this analysis is a critical historical fact: the fourth-century sophists and their Athenian critics were all operating in the wake of a seismic economic change—the collapse of the Athenian empire.

The accounts of Romilly and Kerferd suggest that the first, "great," sophists emerged under economic and social conditions created by the Athenian empire. Fredal argues that the heightened animosity between sophists and their Athenians critics in the fourth century was due to changing economic conditions. It was as a result of the collapse of the socioeconomic conditions that fostered the first sophists that some fourth-century Athenians found themselves in direct competition with these sophists' students. Thus the sophists' economic art of speech was transformed into a political art: *rhētorikē.* A reanalysis of the dual-economy society, sketched by Fredal, reveals that it emerged much earlier—and that it persists, in some forms, to this day. Unfortunately, there are biases and limitations inherent in the available sources. Fredal has already highlighted one problem: most of our sources about the fifth-century sophists who visited Athens during its imperial heyday were written by Athenians who lived in the reduced circumstances of the fourth century.

Almost all accounts or interpretations of the sophists include a cautionary note on the dearth and biases of historical sources.[17] Few of the sophists' own works have survived, and most of these only secondhand; their works—or portions of their works—have been incorporated into the works or collections of later writers. And the earliest surviving accounts of the sophists are often hostile to the characters, views, or practices. Plato's dialogues provide some of the most fully developed portraits of the older sophists, but his bias is clear: Plato wants to discredit their ideas, if not their character. Thus to recover the thinking of the sophists, scholars must often read through or against the texts in which that thinking is presented.

But this cautionary note overlooks an equivalent problem: these biased, even hostile, sources may actually exaggerate the importance of the sophists and their work. Nearly a third of the Platonic corpus, for example, consists of conversations between Socrates and one or more of the elder sophists or of lengthy analyses of their teachings and their implications.[18] No other Athenian author devotes this much attention to the sophists. Only one of Aristophanes' extant plays engages these thinkers and their ideas to any significant degree, and in that play, *Clouds,* he must use the figure of Socrates, a native-born, full-time resident of Athens, to make that effort engaging for his viewers. This suggests a lower public name recognition than that implied by the standard account. A recent study of the extant fragments from the plays of Aristophanes' rivals supports this inference: "[I]n contrast to the presence of Socrates in the fragments of old comedy the silence is so striking that one is inclined to suppose that relatively little attention was paid to the major sophists as individuals" (Carey 2000, 430). In the canon of the standard account, Havelock is the rare author who addresses the possibility that the sophists' fourth-century critics might distort our view of their work in positive ways: "[I]n Plato's eyes the pretension to educate was somehow central to the sophistic profession . . . and that claim cut Plato to the quick. We say in Plato's eyes; for it is again possible that he selected for frontal attack an item which in their programmes was incidental. That is, it was Plato who was obsessed with problems of education and instruction, which he made his own" (Havelock 1957, 162–63). But obsession not only narrows one's focus; it also leads one to return to the object of that focus again and again. Using Plato's dialogues to measure the impact the sophists had on Athens will thus likely lead one to overestimate the sophists' importance.

This points to a second largely overlooked problem with the extant sources: because the vast majority of our earliest accounts of the older sophists are Athenian in origin—or are influenced by Athenian sources—we see how some Athenians viewed the sophists, but we do not see how sophists, or other outsiders, viewed Athenians. Nor do we see as clearly how other cities viewed the sophists, nor whether or how Athenians might have functioned as sophists in other cities. In his account of the Sicilian Expedition, in his life of *Nicias,* Plutarch provides a brief indication of the high esteem in which Athens' tragic poets were held.[19] But because we more typically hear about the intellectual goods flowing into Athens than about similar goods flowing out, Athens appears to have an intellectual trade deficit. And this appearance, too, may lead us to overestimate the importance of the sophists in the intellectual economy of ancient Greece as a whole. In recounting the stories about the day-long conversation between Pericles and Protagoras and about Pericles commissioning Protagoras to draft the constitution for Thurii, for example, scholars attribute the agency and the efficacy to the sophist.[20] But it might be equally valid to argue that Protagoras studied with Pericles on that day.[21] And, for the work of drafting the constitution of Thurii, Protagoras' most important qualification in Pericles' eyes was likely that he was not an Athenian: Thurii was being founded as an "international" city, and another Athenian, Lampon, was already involved in the planning (Hammond 1986, 314; Azoulay, 49).[22] For these reasons, in *Pericles of Athens,* Vincent Azoulay places Protagoras in Pericles' circle rather than vice-versa (91). To better understand the expertise marketed by the older sophists in the late-fifth-century Greek world, then, we must thus recognize that most of our sources are Athenian, from the fourth century, and, in the case of Plato, peculiarly focused on the problems of education and political judgment.

A Dual-Economic Account of the Sophists

A prima facie case has been made for a strong correlation between the formation of the Athenian empire and the emergence of the first sophists. Not merely do most of our accounts place the great sophists in Athens during the age of Pericles, but there are indications that they were drawn there by and their enterprises were predicated on the markets created, both in and outside Athens, by the wealth and order of the Athenian empire. With the collapse of that empire, we would expect these economic conditions to change and with them the social norms predicated on those conditions. Finally, we have been reminded that we are viewing the fifth-century world of the older sophists largely through fourth-century Athenian sources, which may have the paradoxical effect of understating the intellectual agency of the Athenians in the political and economic empire they governed. In order to understand how the older sophists could be so successful in fifth-century Athens (to the extent that they were) and yet be so controversial in fourth-century Athens (in some circles), we must revisit the distinction between the gift and market economies sketched by Fredal. The economic transformation highlighted in Fredal's analysis occurred at the beginning of the fourth century, in the wake of the collapse of the Athenian empire. To place that end-of-empire transformation in perspective, we will examine a similar account of the economic developments that preceded the formation of the Athenian empire and perhaps facilitated or shaped that formation.

In *Warriors into Traders,* David W. Tandy analyzes the works of Homer and Hesiod; the results of recent archaeological digs in Turkey, the Balkans, Greece, and Sicily; and the economic and socio-anthropological histories of Arthur W. H. Adkins, Karl Polanyi, and James M. Redfield, among others, to argue that the emergence of the Greek *polis* marked the end of a turbulent period of social and economic transformation.[23] The bases of power and prestige shifted from the reciprocal obligations of landed wealth *within* a community to the unobligated wealth generated by trade *between* communities (Tandy, 19–130). In the most destructive and dangerous phase of this transformation, the unobligated wealth generated by trade was used, in the form of land-secured loans, to expropriate the family holdings of the poorer members of these early communities (128–35). Hesiod's *Works and Days* and Solon's laws, for example, are attempts to understand and redress these social and economic dislocations, Tandy argues (4–5, 203–27). The compromise struck by Solon set limits on the obligations that unobligated trade wealth could place on landholdings. Thereafter, a wealthy household could still pursue and accrue unencumbered wealth abroad, but that wealth could not then be used to indebt and thereby expropriate the property of one's fellow citizens. In effect, Greeks learned to function in two economies. Often this entailed living in two or more cities. In one's home city, one lived in the social economy of land and lineage. But to generate wealth, perhaps even the wealth necessary to support one's home estate, one periodically lived abroad in order to participate in the mercantile economy.

An important marker of these early economic developments, Tandy argues, is the appearance of "ship-shaped firedogs" in eighth-to-seventh-century burial mounds in Greece, Crete, and other sites in the Aegean. When made of iron, as these were, these practical implements, used to hold firewood off the ground or hearth to improve air circulation, were also symbols of wealth. But more significant for Tandy was their shape: "Thus the firedogs are a reflection of not only how status is asserted but also how it is garnered and maintained—through the acquisition of unencumbered wealth, wealth that stands independent of the community . . . [wealth that is introduced] from the outside *by ship*" (164–65, italics in the original).

In *Money and the Early Greek Mind* (2004), Richard Seaford moves this story forward by showing how iron spits, implements for roasting meat over the fires built on firedogs, evolved from symbols of wealth, to means for exchange, and thereby into the precursors for coinage. And coinage, Seaford argues, prompted and facilitated new levels of abstract thinking. The fact that money, by purchasing goods or by being acquired through the sale of goods, "could be transformed into and from everything else" (11) made it useful as a mental model, even if only unconsciously. Money provided a means for imagining unchanging elements behind or within ever-changing appearances or things.

But coined money also provides a means for organizing and administering large social structures, like empires. It is one means of exercising power at a distance. In a manner analogous to Seaford's metaphysical analysis of money, Darien Shanske describes the "Empire of Logos" the Athenians created with their advanced ships, standard currency, and prescribed courts and procedures (27–31).[24] The Athenians thus oversaw the second economy, the market economy within which most Greeks, including themselves, also operated. In Athens, the Piraeus served as a sort of second city for that second economy; there lived most of the metics who owned or managed the factories and who oversaw Athens' maritime trade with the rest of the Greek world. Citizens of other Greek cities, including landed citizens, came to Athens to make money and to create unobligated wealth for themselves. By the end of the fifth century, Fredal would add, one of the goods traded in that mercantile economy was sophistic "wisdom."

Signs of the Dual Economy in Fifth-Century Greece and Beyond

Elements of the dual economic system described by Tandy—a system of social obligations, of land and lineage, within one's own city, but the freedom to acquire unencumbered wealth by participating in a market economy external to that system of social obligations—persisted beyond the eighth century, facilitating and shaping the professions of the first sophists. Four different sorts of evidence of this dual economy functioning in the late fifth century seem possible. First, the dual-economy model would suggest that the sophists would not in their home cities engage in the money-making activities they engaged in while in Athens and in other city-states of the empire. In this case, the absence of clear evidence of money-making activities in their home cities would count as tentative evidence that the older sophists abstained from such activities. At the same time, second, we should look for evidence that Athenians engaged in such money-making activities while abroad but abstained from them while in Athens. Third, if the sophists are marketing their expertise to clients who are also observing the dual economic rule, then we should expect to see an emphasis on instruction for litigating contracts in courts over instruction for deliberation in the assembly. An enterprising fifth-century Greek family could find itself involved in contractual disputes at home or abroad, but only in their home cities could citizens participate in deliberative assemblies, and few would play major roles in these forums. Fourth, we should look for evidence that reciprocal patterns of exchange were still being observed within home cities—even by sophists and even by Athenians who engaged the services of sophists.

The Segregation of Market Activities: The Sophists

Numerous sources tell us that the great sophists acquired great wealth through the practice of their professions. The dual economic model suggests that this money should have been made outside their home cities. This hypothesis could be disproved if passages from the extant texts show sophists collecting fees in their home cities. For the sophists, the relevant texts have been gathered by Diels and Kranz in *Die Fragmente der Vorsokratiker.* A review of the B fragments provides no evidence that any non-Athenian sophist made any money in his home city.[25] The wealth they earned they made abroad. In Plato's *Hippias Major,* Hippias recalls one of his first successful forays: "Once when I went to Sicily, while Protagoras was visiting there, when he was already famous and an older man, I myself, though far younger, made more than a hundred and fifty minas in a very short time. In one tiny place, Inycus, I made more than twenty. I returned home, took it to my father and gave it to him, much to his surprise and astonishment and that of the other citizens" (242d–e; Gallop, 96). Although

Hippias' fellow citizens marveled at his ability to peddle his intellectual goods abroad, there is no suggestion here that he then offered to sell, or that they bid to buy, those goods. Also, Hippias was able to sell his goods even in very small towns ("in one tiny place"), suggesting that the size of their home communities does not explain the sophists' need to take their merchandise on the road.

The Segregation of Market Activities—Athenians Abroad

By contrast, we have abundant evidence that many Athenians had economic interests outside Athens. Cleruchies, allotments of property in colonies or in allied city-states, were granted to Athenian families as a means to reward military or public service, to mitigate political and economic strains within Athens, and to monitor events throughout the empire (Meiggs, 260–61; Hammond 1986, 306). Other Athenians acquired foreign properties through inheritance or purchase. In Xenophon's *Symposium,* for example, Charmides notes that, as a result of the war, he has lost control of his foreign properties (4.31–32). And in his account of the final stages of the Peloponnesian War, in book 2 of the *Hellenica,* Xenophon explains the strategy behind Lysander's decision to allow Athenians living in the island city-states he "liberates" to return home: When he lays siege to Athens, they will further strain its limited resources (2.2.1–2).

Evidence of the converse, of Athenians wary of participating in the market economy within Athens, is also abundant but less direct. The controversies aroused by the sophists' fees seem more about *what* is being commodified; nevertheless, this unease reflects a general desire to keep the market economy separate from important sociopolitical relationships. In the early plays of Aristophanes—the *Knights* and the *Wasps*—we see and hear the trading economy disparaged by the landed elite. Despite his wealth, indeed because of the *banauson* sources of that wealth, Aristophanes' stand-in for Cleon in the *Knights,* Paphlagon, is mocked (lines 235–37).[26] Making money in this way in one's home city is still somewhat disreputable.

In three short passages in the *Memorabilia,* Xenophon provides vignettes of life in Athens during the siege (2.7.1–4), the civil war (2.8.1), and the rough start of the postwar recovery (2.9.1–8). Heads of noble but now impoverished households—leaders of families whose foreign holdings have been lost and whose domestic lands have been ravaged—must find other ways to support themselves. Socrates advises a man in whose home numerous relations have taken refuge to put his womenfolk to work weaving; although initially reluctant to turn noble women into factory workers, Aristarchus eventually creates a successful family business. Another dispossessed landowner, Eutherus, is advised to offer his managerial expertise for hire at someone else's estate. And in the example cited by Fredal, Socrates advises Criton on how he might set up a noncontractual, but mutually beneficial, relationship with the struggling Archedemus. Initially, each man is shamed by the thought of working for pay or producing and selling commodities within Athens, but with Socrates' help they learn to accept their change of fortune with equanimity. These stories mark the beginning of the seismic shift in Athens' domestic economy at the start of the fourth century.

The Sophists' Products and Services

When the sophists came to Athens, their descriptions of their services were multifaceted and expansive. Many contemporary histories attribute Athenians' interest in the sophists to their political ambitions. But becoming an important figure is not only a matter of public affairs; it is also about gaining and managing wealth. Hippias is perhaps too close to the tradecrafts to make this point, but in Plato's dialogues both Protagoras and Gorgias describe men of affairs—affairs not limited to deliberations in the assembly: "What I teach is sound deliberation, both in domestic matters—how best to manage one's household, and in public affairs—how to realize one's maximum potential for success in political debate and action" (*Protagoras* 319a; Lombardo and Bell, 755); and "I'm referring to the ability to persuade by speeches judges in a law court, councilors in a council meeting, and assemblymen in an assembly or in any other political gathering that might take place. In point of fact, with this ability, you'll have the doctor for your slave, and the physical trainer, too. As for this financial expert of yours, he'll turn out to be making more money for somebody else instead of himself" (*Gorgias* 452e; Zeyl, 798).

That these descriptions are pitched at younger men may also suggest affairs foreign as well as domestic, for young men often spent years abroad, making their way in the world, or to be more specific, making their way in other city-states in the Athenian imperial sphere. In other words, the skills taught by the older sophists seem aimed first at the management of households that have holdings in more than one city-state. And in this work, the sophists themselves are genuine experts. If we read these passages with the understanding that an elite Athenian household oversaw land and lineage in Athens *and* agriculture, trade, and perhaps industry overseas, then members of that household have a need for an expertise the sophists likely possess. They can sell a program for better managing a dual economic life because they themselves are successfully living such lives.

That the smart management of a household and its commerce may have been more central to the teachings of the sophists than politics per se might be also be inferred by the prominence of contractual disputes in the most widespread descriptions of their *technē*. The founding stories of Corax and Tisias feature contractual disputes. Likewise, the exercise in power and bad faith in *Clouds* is not about state affairs but about eluding contractual obligations. Schiappa quite rightly points out that in the play Socrates, Aristophanes' stand-in for the sophists, exhibits interest and expertise in many matters, including astronomy, physics, and biology (lines 70–72). But Strepsiades, Socrates' client, is interested only in escaping his debts. On the question of forensic versus deliberative, then, Schiappa and the standard account could both be right: The sophists may have offered instruction (at least by demonstration) in many forms of speech, but their clients paid their fees in hopes of better outcomes in court. And as any case involving an Athenian, no matter how far flung his holdings or enterprises, had to be tried before an Athenian court,[27] knowledge of Athenian law, politics, and social customs would be valuable to any non-Athenian managing his affairs with Athenians. If Protagoras is observant while visiting the city, then the economic expertise Plato attributes to him may actually have more value abroad than in Athens. And in this context Gorgias' more narrow expertise can be transformed into a physical commodity: the written speech. Logographers, whether native to Athens like Antiphon or transplanted metics like Lysias, prepared speeches for non-Athenians as well as Athenians.[28] A familiarity with Athens' laws and courts, acquired in the course of a visit, would likely have been a selling point.

Vestiges of the Economy of Reciprocal Exchange

From the absence of evidence to the contrary, we have inferred that within their home cities sophists lived within the economy of land and lineage, although those lives may have been heavily subsidized by their earnings abroad. A second silence in the available evidence supports this conclusion. The sophists appear to have performed services for their home cities as a matter of civic obligation. Fees are not mentioned when Hippias discusses his services for Ellis (*Hippias Major* 281a; Gallop, 96) nor when others cite Gorgias' mission to Athens (Diodorus Siculus 12.53.1; Kennedy 1972, 32–33).

Even when these sophists were earning fees, however, they may still have played roles in reciprocal exchanges—between Athenians. Although again neither definitive nor wholly trustworthy, Plato's descriptions of the visits to Athens by Gorgias and Protagoras suggest grand social occasions.[29] Hosting an event with a sophist, as Callicles did for Gorgias and Callias for Protagoras, was very likely as much a display of wealth and power as it was the calculated purchase of an intellectual good.[30] Further, what the host seems to have underwritten for his guests was as much entertainment as it was edification. Displaying one's wealth by entertaining one's friends in an expansive and expensive manner is very much a part of the reciprocal gift culture. Thus we may surmise that the charging of fees—the new economy—often occurred in the context of a far more indirect social culture of giving and receiving, of hosting and visiting.

And by this we should not be surprised. Even today we academics nurture relationships that run the gamut from honorable reciprocity to for-fee market transactions. We go to great lengths to network, to create obligations we can draw on later. To neglect these social relations is to risk limiting one's influence or career. We draw distinctions between by-the-hour seminar leaders, adjunct instructors, and fixed-term, tenure-track, and tenured faculty. We also draw distinctions between for-profit nontraditional degree programs, community colleges, four-year teaching and four-year research institutions. Prestigious institutions go to great lengths to insure that not all who apply are admitted, to maintain rigorous standards (not all who are admitted graduate), and to complicate the line from students' tuition payments to faculty salaries. Despite the many asides in the corpus of the "Standard Account" about the professional debt owed to the first fee-taking sophists, contemporary academics operate within an economic framework that more closely resembles the schools of Plato, Isocrates, or Aristotle.[31]

The New Economy of the Fourth-Century Athenian Critics

Tandy argued that a dual economic system—in which elite households engaged in reciprocal exchanges within their home cities but also transacted business in the market economies of other cities—preceded the birth of the *polis*.[32] This dual system persisted into the fifth century, and the Athenian empire made Athenians advanced players in that system. Athenians had more wealth with which to underwrite the reciprocal exchanges of land and lineage within Athens even as they exploited market opportunities, made possible by their empire, abroad or in specialized market centers like the Piraeus. The sophists who paraded through Athens during the age of Pericles participated in this empire-wide dual economy created by the Athenians. Their most important product was knowledge that households (*oikoi*) could use to acquire, manage, and defend wealth and power within this system. But these sophists also sold more conventional products, public performances, that were purchased by Athenians as displays of wealth within their own networks of reciprocal exchange.

With the collapse of the empire, this system became much more difficult to sustain. Foreign revenue streams for many Athenian families dwindled or disappeared altogether. As a result, these families could no longer keep up the pretense, within Athens, of living solely in the reciprocal exchange economy of land and lineage. In a series of conversations in Xenophon's *Memorabilia,* Socrates counsels men of distinguished Athenian lineages—Aristarchus (2.7.1–4), Eutherus (2.8.1), and, indirectly, Archedemus (the conversation with Criton, 2.9.1–8)—on how to cope with the loss of their lands and incomes. Similar stresses can be heard in Aristophanes' *Wealth* (or *Plutus*). Indeed, the country citizen farmer with whom Aristophanes seems to have identified in all his plays still languishes in hard times. There are references to hard work in barren fields (lines 223, 253–54), to tattered clothes and worn shoes (lines 845–48), and to the flight of professionals from a ruined economy (lines 406–8). Only those who know how to milk the system—demagogues, price-gouging merchants, sycophants, and widows—have prospered; the rest barely eke out a living. Outside of Athens equally dramatic changes were taking place. With the demise of the Athenian empire (and its system for adjudicating contractual disputes), and with the ascendance of the undemocratic Sparta, the broader market for the intellectual goods of the sophists also shrank.

A likely consequence of these changes for the second-generation sophists plying their trade(s) in Athens at the beginning of the fourth century would have been that they were now in direct competition with Athenians who were no longer so reluctant to market their own intellectual goods. Consider Isocrates' description of his own entry into teaching: "For when I was beginning to repair my own fortunes after I had lost in the Peloponnesian War the patrimony which remained to me from what my father had spent partly in rendering himself serviceable to the state and partly in educating me with such care that I was more conspicuous then and more distinguished among the youths of my own age and among my fellow-students than I am now among my fellow citizens—when, as I have said, I began to attach pupils to myself" (*Antidosis* 161–62; Norlin, 275–77). This passage clearly documents the economic strains felt by Athenians after the war. What is not clear is the nature or aim of Isocrates' expensive education before the war. Had he always planned to be a teacher?

Elsewhere in the *Antidosis,* Isocrates notes that foreign students flocked to Athens to study with him—for which he accepted fees.[33] But, perhaps out of deference to the old norms for in-city interactions, he may not have collected "fees" from his Athenian students; we may infer, however, that he was reimbursed for these years of instruction in some way.[34] Thus, contrary to Fredal's argument, the sophists attacked by Isocrates, Plato, and Xenophon are not in the vanguard of a new economy; they are fighting a rearguard battle against Athenians who are creating a new postwar economy in which the two parts of the dual economy are more thoroughly mixed. The schools of Plato, Isocrates, and others are innovations rather than throwbacks, innovations made necessary by the collapse of the imperial economy and the destruction of so much private wealth, both encumbered and unencumbered. Hybrids of traditional educational forms and the for-fee lessons of the periodically visiting sophists of the fifth century, the schools of the fourth-century Athenians are new social institutions. Although, as Tell has observed (23n45), the finances of these new institutions remain obscure, to suggest that the frequent harping on sophists' fees shows that Plato and Isocrates remained mired in the old gift economy is to miss the new buildings for their antique ornaments.

From *Oikonomia* to *Rhētorikē*

The history of Athens may be viewed as a series of efforts to rebalance the conflicting interests of groups—regions, classes, families, professions—contending within the state. According to Tandy, Solon's reforms were implemented in order to protect the ancestral lands of less powerful families from expropriation by families empowered by the unencumbered wealth they had gathered through maritime trade.[35] A second attempt to rebalance the state occurred when, after the overthrow of the tyrants, Cleisthenes reorganized Athenian social relations by creating ten new *phylai* or tribes that each included members from the three districts of Attica: the Pireaus (*paralia*), the city (*astu*), and the rural countryside (*mesologeia*). Through these new groupings, Cleisthenes wove together the separate interests of these distinctly different portions of the populace (Hammond 1986, 189). But sea-derived power later changed Athens in other ways. When Athens' navy, oared by commoners (*thetes*), proved as, if not more, important than its armored soldiers (*hoplites*) or cavalry (*hippeis*), the people (*demos*) could claim a more significant role in the governance of the city. The reforms of Ephialtes readjusted the machinery of the state in response to this new status (Hammond 1986, 288). Finally, the annual tribute paid to Athens by its allies and colonies, for protecting sea lanes and deterring eastern and western aggressors, became a new form of unencumbered wealth that Athens used to ease social tensions within the city and to promote its civic culture and arts (299–310 and 333–44). The unencumbered wealth generated by Athens' sea power greased the new machinery of its democracy.

The great sophists functioned within the world created by Athens' power, both hard and soft power. But their view of this world is from the periphery and, for the most part, pre- or mid-Peloponnesian War. Although we have some evidence that they considered broader political and social themes, such as Panhellenism, the earliest evidence suggests that their best-selling products and services in the age of Periclean Athens were their expertise in managing the affairs of a wealthy household along with the techniques—certain kinds of arguments and arrangements—for executing that expertise within the legal forums and procedures created by the Athenian empire. In the course of transmitting this expertise, sophists likely also shared their observations that local customs were largely accidental, that beneath these lay a more basic physics of power. And these observations may have encouraged Athenians to question cultural constraints on their exercise of power.

Some of Plato's and, to a lesser extent, Isocrates' criticisms of the sophists echo this last point. But their critiques are predicated on their very different standpoints. Instead of from the periphery, the fifth-century sophists' fourth-century Athenian critics viewed the world of Athens' empire from its center—and after its collapse rather than before. For Isocrates, Plato, and Xenophon, the defeat of Athens, the collapse of its empire, and the oligarchic revolution of 404–3 dramatically changed the economic conditions under which they lived and worked. These events also became new facts, new data points, for which any theory of political discourse had to account.[36]

Within Plato's dialogues we can see two different approaches to this problem. In *Gorgias* and the first book of the *Republic,* Plato complicates the logic, the economics, of ambitious fourth-century Athenians. Whereas Callicles imagines he can retain the agency of the *kalokagathos* while stripping away any cultural constraints as quaint fictions, Socrates argues that a unified *demos* can be stronger, and thus in Callicles' terms "better," than the *aristoi* (*Gorgias* 488c–489b). In both books, Plato upends the traditional understanding of the maxim that one should "help friends, harm enemies" (as discussed explicitly in *Republic*

331d–336a; Grube, 975–81).[37] A true friend, Socrates argues, would ensure that one's errors were corrected, one's crimes punished (*Gorg.* 478–81b). Although the intent is clearly to suggest universal standards by which to judge personal behavior, these set pieces—which employ devices similar to those displayed in the anecdote about the countersuits of Corax and Tisias—suggest, at the very least, that private measures of virtue threaten the good order and justice of the city. The city must use its power to constrain the ambitions of its citizens, even its most powerful citizens.

The second way Plato interprets and responds to the history of the Athenian empire is by theorizing about the ways political behavior is determined, or at least influenced, by material conditions. In the *Republic,* Socrates observes that, once a certain standard of living is achieved, a standard that depends on the production of sophisticated goods through complex divisions of labor, a city becomes acquisitive. In seeking the resources it requires for this standard of living, the city will become embroiled in conflicts with other cities, which will result in the injustices of war and domination (372e–373e). In a somewhat similar fashion, the Athenian in the *Laws* argues that the geographical situation of a city will determine, in no small measure, its social and political development. If the goal is a just and moderate city, one should not situate it by the sea (704d–705a).

Fourth-century Athenians lived in a world quite different from that of the great fifth-century sophists, and they viewed that world from a very different standpoint. Living in a world governed by others, the sophists were free to take an agonistic approach to speech—in a variety of different settings. But having observed the failure of the empire and the state their predecessors had governed, fourth-century Athenians were compelled to reflect on the relationships between persuasion (*peitho*) and judgment (*krisis*) and between *oikos* and *polis. Rhētorikē* emerged out of these fourth-century reflections.

Conclusion

The tight correlation between the age of Pericles and the age of the great sophists was not accidental or random. It took an empire, the Athenian empire, to raise the sophists. Through its currency, its court system, and its administrative structures, Athens rationalized, to an unprecedented extent, economic and social relationships within the empire. At the same time, however, an older, more traditional set of social customs still functioned throughout the empire. The older sophists observed the rules of this dual economic system, marketing their intellectual goods and services while abroad but duly performing the functions of elite citizens when at home. For a variety of reasons, techniques for forensic speeches were likely their best-selling intellectual goods, but these sophists were also paid for private performances and competed, in public, for prizes. The elder sophists also offered, likely for even higher fees, extended lessons to those who wanted to practice their profession. On the other side of this economic equation, citizens of Greek cities within the empire, Athenians in particular, had several very different reasons for purchasing the goods and services of visiting sophists. The sophists' expertise in managing the complex affairs of a transnational enterprise would have had direct instrumental value, as would their familiarity with how Athens' legal system operated outside Athens. But the historical evidence suggests that Athenians also purchased sophists' lessons and performances for their symbolic value, as public demonstrations of their wealth, sophistication, and influence.

With the collapse of the Athenian empire, the underpinnings of the first sophistic also collapsed. Many Athenians now entered the market economy and directly competed with foreign-born instructors. These Athenians do seem to have maintained some distinctions in how they were paid for their work, but exactly what niceties were observed is not clear. Nevertheless, it is clear that fourth-century Athenians created new social institutions that had not existed in the fifth. In these longer-term institutions of higher learning, fourth-century Athenians reflected on the dramatic historical (and economic and political) events at the end of the fifth century. Out of these fourth-century reflections on the forces at work in the rise and fall of Athens' fifth-century empire, *rhētorikē* emerged. I concur with Schiappa's assessment of the pre-disciplinary status of rhetoric before Plato but, contrary to Schiappa, I argue that the coining of *rhētorikē* involved much more than Plato's testing the mettle of the sophists. Fourth-century Athenians, Plato in particular, observed that different material conditions encouraged different paths of social and political development. The effective management of the state required that the separate interests and aspirations of different groups, including prominent households, be coordinated. The reforms of Solon, Cleisthenes, Ephialtes, and Pericles were efforts to weave back together threads unraveled by the often conflicting interests of these competing groups and households. When Plato has the Stranger describe how the statesman must weave together the different characters of the citizenry, he is working from a key insight of these earlier leaders (*St.* 309b–311c). A political understanding of *rhētorikē* emerged in response to a critical question about this process: if the goal is a just and durable society, should the teaching of persuasive speaking—to ambitious individuals or households—be promoted, should it be banned, or should it be subsumed in a broader vision of education?

Recurring situations for discourse—situations that may define the future course of a society—are created by material conditions that are often overlooked. We are quick to ascribe agency to transnational agents, like the sophists, but we are slow to recognize the social and political consequences of administrative systems, infrastructures, and technologies.[38] By recognizing the persistence of old norms in new forms, by identifying and measuring contending forces, the energies that separate or individuate versus those that link or connect, by mapping out the structures that channel these forces, and by watching for changes in these underlying conditions, we may become better observers of our own politics.

Afterword

Persistent Questions in the Historiography of Early Greek Rhetorical Theory

Edward Schiappa

The essays in this collection demonstrate that the study of rhetoric before the discipline was formally recognized with the term *rhētorikē* is alive and well. Collectively they represent a wealth of analytical methods and sources of theoretical inspiration brought to bear on a variety of texts by an impressive group of scholars. I am flattered to have been asked to contribute an afterword to the collection and hope that it is not ill-mannered of me to disagree with my colleagues here and there. I believe the most productive manner of engaging them is to identify the persistent questions facing historians of early Greek rhetorical theory and to discuss how the studies contribute to their answer.

The broadest historiographical question is: What sort of overarching framework or meta-narrative should historians use to make sense of the development of language arts in the fifth and fourth centuries B.C.E.? In the past, I have contrasted my revisionist account with what I described as the standard account (1999, 3–13) while drawing a distinction between historical reconstruction and contemporary appropriation (2003b). Robin Reames helpfully describes in her introduction to this volume what she calls the nominal and narratological accounts.

Putting my cards on the table, I want to state unequivocally that I remain committed to the nominal approach as a guiding methodology for writing about early Greek rhetorical theory.[1] At the same time, it may be useful to narrow the gap between the nominal and narratological approaches about "rhetoric" in general. Specifically, I want to distance myself from the extreme version of the nominalist approach attributed to Thomas Cole (1991). Cole wants to deny what might be called *rhetorical consciousness* until the time of Plato, and I know of no other scholar who shares his position. The earliest speakers we have information about—even fictional speakers in Homer's account—show evidence of adapting their message to suit the audience and context in which they find themselves. Thus we can posit that the human capacity for what Roderick P. Hart and Don M. Burks usefully labeled "rhetorical sensitivity" may be nearly universal.

The concept of rhetorical sensitivity is worth a brief digression. Hart and Burks draw from twentieth-century communication theory to note that our speech is both *expressive* and *instrumental*; that is, most of our messages both express our thoughts and feelings *and* seek to accomplish a goal such as to inform, persuade, or entertain. It is the instrumental function of human communication that Hart and Burks call "rhetorical"; thus there is a broad sense in which the rhetorical use of language is as old as humanity itself. For Hart and Burks, rhetorically sensitive individuals adapt the presentation of themselves and of their messages to specific audiences and circumstances. Such adaptation need not be especially sophisticated, let alone informed by explicit training or theory; even a child who knows how to adapt a request when making it to one parent versus the other is demonstrating rhetorical sensitivity. Whether seeking a favor or asking for directions, most people will present a slightly different "self" and message to those they already know well versus strangers, or addressing those with more or less power and authority.

Thus, the nominal approach does not need to entail the metaphor of magic, whereby Plato brought the discipline of *rhētorikē technē* into being out of the void by uttering the word *rhētorikē.* Rather, both the nominal and narratological approaches can embrace the metaphors of *evolution* and *development.* As I have tried to illustrate with Protagoras, Gorgias, and other fifth-century B.C.E. authors, theories of *rhētorikē* were preceded by theories of *logos.* Compared to the fully "disciplined" understanding of *rhētorikē* in Aristotle and arguably in the *Rhetorica ad Alexandrum,* theories concerned with *logos* had a broader scope, involved a more diverse set of means of expression (including discussion and question/answer), aimed equally at truth and success, and applied both to political and nonpolitical speakers and contexts (Schiappa 1999, 75). Despite these differences, it is clear that much of what was going on vis-à-vis the discourse practices and theories of the fifth century are relevant to what we now call the history of rhetoric. My point throughout my career has been that we need to take note of the *differences* between theories and pedagogies of *logos* and of *rhētorikē* as well as noting their similarities as we assemble our narratives of the beginnings of "rhetoric."

Robin Reames' essay advances the case that Heraclitus should be added to our list of important pre-Socratic *logos* theorists.[2] Against my earlier published claim that Heraclitus did not address language as an object of inquiry, Reames provides a compelling case that *logos* in the fragment believed to mark the beginning of Heraclitus' book is crucial for understanding Heraclitus' project overall, and can be read as prefiguring a specific formulation of contrasting *logoi* rather than advancing a "metaphysical" account of logos as reason, divine mind, or eternal fire. Mining the philological evidence that the verb from which *logos* is derived (*legein*) has an early sense of "to lay" and "to gather," Reames proffers a Heraclitean account of *logos:* "For those who are heedful to what *logos* both gathers and lays, both shows and hides, it will lead to wisdom."

Reames' account narrows the conceptual leap between Heraclitus and Protagoras and enhances my account of the Heraclitean roots of Protagoras' claim that "two *logoi* are present about every 'thing,' opposed to each other" (2003b, 100).

Evolutionary or developmental metaphors are useful for understanding the emergence and transformation of writings about topics later united under the sign of rhetoric, including persuasion, reason, speech, deception, and truth. For example, John T. Kirby and Jenny Strauss Clay have demonstrated that the writings of Hesiod can be mined for nuggets that can, in turn, be fashioned into an implicit or undeclared "theory" of persuasive speech. Similarly, Wilfred E. Major's account of Aristophanes concludes that, while the playwright's works do not provide direct evidence of a fifth-century "discipline" of rhetoric, as some scholars still insist, they nonetheless contain a wealth of insight as to how Aristophanes thought about such topics as sophistic/philosophical pedagogy, democracy, and the problems of Athenian political debate (see also Larson). David Sansone pushes the point further, controversially arguing that life imitated art in the case of Greek drama and that early rhetorical practice was significantly influenced by techniques that would-be orators learned from the stage.

The evolution/development metaphor is also a useful way to think about changing modes of composition and reasoning that occurred during the fifth and fourth centuries B.C.E. The fact that new modes of expression and models of explanation emerged during this period of time should not lead us to paint predominantly oral cultures as "irrational." Forms of rationality changed over time, but David C. Hoffman is clearly right to chide those who implicitly or explicitly claim an overnight revolution in how humans thought. His description of *mētis* as a form of "context-bound" or "strategic rationality" reminds us that what Gorgias would later call "reasoning" (*logismos,* in *Helen 2*) and "logic" in Plato and Aristotle (*logikē*), certainly had recognizable antecedents. It is no surprise that the rhetorically sensitive Odysseus was described as *poly-mētis;* the naming of an art of logic should not imply no one was logical prior to Plato, just as the naming of an art of "rhetoric" does not mean no one was rhetorical prior to Plato.

Similarly, Marina McCoy is surely correct to identify what she calls "proto-technical" strategies in Homer. The status of implicit rhetorical theory in Homer is a topic with a long history (Roisman; Knudsen), and there has been a tendency to see the issue in black and white. McCoy does not use the word "evolution" but "development," a key theme in her analysis. What she finds in the discourse of the fictional character of Odysseus is described as strategies that would later be developed as the rhetorical concepts of *ethopoiēsis* (character or *persona*), and *kairos* (appropriateness), and a possible instance of *prosopopoeia* (speaking as another). If I may refer to my earlier introduction of the concept of "rhetorical sensitivity," McCoy here seems to be documenting such sensitivity in Homer.

Further theorizing on the concept of rhetorical sensitivity posited a range of people's willingness to adapt themselves or their messages—from "Noble Selves" who resist variation from their personal norms to "Rhetorical Reflectors" who have no "Self" to call their own (Darnell and Brockriede, 175–82). Subsequent empirical investigation by Hart, Robert E. Carlson, and William F. Eadie found that people vary greatly in their attitudes concerning adapting the presentation of themselves and of their messages. Unsurprisingly, these researchers found that there are identifiable demographic, familial, and cultural variables that are associated with different levels of rhetorical sensitivity. To be sure, it is hazardous to project the modernist sense of "the self" from Hart and Burks backwards to pre-Socratic times, as a number of classical scholars have noted (Snell; Gill; Long; Williams). The argument could be made, however, that historians of rhetoric might be well positioned to contribute to the ongoing debate about Greek conceptions of self precisely by examining how individual selves are performed through discourse. To me, this is the most significant insight provided by McCoy. The account given of Odysseus nicely challenges a too-narrow understanding of the Homeric self, as she documents the relevance of Hart and Burk's conceptualization of rhetorical sensitivity in Odysseus' varied rhetorical performances.[3]

Historians who have only texts or fragments available must decide at what point demonstrated rhetorical sensitivity provides sign evidence of an underlying *theory* (or even "proto-theory") of rhetoric. My nominalist position admittedly sets a high bar by requiring evidence of a theoretical vocabulary. This is because my scholarly interests are particularly narrow. One could argue that, just as the scope of rhetorical theory has increased in the past century, what has "counted" as relevant to rhetorical theory in classical Greece has also increased. For example, as the rhetoric/philosophy binary was challenged by various twentieth-century theorists, it became somewhat easier to argue that the same binary was problematic when classifying certain texts of the fifth and fourth centuries B.C.E. What we find as relevant evidence for "theory" is a function of our particular values and interests, and I would be the first to acknowledge that other scholars have quite different interests from my own, leading them to see "theory" where I see nascent or implicit theorizing or contemporary appropriation.

My narrow focus has not prevented me, however, from writing at length about such figures as Protagoras, Gorgias, and Isocrates, as their preserved texts and fragments are clearly relevant to the development of theories of discourse, including rhetorical pedagogy and theory. Just as they promised, this book's authors have demonstrated the relevance of other authors to the history of "rhetoric" as well.

The scare quotes around the word "rhetoric" gesture to what I see as the second persistent question facing historians, which is simply, "What is rhetoric?" When we talk about the beginning or development of "rhetoric" in the fifth century B.C.E., to what are we referring? Put less platonically, what "counts" as *rhetoric* for the historian of classical Greece?[4]

The question is persistent because there is an excessively wide range of phenomena to which the labels "rhetoric" and "rhetorical" have been applied in classical Greek scholarship (Schiappa and Hamm), and once such terms are introduced, inferences made about rhetorical *theory* or *strategy* seem much easier to make. Some scholars take "X speaks persuasively" as coterminous with "X speaks rhetorically" and from that premise it is reasoned that, "*If* X speaks rhetorically, *then* X must be informed by an implicit or explicit rhetorical theory." The problem with such reasoning should be obvious: All humans engage in informal or formal persuasive speaking, but we hardly want to claim that all humans are guided by "rhetorical theory" unless we are willing to give up any distinctive explanatory power to the phrase.

The key equivocation enters a historical narrative through a deceptively simple locution, such as "X's rhetoric." But what precisely does the word "rhetoric" denote here? Does it refer to X's discourse in the same manner as the word "oratory" (*rhētoreia*) refers to a speech? Or does it refer to the persuasive content of the discourse? If a scholar has one of these first two senses of "rhetoric" in mind, I hope we can agree that the introduction of the word "rhetoric" is imprecise and potentially misleading, because "rhetoric" can also imply a sense of artistry (self-conscious or not) or a sense of strategy. The strategic sense of "rhetoric," in turn, implies deliberate choice that may be guided by imitation, training, or even theory. The essays in this collection are most useful when the word "rhetoric" is used cautiously and its denotative meaning made explicit.

If my second persistent question amounted to a plea for clarity, the third and fourth involve a methodological and theoretical challenge, respectively: What counts as a "rhetorical stratagem"? And when can one infer "theory" based on their use? The questions are related but distinct.

The appearance of what we would now identify as a rhetorical stratagem does necessarily imply its user thought of it *as* a stratagem. Children learn how to use nouns, verbs, and adjectives to do all sorts of clever things with language long before they ever learn the words and concepts of "nouns, verbs, and adjectives," just as they learn to tell stories before they ever hear anything about "narrative" or "plot." If an ancient Greek had turned a story told by a child into a text and buried it for 2,400 years, that text would hardly stand as proof that the author had a theory of grammar or narratology, even if the text contained components we now associate with such theories. Just as children learn to use language in remarkably sophisticated ways prior to learning a vocabulary that describes what they are doing, adult speakers may use a variety of linguistic and argumentative devices without being taught, for example, Aristotle's three modes of proof or the difference between argument by analogy and argument from example. In other words, even though it is a very common form of argument, the ability of a historian to point to X or Y feature in the text does not prove that X or Y was recognized at the time as part of an art or *technē*, or was the result of training or theory.

So how do we know when there is "theory" at work? Influenced by historians as diverse as Thomas S. Kuhn and Eric Havelock, I have argued previously that the clearest evidence of what we can describe as "theory" is the emergence of a metalinguistic vocabulary used to classify, to conceptualize, and to teach that which is being described. For me, this is also one of the most fascinating aspects of early Greek philosophy and rhetoric—the emergence of a technical vocabulary, including the labels "philosophy" and "rhetoric" themselves. The simultaneous grappling with language and reality is missed if we supply a later-developed vocabulary too soon into our historical narratives. For example, when scholars have tried to describe two different periodic styles of prose composition in his *Rhetoric* (3.9.1), Aristotle's two categories, *eiromenē* and *katestrammenē*, have been translated as "extended and conjunctively united" and "antithetic" by Lawson-Tancred (232) and as "continuous and united" and "periodic" by Freese (387). But George A. Kennedy's more literal translation of *eiromenē* and *katestrammenē* as "strung-on" and "turned-down" reminds us of the on-going challenge to Greek intellectuals to develop a conceptual vocabulary, in this case by metaphorically extended terms not typically used to describe language use (2007, 214).

It is possible that the appearance of a rhetorical stratagem in a text is the result of the speaker/author having *learned* when and how to use such a stratagem. Where historians find evidence for such instruction, then we certainly have ample cause to claim such activities as part of the history of *rhetorical pedagogy*. The problem is that the available evidence concerning such pedagogy prior to the fourth century B.C.E. is remarkably scant. Despite the later claims that the "sophists taught rhetoric," we have very little idea prior to the fourth century just what they taught or how. The available evidence suggests that their instruction was much broader than what is later codified as "rhetoric." Michael Gagarin goes so far as to argue that, not only did the sophists not teach *rhētorikē technē*, their focus was far from limited to persuasive speech: "The Sophists have a fluid, multi-faceted understanding of *logos*, in which persuasion was but one feature, and not necessarily the most important" (2005, 290). He concludes: "For the Sophists, *logos* was more a tool for thinking than for persuading" (291).

The available evidence does not support the claim that fifth-century sophists taught speech composition and performance conceptually, but rather primarily and perhaps exclusively by example. I agree with Cole's conclusion that references to early *technai* were references to collections of speeches, not to treatises of the sort we see emerging in the fourth century B.C.E., such as Aristotle's *Rhetoric*.

Thus, the ability to identify a rhetorical stratagem is a far cry from establishing the existence of a "theory of rhetoric." For this and other reasons,

Robert Gaines' argument for Theodorus having successfully taught a twelve-part scheme of speech parts highlights the difficulties of inferring theory from practice. As Michael de Brauw (2010), David Timmerman and I (141–42), and Wilfred E. Major, have argued, one cannot document a consistent pattern of even a four-part division of speeches until decades after the fifth century B.C.E. Even the words used to describe an "introduction" (*prooimion*) and "conclusion" (*epilogos*) do not appear to have been used to describe speeches or prose compositions until the mid-fourth century B.C.E. (Timmerman and Schiappa, 146–52). The standard account that the division of speeches originated with Corax and Tisias is notoriously unreliable (Schiappa 1999, 34–47). Even those speeches that can be claimed to have three parts (introduction, argument, and conclusion) may be more the result of an imitation of the pattern of "ring composition" inherited from oral modes of composition than a result of a recognized rhetorical pedagogy.

The earliest evidence we have of efforts to create a prescriptive formula for speech composition is from Plato's *Phaedrus* (266d), and there he uses the phrase *logōn technē* to describe the "books" that supposedly teach such parts. It is possible that Theodorus advocated a twelve-part framework for forensic speeches, but if he did I suspect that it was advanced in the fourth rather than the fifth century B.C.E., and there is no evidence as to when or if anyone ever composed a speech using it.[5] Though Gaines cites a speech known as *(pseudo-) Lysias 6,* the speech at best contains only five of the twelve parts, despite our supposedly having as much as 85 percent of the speech. The other seven parts, we are asked to believe, either were crammed into the remaining text or were left out deliberately because it was a "supporting" speech *not expected to follow standard prosecution procedure*—raising the obvious question of how we can draw inferences from it about the status of typical oratorical practices. Since we know nothing of what Theodorus meant with such labels as *pistōsis* and *epipistōsis* (the latter of which appears only once in all of Greek literature), to describe as "speculative" any inferences made as to whether a text illustrates them would be generous. Gaines concedes that it *seems to him* that portions of the speech constitute "confirmation" and "additional confirmation," but such passages could just as well be labeled as instances of amplification, an extended set of proofs, or even (looking at §§20–30) an out-of-order narrative (*diēgēsis*). Gaines is able to hypothesize possible theoretical meanings for *pistōsis* and *epipistōsis* that conveniently correspond to what he finds in the text, but his analysis illustrates the difficulty facing historians who want to infer theory from practice: There is simply no way to confirm such inferences without some form of corroboration.

As McCoy's reference to music nicely underscores, the more appropriate parallel case for understanding an emerging and evolving set of discourse practices is art, not science. The practice of music outstrips theory, and one can have a flourishing musical culture with nary a musicologist in sight. The relationship between observable practice and implicit or inferred "theory" continues to challenge historians of rhetoric, as several essays of this volume illustrate. The level of artistry achieved in Greek oratorical practice is admirable, but as the analogies with language acquisition and musical practices suggest, does not by itself prove the existence of rhetorical theory, narrowly defined.

The fifth and final question I wish to revisit is what sort of disciplinary labels are appropriate for the texts of the fifth and fourth century B.C.E. that are of interest to this volume's authors? As Professor Reames' introduction asks, "What are we to call the practices of eloquence and oratory before they were formulated explicitly by the art called *rhētorikē*?" And at what point do we distinguish among rhetorical art, pedagogy, and theory? At times, the academic debate over the disciplinary status of rhetoric during this time period has resembled a variation of the game Capture the Flag, with nominalists like myself seeking to deny the flag of rhetorical theory to certain texts pitted against other scholars seeking to reclaim that flag. Fortunately, as some of this book's essays illustrate, it is easy enough to create more flags. That is to say, it is simple enough to stipulate a conceptual apparatus that includes rhetorical practice, pedagogy, and theory as the salient categories, and then chart how these categories change over time, especially as fourth-century authors impose their particular disciplinary vocabularies on them.

With regard to rhetorical practice—stipulated here to mean formal public speaking in forensic, deliberative, or ceremonial settings—there are endless ways to analyze the surviving texts of the classical era. Terry L. Papillon's insightful analysis of schismogenesis in the discourse of Isocrates is an excellent example. Papillon does not attempt to advance claims regarding an implicit Isocratean "rhetorical theory," but points out that the linguistic devices at work in Isocrates' discourse represent recurring patterns of thought that can be found in Thucydides and elsewhere in Greek literature. Papillon's analysis helps us to understand not only the strengths and weaknesses of Isocrates' argumentative choices in his own era, but also our own.

With what disciplinary categories shall we describe the pre-Platonic authors we now place in the history of rhetoric? Carol Poster's method for addressing such issues is reminiscent of Catherine Osborne's critique of those who wish to focus on the *ipsissima verba* of the pre-Socratics; what interests Poster is not the correct classification of Gorgias or his text *On Not Being* but their various receptions over time. Thus Poster wisely sidesteps the question of whether to categorize Gorgias' activities as "sophistic," "rhetorical," or "philosophical" and instead asks *according to whom?* Did author X consider Gorgias *this* or *that,* and why? The answers, both in classical times and in our own, may say as much or more about those doing the categorizing as they do about Gorgias. As Poster puts it, how Gorgias is characterized "appears to depend on the individual knowledge, interests, and aims of particular sources." In short, there is no timeless essence of Gorgias or his texts, but a range of activities and textual performances that can be labeled in hindsight according to what we find to be most salient about them given our specific needs and interests. Her creative phrase "philosophical sophistic" does precisely the sort of synthesis that we need to understand the status of works by intellectuals active before Aristotle's disciplinary labels take hold.[6]

Similarly, Thomas Rickert's essay can be read as deconstructing long-held habits of interpreting Parmenides. Rickert's project exemplifies both historical reconstruction and contemporary appropriation (Schiappa 2003b). He makes the historical case for challenging the traditional categorization of Parmenides as a philosopher, narrowly understood. His historical account of Parmenides as (in my terms) a "predisciplinary" philosopher and theorist of persuasion, not to mention (in his words) a performer, healer, and "skywalker," is a powerful reminder of how, when we take our "received categories" and read "them back into the past," those interpretive categories can lead us not to appreciate the complexity of the "Other" behind preserved texts. But Rickert does not stop with historical reconstruction, as he also suggests that an enhanced appreciation of Parmenides invites us to consider "what philosophy, sophistry, or rhetoric is, or could be."

Michael Svoboda's essay tackles the issue of categorization in a refreshingly new way. He concedes that it is not clear exactly who should be included within the category of fifth-century "older" sophists other than Protagoras and Gorgias, and presumably Hippias and Prodicus. Svoboda then approaches his analysis of how the sophists functioned in the democratic political economy of the Athenian empire. Svoboda argues, partly following James Fredal's work, that the changing economic and political fortunes of the Athenian empire along with the shift from a gift-exchange to a market economy combined to create a context that was ideal for the rise of a professional class of teachers. Moreover, Svoboda reminds us of an often-overlooked dimension of at least some of the fifth-century sophists' training—the management of households. How far we have come from the stereotype of the older sophists as teachers of rhetoric-and-only-rhetoric!

A number of scholars have struggled to explain the differences between fifth- and fourth- century sophists. Most, including myself, have adopted a developmental or evolutionary metaphor that sees increasing specialization as progress. Svoboda adds an interesting dimension to such accounts, however, as he notes that the fall of Athenian economic and political hegemony *necessitated* a different "business model" (my term) for education as well as a reconsideration of the strengths and weaknesses of public deliberation.

The questions I have identified as persistent—the larger framework guiding our historical approach, the definition of "rhetoric," what counts as a "rhetorical stratagem," when one can infer "theory" from a text, and what sort of disciplinary labels are appropriate for the texts of the fifth and fourth century B.C.E.—persist because there is no simple way to resolve differences of opinion.

While something of a consensus has emerged over the years since 1990 about the narrow historical question of the timing of the emergence of the word *rhētorikē,* what one does with that "fact" depends on one's values and interests; hence, there will continue to be different answers and thus different historical narratives about early Greek rhetoric.

Thus, I end this afterword as I began it, by praising my colleagues for adding a fascinating array of theories, methods, and texts to the growing body of work on pre-Platonic rhetoric. Even though I have quibbled with particular directions or stopping places along the way, I know that readers of this volume will benefit from the intellectual journey.[7]

Appendix A

A Timeline of the Life of Gorgias of Leontini

Carol Poster

Birth

According to the major sources, Gorgias was born in approximately 480 B.C.E. (DK82a6 = pseudo-Plutarch, X orat. 832f, and somewhat imprecisely corroborated in DK82a10 and DK82a14). DK82A2 (= Suda) states that Porphyry thought Gorgias was born in the eightieth Olympiad (460 B.C.E.), but adds (correctly) that an earlier date is more probable. Sources are unanimous in assigning his birth and early career to Leontini. Pseudo-Plutarch and Photius place Gorgias as slightly older than Antiphon (DK87a3 and 4), confirming a birthdate of approximately 480 B.C.E.

Early Studies

Several sources describe Gorgias as a student or follower of Empedocles, including DK82a2 (= Suda), DK82a3 (= DL VIII.58–59, information attributed to Satyricus), DK82a10 (= Olympiodorus, *in Grg.* 0.9, 14.12), and DK82a14 (= Quintilian, *Inst.* III.1.8). In the absence of formal credentials, terms like "student," "follower," or "admirer" are inherently imprecise; without additional evidence it is not possible to determine whether this implies that Gorgias attended a few public displays by Empedocles or had some more substantial relationship.[1] Some degree of familiarity or association is not improbable. Testimonia point to a period somewhere between 460 and 430 for this phase of Gorgias' life, but it cannot be pinpointed more accurately.

On Non-Being

Isocrates, Sextus Empiricus, Olympiodorus, and MXG attest to Gorgianic authorship of "On Non-Being." Olympiodorus (*In Grg.* 0.9) dates the treatise to the eighty-fourth Olympiad (444–441 B.C.E.). This date is suspiciously close to Gorgias' flourishing (assuming a 480 birthdate) and unconfirmed by other sources. Given that the treatise engages Eleatic ontology, it is probable that it was written in Italy sometime between Gorgias' early studies and his embassy to Athens; the eighty-fourth Olympiad would indeed fall in the center of that period.

Early Italian Career

Little is known of Gorgias' activities (other than association with Empedocles) prior to his arrival in Athens. His being selected for such an embassy may have been due to his reputation as an eloquent speaker, but distinction in wisdom (*sophos* in its archaic sense), rather than specific oratorical talent, was a traditional criterion for such roles.[2] Plato, in summarizing the start of the rhetorical art at the end of *Phaedrus,* associates Gorgias with Tisias in viewing probabilities as more esteemed than truth (267a), but the conjunction seems ideological rather than chronological. Cicero (DK87a7 = *Brutus* 12.47) stated that Aristotle gave an account of rhetoric beginning with Corax and Tisias and continuing with Gorgias, Antiphon of Rhamnus, and Lysias.[3] This relative chronology, while shedding some light on the Sicilian foundation account of the history of rhetoric, lacks precise dates. Diodorus (DK82a4) is the main source for Gorgias' distinction as a speaker before 427, but this may imply a reputation for eloquent speech on philosophical topics rather than strictly "rhetorical" activities if, in fact, subject matter rather than occasion or approach can serve to define a speech as "rhetorical" or "philosophical." As there is no report of a distinctive break with Empedocles or a "conversion" to sophistic, Gorgias' pre-427 activities could have been purely "philosophical" (albeit distinguished for eloquence), have been shifting gradually from youthful studies in philosophy to rhetoric/sophistic, or have combined the two in some manner.

Athenian Embassy

Diodorus Siculus discusses Gorgias' role in the embassy from Leontini to Athens in 427 B.C.E. (corroborated by epigraphical evidence), describing Gorgias as already eminent as an orator, and much admired in Athens for the novelty of his style (DK82a4 = XII.53.1). Dionysius of Halicarnassus corroborates Diodorus' account of the embassy and Gorgias' impact on Athenian audiences without mentioning the specific date of the embassy (*Lysias* 3), as does Plato (or pseudo-Plato) in *Hippias Major* (282b).

Subsequent Athenian Activity

Diodorus stated that Gorgias returned home to Leontini after the Athenian embassy, which, if accurate, would require a second visit to Athens at a later date to account for activities described by other sources (DK82a4 = XII.53.1). Philostratus (DK82a1 = VS 493) talks of Gorgias, as an old man, being admired in Athens for his improvised speeches. Plato's *Gorgias* and *Meno* portray Gorgias as a relatively old man being well known and still active in Athens, but neither dramatic nor compositional dates of the dialogues are certain.[4] *Apology* 19e (= DK828a) suggests that Gorgias was well known to Athenians as a teacher of rhetoric in 399, although the text does not contain sufficient detail to confirm Gorgias' presence in Athens at that specific date with any certainty. Comic poets confirm that Gorgias was well known in Athens as a strikingly eloquent speaker with a distinctive style, albeit without contributing detailed information about the dates or nature of his activities.[5]

Wealth

There are numerous references to Gorgias having become wealthy through his activities as a sophist/rhetorician. Isocrates is an early source for Gorgias' wealth (DK82a18 = 15, 155). Suda (= DK82a2) mentions that Gorgias charged his students one hundred minas (whether the precise sum is trustworthy, the general impression of high fees is well confirmed). Xenophon (DK82a5 = *Anabasis* 11.6.16) probably implies a substantial fee paid by Proxenus to Gorgias. The solid-gold statue Gorgias erected of himself at Delphi is frequently cited as evidence of the extent of his wealth (DK82a7), in sources as diverse as Pausanias (VI.17.7), Athenaeus (XIX 505d), Cicero (*de Oratore* III.32.129) and Philostratus (DK82a1 = *VS* 1.4). Pliny, in his *Natural History,* dates the dedication (obviously incorrectly) to the seventieth Olympiad (XXXIII.83).

Appendix A: Timeline of Gorgias

Extensive Travels

Philostratus mentions declamations at various festivals (DK82a1 = *VS* I.9). Isocrates also describes Gorgias as "not inhabiting one city steadily" (DK82a18 = 15.155). Multiple sources place him in Thessaly.

Late Career (and Probable Death) in Thessaly

Isocrates mentions Gorgias' residence in Thessaly, but is vague as to when it occurred (DK82a18 = 15.155). Philostratus also mentions Gorgias as having been active and extremely influential as a sophist in Thessaly (DK82a6 = *VS* 481, also DK88a1) without specifying dates, as does Plato (*Meno* 70b).[6] Pausanias stated that Gorgias was admired by Jason, ruler of Thessaly (ca. 380–70) and moved there at his behest (DK82a7 = Pausanias VI.17.7 sq.)

Longevity

Our sources testify unanimously to Gorgias' longevity, some of which claim he reached the age of 105 (DK82a1, 7, 11, 12, 13, 14, 15).

Associates

Numerous followers, admirers, pupils, and imitators of Gorgias are mentioned in testimonia, although the various terms used to associate people with him convey little information about the precise nature or duration of the relationships. Moreover, an awareness that degrees of association may be overstated is necessary to compensate for the general tendency of doxographers to group thinkers into schools and successions. Philostratus (DK82A1 = VS 492–94) mentions that Gorgias was admired both by young (Critias, Alcibiades, Agathon) and old (Pericles, Thucydides).[7] However, this may reflect anything from stylistic imitation through frequent attendance at epideictic displays (or perhaps social events like the ones portrayed in Plato's *Protagoras* and *Gorgias*) to (in the case of the younger group) possibly some sort of educational experience.[8] Philostratus' *Epistle* 73 (= DK82a31), a letter to Julia Domna purportedly defending Gorgias against the attacks of Plutarch, describes how the style of Gorgias influenced many notable Athenians, even Plato, but at issue is stylistic influence, not personal association.[9] Suda (DK82a2) lists Polus, Pericles (improbable), Isocrates, and Alcidamas as pupils. Plato (*Phaedrus* 238d = DK82a4) lists Licymnius and Polus as associates of Gorgias, and Xenophon adds Proxenus of Boetia as a pupil (*Anabasis* II.6.16 = DK82a4; repeated in Diogenes Laertius *VP* II.49). Isocrates is mentioned as a pupil of Gorgias by Cicero, Quintilian, and (indirectly) pseudo-Plutarch (DK82a12, 16, 17, 32). Diogenes Laertius also adds Antisthenes as a pupil (*VP* VI.1; no confirming evidence) and Aeschines as a stylistic imitator (*VP* II.63).

Appendix B

A Summary of Gorgias' Work and Activity

Carol Poster

Name	**Date**	**Categorization of Gorgias**
Aristophanes	*Clouds,* 423 B.C.E.	Sophists in general as physicists as well as clever speakers
Isocrates	436–348 B.C.E.	Philosophical/eristic sophist
Xenophon	ca. 430–ca. 350 B.C.E.	Physicist/sophist, teacher, and clever speaker
Plato	ca. 425–347 B.C.E.	Rhetorician, sophist, teacher
Aristotle	384–22 B.C.E.	Sophist, orator
Philodemus	ca. 110–40 B.C.E.	Sophistic rhetorician
Cicero	106–43 B.C.E.	Sophist, orator, rhetorician
Diodorus Siculus	flourished 60–30 B.C.E.	Orator
Dionysius of Halicarnassus	60–7 B.C.E.	Philosophical sophist
Quintilian	35–ca. 100 C.E.	Orator, rhetorician
Aelius Aristides	117–181 C.E.	Plato's Gorgias
Sextus Empiricus	ca. 160–210 C.E.	Natural philosopher
Philostratus	ca. 170–250 C.E.	Philosophical sophist
Diogenes Laertius	flourished third century C.E.	Orator, rhetorician
Iamblichus	ca. 245–325 C.E.	Pythagorean rhetoric
Themistius	born ca. 317–388 C.E.	Sophist (following Plato)
Syrianus	died ca. 437 C.E.	Rhetorician
Olympiodorus	ca. 500–570 C.E.	Sophist

Appendix C

A New Testimonium of Theodorus Byzantius

Robert N. Gaines

Among the Theodorean testimonia collected by Radermacher, Theodorus is mentioned among authors of books on the art of speeches by Plato (*Phdr.* 266d [B XII 5]) and as an author of more that one treatise on rhetoric by both Aristotle (*Rh.* 2.23.28 (1400b) [B XII 11], Grimaldi, 333) and Dionysius of Halicarnassus (*Is.* 19 [B XII 4]). To these witnesses we may now add a previously unnoticed testimonium in Phld. *Rh.* 4, *P. Herc.* 1007, col. 5a.9–22 (preliminary text, critical apparatus, and translation are my own).

Preliminary Text

. . . μηδὲ]ν ἐ̣[πιβε|βλ[έ]φθαι τῶν γ[ι]ν̣ο̣[μέ]ν̣[ων | τ[ότε] πρὸ αὐτῆς ἀμ[α]θήτων | οὐ π̣[ολ]ειτι[κ]ῶν μ[ό]νων ἀλ|λ]ὰ καὶ φιλοσόφ[ω]ν καὶ τῶν | κ̣α̣τ' ἄλλας μαθήσεις καὶ | διαν]οήσεις [π]ερι̣[σήμων | πρὸ] Θ̣ε̣οδῷρου κα[ὶ] Ἀντιφῶν|τος] καὶ παντὸς ἁ[π]λῶς τε|χνογράφου διαπεφευγό|των οὐ μόνον τὰς̣ οὕτω | προχείρους ἐν ταῖς ἑρμη|νείαις ἀτοπίας̣ ἀλλὰ σχε|δ[ὸ]ν καὶ πάσας.

Critical Apparatus

P. Herc. 1007 col. 5a = col. VI Spengel, Gros; col. Va Sudhaus

Fontes: *P* = Papyrus Herculanensis; *O* = Apographum Oxoniense; *N* = Apographum Neapolitanum

9 μηδὲ]ν Sudhaus **9–10** [ἐπιβε|βλέφθ]α[ι] Sudhaus post [βε|βλ[ά]φθαι Spengel **10** φ *O:* φ vel θ̣ *P,* deest *N* θ *O:* θ̣ vel ε̣ *P,* deest *N* γ vel π̣ *PON*]ν̣ vel]η̣,]τ̣,]π̣,]μ̣ *P:* deest *ON* ο̣ vel θ̣, ρ̣ *P:* deest *ON* ν̣[vel λ̣ι̣[, α̣ι̣[*PON* γ[ινομέ]ν[ων Sudhaus **11**]π *ON:*]π̣ vel]τ̣ *P* post τη c *ON:* ς̣ vel γ, ε̣ *P* ante ητ θ *ON:* θ̣ vel ο̣, ε̣, ς̣ *P* τ[ότε] Sudhaus ἀμ[α]θήτων Scotti **12** π̣ vel γ *PO:* deest *N* ante νμ ω *O:* ω̣ vel μ̣ *N,* ω̣ vel υ̣ *P* post νων spat. vac. [πολ]ε̣ι̣τι[κ]ῶν Sudhaus post πολ]ιτι[κ]ῶ[ν] Gros μ[ό]νων Spengel **12–13** ἀλ|λ]ὰ Scotti **13** post]α κ *ON:* κ̣ vel χ *P* fin. ν *ON:* vestigium *P* φιλοσόφ[ων] Scotti **14** κ̣ vel ν̣, η̣ *P:* deest *ON* α̣ vel λ̣, δ̣ *N:* vestigia *P,* deest *O* post κ̣α̣ τ *ON:* τ̣ vel π̣ *P* post λα c *ON:* ς̣ vel ε̣ *P* **15** ante ρ ε *N:* ε̣ vel ς̣, τ̣, γ, π̣ *PO* ι̣ vel ο̣, ς̣ *P:* deest *ON* διαν]οήσεις Scotti [π]ερ[ισήμων Sudhaus **16–21**]ω̣ρουκ[|]π̣αντο̣[|]ουδιαπ̣[|]ονον[|]υ̣σε[|]ας̣[disiunctum fragmentum in sinestera margine *O,* coniunxit Spengel **16** θ̣ vel ς̣, ο̣, ε̣, ω̣ *P:* deest *ON* ε̣ vel ς̣ *P:* deest *ON* ω̣ vel μ̣, υ̣ *O:* deest *PN* πρὸ] Sudhaus post καὶ πρ]ὸ Scotti κ]α[ὶ Sudhaus Θ̣ε̣οδῷρου legi: [Ζωπύρου] Sudhaus **16–17** Ἀντιφῶν|τος] Scotti **17** ἁ[π]λῶς Scotti **20** fin. η *N:* η̣ vel ν̣, ι̣, ω̣ *P,* ν *O* post 20 paragraphus **21** ς̣ vel γ, τ̣ *PON* **21–22** σχε|δ[ὸ]ν Scotti.

Translation

(*top of col., ca. 22 words missing*) . . . in no way observed when the uneducated born at a time before him,[1] not politicians alone, but also philosophers, and those notable in other disciplines and pursuits before Theodorus and Antiphon and simply every writer on the art of rhetoric, completely escaped not only just ordinary ineptitudes in their expression but also almost all <ineptitudes>.

This passage mentions Theodorus and Antiphon as representatives of a group consisting of "simply every writer on the art of rhetoric."[2] The discussion in which the passage arises would appear to address a claim that rhetorical studies prescribed how to discourse in an educated or uneducated fashion (see Sudhaus 1: 186, 188; *P. Herc.* col. 4a.16–21, col. 6a. 8–12).

Notes

Introduction

1. This can be seen from the outset of both works. Herodotus began, "Here is the showing-forth of the inquiry of Herodotus of Halicarnassus, so that neither what human beings have done might disappear in time, nor the deeds great and admirable, partly shown forth by Greeks, and partly by the barbarians, might be without fame" (I.1; Mensch, 3). Thucydides begins similarly: "Thucydides of Athens wrote this history of the war fought against each other by the Peloponnesians and the Athenians. He began his work right at the outbreak, reckoning that this would be a major war and more momentous than any previous conflict" (I.1; Hammond, 3). Throughout both works, the authors express a distrust of secondhand accounts and the oral record that mirrors neatly their own desire to set their firsthand accounts in writing.

2. It is clear from Aristotle's account of Corax in *Rhet.* 1402a and of Tisias in *Soph. Elench.* 183 that both had written books on the subject. Plato refers at length to a written work on rhetoric by Tisias at *Phaedrus* 273a–274a. And Quintilian in *Inst. Or.* III.8–9 states explicitly that "the earliest writers of text-books are the Sicilians, Corax and Tisias, who were followed by another from the same island, namely Gorgias of Leontini, whom tradition asserts to have been the pupil of Empedocles. He, thanks to his length of days, for he lived to a hundred and nine, flourished as the contemporary of many rhetoricians, was consequently the rival of those whom I have just mentioned, and lived on to survive Socrates" (Butler, 375).

3. Charlton (1985) explains how what we identify as academic disciplines did not emerge until the third century in Alexandria (47).

Unity, Dissociation, and Schismogenesis in Isocrates

1. The current chapter is submitted in remembrance of Professor Mackin, who passed away in August 2011.

2. The opportunities to turn back are few; the choice for leniency only barely succeeds in Corcyra (Thucydides 3.70–85), and fails with Melos (Thucydides 5.84–114). Though there may also have been an opportunity for reconciliation during the peace of Nicias, Thucydides makes it clear that it was not viable.

3. Mackin's words come from late in his conclusion, where he broadens his scope and considers the lessons of his observation for modern discourse. Perceptively, he does not fault Pericles for his ignorance of the larger ramifications of his words (258).

4. See, for example, Gomme (vol. 1: 236), Romilly (1963), Hornblower (1987), Forde (1989), Price (2001), Kagan (2003), Stahl (2003), Sahlins (2004), Hanson (2005), Foster (2010), Harloe and Morley (2012), Morley (2013), and Hawthorn (2014).

5. The Melian Dialogue (*Peloponnesian War* 5.84–114) provides a most vivid example when Athens confronts Melos in 416 B.C.E. Euripides may have commented on the violence of this event in his play *Trojan Women* of 415.

6. For example, Schiappa (1985), John Poulakos (1995), Takis Poulakos (1997), and Papillon (1996 and 1997).

7. It also derives from the political work of Lewis Fry Richardson (1939).

8. To explain how the styles between women and men can drive each other to more exaggerated forms of behavior, Deborah Tannen (1993, 177–84; 1994, 234–36; 2001, 103–5) explains how the split is created in a complementary way. Two people who have different styles (of communication, personality, behavior) end up exhibiting more exaggerated forms of that different behavior than they would if they were not encountering someone with an opposite style.

9. Bateson is more guarded about this in the conclusion to the second edition of *Naven* (1958).

10. See also Perelman 1982, 126–37.

11. See for example Romilly 1958.

12. The difficulties of the year 339, before Chaeronea, left him with no choice: his frustration with Philip meant that he could only return to Athenian leadership. Later on, after Philip's victory, Isocrates realized the inevitability of Philip's leadership and wrote his last work, the second epistle to Philip, in which he tried to make the best of a (to him now) bad situation by calling him to lead the Greeks again.

13. Or perhaps a "re-newed" sense. He uses the Trojan wars and especially the Persian wars as a way to show precedent for a pattern of Greeks against Easterners (4.85, 158, 181, 186; 12.42–52). It is significant, I think, that Pericles does not use this early history in his argumentation (Mackin, 254).

14. On Isocrates' death, see pseudo-Plutarch *Moralia* 837e–f and Edwards 1994, 26–27.

Theodorus Byzantius on the Parts of a Speech

1. On Theodorus' dates see Solmsen cols. 1839–42. Evidence regarding Theodorus' life and works is collected in Radermacher [BXII] 106–11.

2. Pl. *Phdr.* 261, 266–67; Arist. *S.E.* 34 [183b]; D.H. *Amm.* 1: 2; cf. Them. *Or.* 26, 328.

3. Pl. *Phdr.* 266d; Arist. *Rh.* 2.23.28 (1400b), following Grimaldi 333 [1400b.15–16]; D.H. *Is.* 19; Phld. *Rh.* 4, *P. Herc.* 1007, col. 5a.10–21 (see Appendix C).

4. Arist. Τεχνῶν συναγωγή ap. Cic. *Brut.* 48.

5. Pl. *Phdr.* 266d–267e; Arist. *Rh.* 3.13.5; Mart. Cap. 5.552.

6. Especially Pl. *Phdr.* 266d-267e; Arist. *Rh.* 3.13.4–5 (1414b).

7. Hamberger, 73–80; Solmsen, cols. 1844–45; cf. similar reductions in Kennedy 1994, 32; Heitsch, 38; Theobald, 284n16; Schirren, 1516; De Brauw, 188–90.

8. The standard scholarly view is that *Oration* 6 in the Lysianic corpus was not authored by Lysias (hence "pseudo-Lysias"); see, e.g., Usher 1999, 113; Todd 2000, 63–64. Accordingly, to avoid confusion, I refer to *Oration* 6 as pseudo-Lysianic and its author as pseudo-Lysias.

9. For the date of the work, I follow Todd 2007, 407–8, who argues that "what we have is in origins and in essence a genuine speech delivered at the trial [of Andokides]," though the text "may represent post-trial revision." This view places the composition of the speech in 400 (or 399) B.C.E.

10. For the text of Plato's *Phaedrus,* I follow Burnet 1901. With reference to present passage (i.e., *Phdr.* 266d5–6), the translation is my own.

11. This is the Fowler 1914 translation (537, 539), partly revised.

12. Cf. Mirhady 2007 6 who omits only the speech-conclusion in his list of speech parts attributed to Theodorus at *Phdr.* 266d–267a. Out of the speech parts mentioned, confirmation, additional confirmation, refutation, and additional refutation are assigned

to Theodorus by name; remaining parts are attributed to him as one of the writers of rhetoric books, since Plato deliberately summarizes "the things that have been written in books on the art of speeches" (*Phdr.* 266d; cf. Vries [266d5–6, 266d7] 221). The speech-conclusion is expressly attributed to all the rhetoric book writers—Theodorus included—in the clause, "But all seem to be in agreement concerning the conclusion of discourses" (267d; trans. Fowler 539; cf. Vries [267d3–4] 226).

13. See, e.g., Hackforth, 138; Vries, 221; Leeman and Pinkster, 180; Cole 1991, 23; Romilly, 60; Heitsch, 37–38; Mirhady, 6; Schirren, 1516.

14. Yunis (on *Phdr.* 266d5–267d9) stresses Plato's grasp of details in the early rhetoric books: "S.'s surprisingly extensive knowledge of the sophists' books reveals an ability to engage his interlocutor in the most opportune manner. Plato thereby also shows that his critique of sophistic rhetoric is based not on ignorance but on close familiarity" (2011, 200).

15. For the text of Aristotle's *Rhetoric,* I follow Kassel. The translation is my own, following Kennedy 2007, 231.

16. Kühner and Gerth, 662–63 [§470.2]; Cooper and Krüger 1: 549 [51.16.2]; cf. Pl. *Phdr.* 265a: μανίαν γάρ τινα, *Prot.* 313c: ὁ σοφιστὴς τυγχάνει ὢν ἔμπορός τις ἢ κάπηλος.

17. The proximity of Theodorus' dates to the trial of Andokides for impiety along with evidence in *Suidas* (θ.145) for a Theodorean speech *Against Andokides* has engendered several proposals that Theodorus was the author of Ps. Lys. 6; see, e.g., Bergk, 357 ("vielleicht"); Roegholt, 12; Drerup, 337–40; Schneider, 372. However, the evidence for these proposals is not decisive, and the Theodorus-authorship thesis has not figured significantly in scholarship on *Oration* 6 for about a century.

18. Here and elsewhere for the text of Ps. Lys. 6, I refer to Carey 2007.

19. My translation; on δὲ καὶ, see Denniston and Dover, 305 (s.v. καὶ, II.B.7.ii).

20. My conjecture and translation, following Todd 2007, 469–70.

21. See, e.g., Bergk, 357n80; Jebb 1: 280; MacDowell, 14; Todd 2007, 405, 463.

22. Todd (2007, 463) offers a specific example of what he recognizes as a "structural weakness" in *Oration* 6, namely use of an anticipatory topic ("I hear he will say") in two places within the speech (§13 and §35). However, this double use of the topic becomes explicable once it is considered that the anticipations serve distinct purposes in speech parts that have different functions. At §13 the anticipation allows the speaker to insist that those who fail to punish impiety are guilty of impiety (§13) and that Andokides admitted to profaning the Mysteries (§14). Both of these assertions are relevant to the speech part where they arise, confirmation (πίστωσις). At §35 the anticipation allows direct rebuttal of four possible arguments in Andokides' possible defense (§35–45). These rebuttals relate directly to the speech part in which they arise, refutation (ἔλεγχος).

23. I here follow the Ross text.

24. This is a slight revision of the Forster translation in Forster and Furley, 153, 155.

25. Cole 1991, 28; 2007, 46. Schiappa 1999, 25.

26. Schiappa 2003b, 49–54; 1999, 45–47. Cole 1991, 22–26, 82.

27. Cole 1991, 2, 98–99. Schiappa 1990, 457–70; 1999, 40–49.

28. See, e.g., Usher 1992, 58–60; 1999, 2n3; also Gaines, 500–503; Gagarin 1994 65–66n6; Hesk, 60–61; Reinhardt, 87, 102–3.

29. For some time evolutionary historians have posited that theoretical arts of speechmaking or rhetoric were commonly available in the fifth century B.C.E., but that they were rendered obsolete by Aristotle's *Collection of Arts* and thereafter forgotten—a circumstance which explains why they have not survived; see, e.g., Kennedy 2007, 302–6. In response to the evolutionary explanation for the non-survival of fifth-century arts, Schiappa insists, "A more likely explanation is that there were no theoretical 'Arts

of Rhetoric' written in the fifth century B.C.E." (1999, 45). In the same connection, Cole rules out the possibility of theoretical "arts" less directly. He first concludes that any fifth-century handbooks must have contained only specimens of discourse: "The balance of the evidence suggests that . . . practice and demonstration texts were, to begin with, the only, or at any rate the most characteristic, and most influential compositions of those teachers whose written *technai* came to be regarded as the beginnings of rhetoric" (1991, 82). Regarding such *technai,* Cole then conjectures that they were not analytical, and therefore not theoretical; authors whose works are subjected to this conjecture specifically include Evenus, Theodorus, Polus, and Licymnius (82–84). In my view, the crucial question obscured in this dispute is whether there existed specialized theoretical instruction regarding composition of practical discourse before Plato and Aristotle actively participated in the development of rhetorical theory. It is for this reason that I have framed the "lingering problem" for the evolutionary view as I have.

30. The case of Theodorus would appear to satisfy Schiappa's revisionist criteria for emergence of the theory of an activity (as articulated in Schiappa 1999, 22).

Gorgias' "On Non-Being"

1. Earlier drafts of this paper were presented at meetings of the International Society for History of Rhetoric (Montreal, July 2009) and the Canadian Society for the Study of Rhetoric (Waterloo-Kitchener 2012). Thanks are owed to York University for research and travel support, and to Robin Reames for her work on this project from inspiration to fruition. All references not specifically cited were taken from the online *Thesaurus Linguae Graecae* database.

2. For scholarship concerning the generic category of "On Non-Being," see Kerferd (1981), Wardy (1996), Schiappa (1997), Consigny (2001), and McComiskey (2002). See Poster (1994) for discussion of problems of genre and Eleatic ontology.

3. Schiappa (1997) characterizes the major contemporary schools of thought concerning "On Non-Being." See Whedbee (2008) for portraits of sophistic in the eighteenth and nineteenth centuries. McComiskey (1994) summarizes the revival of interest in sophistic in contemporary US composition and communication studies.

4. Isocrates and the Callicles of Plato's *Gorgias* consider a transition from metaphysical speculation to political action (or speech) a putting away of childish things, but Isocrates rather specifically cites "On Non-Being" as an example of puerile metaphysical speculation and a spectacular falsehood (*Helen* 3; *Antidosis* 268). Later biographies of philosophers frequently portray conversions to philosophy after rhetorical education. A common career pattern involved teaching rhetoric to earn a living while waiting for one of the rare municipal rhetorical chairs to open up, just as English professors right now may teach first-year writing to support themselves while applying for jobs as medievalists or literary theorists. Aristotle, Porphyry, Iamblichus, and Proclus are among the many notable philosophers who taught rhetoric early in their careers.

5. DK numbers are used for most citations, with original sources supplied parenthetically where significant. See Buchheim for comprehensive fragments and testimonia, and Sprague for English translations of DK fragments and testimonia.

6. Pythagoras, Parmenides, and others are also portrayed as conducting such embassies. In a later period, this tradition continues with the appointments to the Museum in Alexandria, embassies, and the post of ab Epistulis, often reflecting general distinction rather than specific technical skill (Lewis).

7. See Swain for the point that Philostratus is not engaged in straightforward biography, but rather a historical discussion of a certain model of display oratory, and while

not deliberately creating fiction, he should not be read as concerned primarily with the accuracy of minute historical details. He would have been more concerned with stylistic influence than precisely the number of hours and the contexts in which admirers would have been in contact with Gorgias. Moreover, he was writing over five hundred years after the events in question, and the reliability of his sources is not guaranteed.

8. Athenaeus' mention of Gorgias having read Plato's dialogue (11.505d–e), if reliable, does not suggest a personal encounter or significant acquaintanceship. Unfortunately, the precise chronology of Gorgias' activities (other than the 427 embassy) is unknown, and therefore, we cannot rule out Plato having encountered Gorgias in Athens sometime between ca. 404 and 399. On the other hand, Plato's travels after Socrates' death and Gorgias' residence in Thessaly leave a very narrow window for a possible meeting. Olympiodorus (*In Gorgiam* proem 9) may be implying that Plato was personally unacquainted with Gorgias, but the sense of the phrase is unclear, especially in light of the subsequent proof that Gorgias and Plato were contemporaries.

9. Aristotle mentions Gorgias five times (*Pol.* 1260a28 and 1275b26 and *Rhet.* 1405b38, 1406b9, and 1408b20); four of the mentions refer to his style, commenting on quotations from unidentifiable works, and one to his definition of the virtues.

10. Schenkeveld (1992) and Too (1995) are among a small minority arguing that the evidence for Isocrates studying with Gorgias is weak, but their arguments seem less than compelling given the sheer mass of ancient attestations.

11. The text here is not entirely clear, but emphasizes that different topics are appropriate to the two genres.

12. Twenty- and twenty-first-century scholarship traditionally questions whether the distinction may be Platonic anachronism, importing a distinction Plato intends to make between himself and the rhetorical schools of his own period to the fifth century, in which there was no clear distinction among the various types of "clever people." The Socrates of Aristophanes' *Clouds* is, I think, likely to have portrayed a type of verbal agility and speculative cleverness that Athenians of the period would have attributed indifferently to Socrates, Protagoras, or Gorgias.

13. Isocrates uses the term *rhētorikē* twice, in *Nicocles* and *Antidosis,* but not of Gorgias.

14. Isocrates identifies his sophists as "men who care for nothing but enriching themselves at the expense of the youth [by means of] eristic disputations" (*Helen* 10.6) in a passage strikingly reminiscent of the definition concluding Plato's dialogue, that the sophist is "nothing else, apparently, than the money-making class of the disputatious, argumentative, pugnacious, combative, acquisitive art . . ." (*Sophist* 226a; Fowler 2006, 299). See also Xenophon, "for the sophist is a hunter after the rich and young, the philosopher is the common friend of all . . . " (*Cyn.* XIII.9; Dakyns, 124).

15. Alcmaeon, unlike the others in the list, was probably a Pythagorean rather than an Eleatic, but his work on sensation and his physics have certain similarities to material found in Empedocles. Although Raven's hypothesis concerning Parmenides as a dissident Pythagorean is not sustainable, the approaches of the two schools to natural philosophy are similar in being rational rather then empirical, employing mystical or mythical elements, and searching for unified accounts of limited transcendent causes behind the superficial multiplicity of the phenomena.

16. Given that Empedocles appears to have given popular recitations of poems about natural philosophy, it is not improbable that Gorgias modeled "On Non-Being" on his teacher's performances, albeit employing poetic prose rather than verse. See Kingsley (1995) for account of Empedocles as charismatic performer.

17. My translation.

18. The term *sunousia* is particularly interesting as the paid sophistic education is normally (see Robb) contrasted with an older tradition of *sunousia,* but here Gorgias is portrayed as operating within the older framework of association, but for money.

19. See Gray for a strong argument in favor of the authenticity and unity of "Cynegeticus." Aristophanes' *Clouds* was initially produced in 423 B.C.E. The revised version, which is the one that has been preserved in the manuscript tradition, was written a few years later (the precise date is uncertain) and circulated in manuscript form. Given that Xenophon would have been approximately seven years old at the initial production, acquaintance with the revised version is more probable than familiarity with the initial performance. See Hubbard for discussion of dates and versions of the *Clouds.*

20. Dionysius of Halicarnassus examines Lysias' speeches as models useful to students of oratory in a manner which suggests that by the Hellenistic period, as whatever putative forensic issues were involved would have been long ago resolved, they were read as displays of oratorical skill. In this sense, one might say that any deliberative or forensic oration, published and read by later generations, becomes viewed as epideictic—Demosthenes' crown, the actions of Eratosthenes, or the guilt of Milo are no longer active concerns of subsequent readers, and thus, no matter what the original intentions of the authors, the works no longer function to persuade subsequent audiences but instead to entertain, to satisfy intellectual curiosity, or to serve as models for composition; that is, all speeches on deliberative or forensic subjects survive by being received as epideictic.

21. For discussion of Philostratus and Hellenic paideia, see Brown (1992) and Anderson (1986 and 1993).

22. Translation amended.

23. This passage comments on the very end of Iamblichus' *De vita Pythagorica,* which is simply a list of notable Pythagoreans, organized geographically. Iamblichus himself lists Empedocles and Parmenides (and Melissus as well), but not Zeno, Tisias, Corax, or Gorgias.

24. No source is given in the book, nor could I find anything in a *Thesaurus Linguae Graecae* search that seemed relevant to this claim. Tarrant (personal communication) does not remember what specific source the author of this section of the introduction may have had in mind some fourteen years ago.

25. See Heath for discussion of this distinction.

26. For a summary of the ways in which Gorgias' work and activity are described by the ancient testimony, see Appendix B.

27. His description of following his brother (assuming it is true) suggests some curiosity about medicine. His claim to be able to speak on any topics proposed suggests at least superficial knowledge of likely topics, His extant speeches suggest familiarity with major trends in ethical, physical, and rhetorical ideas of his period.

28. The repetition is intentional as teaching is an activity characteristic of both rhetoric and sophistic, although rhetorical teaching would eventually, as discussed by Heath, focus on more technical matters (argument, issue theory, parts of oration) and sophistic on style, performance, and imitation of models. This distinction was not fully developed until well into the Hellenistic period; when reading post-Platonic testimonia, we need to remain aware that clear distinctions between sophistic and rhetoric may reflect terministic biases of later writers rather than fifth- or even fourth-century standard usage.

29. Shakespeare, *A Midsummer Night's Dream,* Act 5, Scene 1.

Parmenides

1. The translations by Ustinova and Kingsley differ slightly.

2. Hoffman in this volume also addresses problems with the myth-to-reason framework structuring much rhetorical history.

3. Edward Schiappa (1990, 457; 2003b, 40–41) argues compellingly that the term *rhētorikē* is Plato's, or at the least a fourth-century and not fifth-century B.C.E. usage (although the root term, in various formulations, is older). The term "sophist" is also contested, but I cannot delve into that issue here.

4. A partial list would include the following. Glenn and Lunsford help rectify the masculinist bias in the rhetorical tradition by reincluding women rhetors. Vitanza (1994) and Ballif (2013) call attention to historiography, or how history is produced and written, noting its assumptions and limitations. Kennedy (1998) was one of the first to produce an ambitious comparative rhetoric that included attention to nonhuman and early human rhetorics, as well as cross-cultural rhetorics. This work has since been followed by Lipson and Binkley's (2004, 2009) two edited collections on ancient rhetorics outside the Greek orbit, and by Baca and Villanueva's collection that situates ancient and alternative rhetorics in the Americas. Enos and Walker significantly revise the field's standard rhetorical history. Finally, there have been two recent special issues of *Rhetoric Society Quarterly*, one on historiography edited by Michelle Balliff (44.3, 2014), the other on comparative rhetoric edited by LuMing Mao (43.3, 2013) that speak to the expansion and deepening of the understanding of rhetoric's sources and origins.

5. I rely on Graham, unless otherwise noted, for translations of Parmenides' fragments.

6. The Greeks considered parricide one of the greatest crimes.

7. Aristotle thus saw Parmenides and other, earlier thinkers as grasping at ideas and arguments not perfected as *philosophy* until later; we can see this, for instance, in his charge that Parmenides (and Melissus) argue sophistically (*Physics* 185a7–12, 186a4–10).

8. In his new translation of Parmenides and the pre-Socratics, Waterfield acknowledges that Parmenides was more than just a philosopher but still complains about the "somewhat tortured verse" (50).

9. Burkert states that German scholarship reads the proem as primarily symbolic of an ascent to the light, despite the contrary evidence (86–87).

10. Palmer argues that Parmenides is not advocating strict monism nor primarily refuting earlier, Ionian cosmologies (49–50).

11. See Jarratt, 11, 43; Vitanza 1997, 176, 181, 253–54; Ballif 2001, 40–42, 93, 120–21, 131; and Enos, 128–29. Ballif, Jarratt, and Vitanza have already done much groundwork that challenges the kinds of easy categorization determining Parmenides' philosophic reception.

12. Rohde remarks that the legend that Pythagoras descended to Hades is untrue, even though the legend is quite old.

13. Translation modified.

14. Patton emphasizes that the practice was widespread in the ancient world and that it involved special, sacred places—particularly caves and underground sanctuaries. Incubation was picked up by Christianity, and in many places it is still practiced today. A defining feature of incubation is that the dream is divinely given, not humanly achieved.

15. According to Patton, the god allows the summons (199).

16. Kingsley notes that verb forms of "carry" are used four times in the opening verses.

17. Older textual editors, following Diels, had adopted the variant *eukykleos* ("well rounded"), from Simplicius' manuscript; however, modern editors now accept *eupeitheos* as more likely, based on manuscript traditions and internal evidence from Parmenides' poem. See Mourelatos 2008, xxxiv, 154–55, 157; also note Mourelatos' argument that the meanings of *eupeitheos* and *eukykleos* are related.

18. See Burkert, 90: "Parmenides plays with allusions, revealing and concealing at the same time."

19. See also Burkert, 99.

20. Orpheus and Heracles also meet Persephone when they journey to the underworld, and in paintings, she greets them as Parmenides is greeted, with the outstretched right hand (Kingsley 1999, 94). Kingsley is not the only one to identify Persephone; see also Gemelli Marciano, 35.

21. According to Kingsley, the term *kouros* is ancient; it indicates a young boy or an initiate, and is frequently a term used to designate someone who will be a hero, as, for instance, with Herakles (1999, 71).

22. The authors demonstrate that the placebo effect, which is already widely recognized as having beneficial effects, does not even need to be hidden, as previously thought.

23. It has been reported that recitation of hexameter rhythms has concrete effects on the human body, synchronizing heart rate and respiration in a therapeutic manner. See Cysarz et al., H579.

24. According to Michael Winkelman, "Shamanism involves social adaptations that use biological potentials provided by integrative altered states of consciousness (ASC) to facilitate community integration, personal development, and healing" (194). William Covino likewise argues that "magic is a social act whose medium is persuasive discourse" (11).

25. On this point, see Guthrie 1965, 1, 9. See also Hoffman in this volume.

26. The power of rationality to stun and bind is not as odd as it might appear; consider Sloterdijk's account of a pupil reading Kant for the first time, who felt "as if an old bony hand were slowly screwing his brain out of his head[;] . . . sweat stood on his brow" (qtd. in Sloterdijk, xxxi).

27. This statement, about how categories bind and constrain, in turn reflects upon historiography—and hence is equally applicable to how we think about rhetorical history and prehistory.

28. See for example Ioannidis; Stroebe, Postmes, and Spears, 670, 688; Haidt; and the *Economist.*

Heraclitus' Doublespeak

1. This numbering system for the pre-Socratic fragments is from Hermann Alexander Diels and Walther Krantz, or Diels-Krantz (DK). In this system, each pre-Socratic author is identified by a number—Heraclitus is 22—and the fragments are either "A fragments" or "B fragments" (testimonia or exact quote, respectively). Hence Heraclitus' first fragment is designated "DK22b1."

2. Although Heidegger also devoted a late lecture course entirely to Heraclitus in 1966–67 (Heidegger 1979), because of the brevity and narrowness of focus on Heraclitus' *logos* fragments in the essay on DK22b50 and *Introduction to Metaphysics,* I have confined my analysis to these texts. Heidegger also briefly discusses Heraclitus' *logos* in *Basic Concepts of Ancient Philosophy,* which was originally a lecture course from 1926 (2008, 48–50).

3. Fragment 48 is as follows: τῷ τόξῳ ὄνομα βίος, ἔργον δὲ θάνατος; "The name of the bow is life; its work is death" (Kahn 65). For translations of the fragments, I have

consulted Burnet 1930, Kirk 1962, Kahn, and Barnes 1982 and 1987, with some changes as noted. For the translation of the first fragment, I use George Kennedy's translation of Aristotle's Rhetoric (1991), since it preserves in its word order the grammatical ambiguity. For other works by Aristotle, I have consulted the Barnes edition of his complete works (1984), with adjustments.

4. This view represents a significant change from Poster's 1996 paper, in which she interprets Heraclitus' *logos* as though it were outside the radical instability of the world.

5. That this is the opening line of Heraclitus' book is widely attested to by various ancient sources. Cf. Sextus Empiricus *Adv. Math.* 7.132 (Bury, 73); Aristotle *Rhet.* 1407b. For a complete record of the ancient testimonia on the first lines, see Kirk 1962, 33–34.

6. The presumption that Heraclitus' *logos* must be metaphysical in nature appears throughout late ancient and medieval receptions of Heraclitus. Cf. Sextus Empiricus *Adv. Math.* 7.126–32 (Bury, 68–73); Hippolytus *Ref.* 9.3–5 (Litwa 626–31); Clement of Alexandria *Strom.* 5.14 (Wilson, 283–88). For useful summaries of this tradition, see Adam and Inge. The overtly metaphysical view of Heraclitus' *logos* appears less frequently in recent scholarship, but nevertheless remains in circulation. Its fuller articulation can be found in English, Frankel, Darcus, Miller, and Adomenas. In other cases, the Stoic *logos* more insidiously infects interpretations of Heraclitus' *logos.* For example, I suggest along with Hoffman (2006) that Kirk's (1954) and Guthrie's (1962) contention that the *logos* is quite literally fire or a fire-like substance is too reliant on the Stoic concept of *ekpurōsis* or "divine fire." For more on the critique of this kind of anachronism that finds Platonist metaphysics and reason in Heraclitus' *logos,* see Burnet 1892, 133n; Minar, 327; Glasson, 231–38; and Heidegger 2000, 133–43.

7. This suspicion of Aristotle dates back to Harold Cherniss' 1935 monograph, where he argues that Aristotle's view of the pre-Socratics is not to be trusted because he so transparently remolds their thought for his own purpose. Similar distrust pervades modern scholarship on this issue. Cf. Cherniss 1951, McDiarmid; Jaeger 1947 and 1948; Stevenson; Miller, 164; and Cole 1991, 27. I believe this distrust is misplaced, not only because, unlike us, he had access to Heraclitus' entire work, but more importantly, because Aristotle was chronologically unadulterated by the hermeneutic traditions that read backward into Heraclitus' *logos* a mystical prototype of Stoic, Platonist, and Christian metaphysics that for two millennia have dominated our understanding. For a reconsideration of Aristotle as a commentator on the pre-Socratics, see Collobert.

8. Although I believe the purpose of Aristotle's example shows him to be disinterested compared to later interpreters who stress the religio-metaphysical properties of the *logos* of the first fragment, Miller critiques Aristotle for the same point: "That the metaphysical Logos concept so central to the thought of Heraclitus should appear totally unknown to Plato and Aristotle (the latter quotes the opening of Frg. 1 [*Rhet.* 1407b 11] only for the purpose of making a grammatical point) is something of an enigma to students of classical philosophy, but a fact to be reckoned with no more nor less than the fact that we today quite simply know more about the pre-Socratics than did the ancients themselves" (164).

9. Kirk, for example, treats this lack of resolution as though it were an argumentative paucity on Aristotle's part as opposed to an intentional and necessary preservation of Heraclitus' indeterminacy, and attempts to resolve that indeterminacy by assigning ἀεὶ to modify either "always" or "ignorant" but not both. He suggests that "ἐόντας expects a predicate, but . . . τοῦδ' forms such predicate" (1962, 34) and therefore, that ἐόντας modifies ἀξύνετοι. However, the likelihood that τοῦδ' serves as the predicate for ἐόντας ("though this logos is this . . . ") does not rule out the possibility that Heraclitus employed ἀεὶ to serve two functions in the sentence: "Though this logos is this always

uncomprehending are men." Kirk's resolution of Heraclitus' grammar on this point does not disambiguate the paradox, despite his treatment of the paradox as a grammatical problem in need of resolution. Kahn provides a succinct and useful summary of the dispute between those who claim aiei modifies eontos and those who contend aiei modifies axunetoi (93).

10. Translations modified.

11. Aristotle refers to the paradoxes that all things are one and the harmony of opposites in *Top.* 1.104b and 8.159b, *Phys.* 1.185a–b, *Univ.* 396b, *Met.* 5.1012a, 11.1067a, *Nic.* 8.1155b, and *Eud.* 7.1235a; and the paradox of the flux and flow of the universe in *Heav.* 1.279b and 3.298b, *Soul* 1.405a. Although the authorship of *On the Universe* and *Problems* is doubtful, the references to Heraclitus contained there are consistent with the rest of Aristotle's work, and for this reason I have not excluded them from this list.

12. Translation amended.

13. For example, in his landmark first edition of *Early Greek Philosophy,* Burnet wrote: "I have no hesitation in understanding the word λόγος . . . simply as 'argument,' 'discourse,' . . . or the like. The Stoic interpretation, as we find it in Marcus Aurelius, iv. 46 must be rejected altogether; the word λόγος did not mean Reason at all in early days" (1892 133n). Burnet tempered somewhat this monistic reading of the λόγος in the second (1908) and later editions: "the λόγος is primarily the discourse of Herakleitus himself; though as he is a prophet, we may call it his 'Word.' It can neither mean a discourse addressed to Herakleitus nor yet 'reason" (146n). As Kirk notes, "This view, in all its simplicity, has not won acceptance for the good reason that in fr. 50, where plainly the same kind of λόγος is under discussion, λόγος is formally distinguished from the speaker" (1962, 37). See also Miller, 168; Kirk, Raven, and Schofield, 187. Catherine Osborne has pointed out that *logos* in fr. 50 is a correction by Bernays, and that the original word was *dogmatos* (doctrine). Although she is not persuaded by Marcovich's argument in favor of the correction, she concedes in a footnote that "it does seem plausible that *dogmatos* might have originated as an explanation of what *logos* meant in this context, and took the place of *logos* in the text as a result" (147n45). Ultimately, it is uncertain whether the original term in DK22b50 was *logos* or *dogmatos.*

14. Translation amended.

15. For a longer explanation of proem conventions of Heraclitus and his contemporaries, see the discussion in note 30, below.

16. Translation amended.

17. For more on this critique, see Burnet 1892, 133n; Minar, 327; and Glasson, 231–38.

18. Translation amended.

19. Translation amended. This fragment contains another excellent example of Heraclitean wordplay, in the subtle replacement of ξυνὸς for κοινός. I believe this change in terminology is a further indication that the two fragments, 2 and 114, should not be treated interchangeably.

20. Robinson notes that 114 contains a pun that does not translate: "To speak 'with insight' (ξὺν νόῳ) is to base oneself on 'what is common' (τῷ ξυνῷ) (a favourite Heraclitean word: see fragments 80, 103, and perhaps 2)" (156). Here, Robinson seems to be acknowledging that the pun in 114 linguistically distances the *xunon* of 114 from the *xunon* of 2 (see note 19, above). At the same time, however, he implicitly equates the *logos* of fr. 1 with the universal *nomos* that is the "blueprint" for all the cosmos. He presumes this consonance even though the pun challenges this consonance.

21. Chaïm Perelman and Lucie Olbrechts-Tyteca have analyzed the argumentative effect of the transformation from analogy to example or illustration: "In the ordinary course

[of an analogy], the *phoros* is better known than the theme of which it should clarify the structure or establish the value, either its value as a whole or the respective value of its components. . . . When the two relations encountered belong to the same sphere, and can be subsumed under a common structure, we have not analogy but argument by example or illustration" (373). By collapsing the distance between the theme and the *phoros, nomos* serves not as an analogy for what is common, but as an example of *logos.*

22. Even when scholars have critiqued the mishandling of this analogy, the critique has had little impact. For example, Mourelatos (1965) correctly identifies human and divine laws as merely a "convenient analogue" (259) according to Heraclitus, but not identical to *logos.* Nevertheless, Mourelatos' challenge affected none of the major monographs on Heraclitus in the decades that followed the publication of his article.

23. Cf. Kirk 1954, 53 and 396; Guthrie 1962, 427–32; Hoffman 2006, 10.

24. The material cause of the universe was one category of the four causes identified by Aristotle in his work on nature. In addition, he identifies the so-called formal cause (explained not through recourse to matter alone, but through recourse to *logos,* to the composition or form of matter: *Met.* 983a), efficient cause (the movement that causes change or transformation), and final cause (the cause opposed to the movement—"that for the sake of which" or "the good (for this is the end of all generation and change)" [*Met.* 983a; Barnes 1984, 1955]).

25. All of the early philosophers, Aristotle suggests, were able to conceive of only two of the four categories of causes. He wrote, "These thinkers, as we say, evidently got hold up to a certain point of two of the causes which we distinguished in our work on nature—the matter and the source of the movement—vaguely, however, and with no clearness, but as untrained men behave in fights; for they go round their opponents and often strike fine blows, but they do not fight on scientific principles, and so these thinkers do not seem to know what they say; for it is evident that, as a rule, they make no use of their causes except to a small extent. . . . Regarding the two causes, then, as we say, the inquiry seems to have been pushed thus far by the early philosophers" (*Met.* 985a; Barnes 1984, 1558). Although this is one of the more controversial passages, often cited as evidence of Aristotle's demeaning and dismissive perspective on the pre-Socratics, the idea that Heraclitus' thought was necessarily bound to materiality is noncontroversial.

26. See note 6, above.

27. T. F. Glasson wrote: "Plato in his treatment of the Heraclitean school does not mention the Logos. Nor does Aristotle in his account of Heraclitus. This would be most surprising if it really were the case that the doctrine of the Logos was his central message. Again, it is highly significant that no instances can be quoted of the use of Logos as a cosmic principle in the period which lies between Heraclitus and the Stoics" (236).

28. For a fuller development of this argument, see Minar.

29. From Aristotle's commentary, this seems to be an appropriate and standard proportion of the text. Citing several pre-Socratic texts as examples, he wrote that the introductory remarks are not always necessary in shorter speeches, and are only used when the topic of the speech is particularly controversial (*Rhet.* 1414a–b).

30. Not only the topics of the fragments, but also the quantity of terms related to speaking, discourse, listening, hearing, and so forth indicate an unusual focus on speech and discourse in Heraclitus' work on nature. Through a freeware concordance application (Antconc, available at http://www.antlab.sci.waseda.ac.jp/antconc_index.html) I found that terms for speech and discourse occur twenty-two times (*logos-legein, eposepein, stomata, homologein* and others; see DK22b1, 19, 50, 92, 93, 107, 108, 114), hearing and listening occur twenty-seven times (*akousai,* etc.; see DK22b1, 17, 19, 34, 50, 55, 101),

and misunderstanding and understanding occur more than twenty times (see DK22b1, 17, 19, 34, 55, 73, 108, 114). In total, these terms constitute roughly 5 percent of the total vocabulary. This may be contrasted with the other four pre-Socratic authors of works on nature from which we still have a substantial amount (over twenty) of surviving fragments (Xenophanes, Parmenides, Anaxagoras, and Empedocles). In these fragments, occurrences of such terms constitute at most 3 percent (Xenophanes) and at least less than 1 percent (Anaxagoras). The most striking contrast is found in the terms that refer to the audience's hearing and listening to the discourse, which are very little treated in the other texts. This basic lexical comparison reveals that Heraclitus treated rhetorical themes far more extensively than did his contemporaries.

31. This observation of the importance of language as a theme in Heraclitus' discourse is reinforced by Kirk 1962, 7; Kahn, 9; Osborne, 146; and Poster 1996, 5, and 2006, 20. Guthrie concurs with Gigon that these references to speaking, hearing, listening, and understanding are common themes of *proemia*, but neither acknowledges the exceptional proportion devoted to these themes in Heraclitus' discourse. See Guthrie 1962, 419 and 427; Gigon, 47.

32. In addition to Guthrie and Kirk's fire hypothesis, Minar is also worthy of mention for his material understanding of *logos*. He notes on the one hand that any meaning hidden within Heraclitus' *logos* must at least contain the idea of verbal expression, and on the other hand that the hidden meaning should not be sought through reference to such "exceptional" fragments that refer to god or the divine. Rather, it should be sought through reference to the fragments that are more in line with the basic interest of the work as a whole—the natural world. And, Minar emphasizes, this material world was not viewed as something separate from the world of human thought, life, and observation. Minar wrote: "Neither the division of reason from sense nor the concern with a criterion of truth is as early as Heraclitus. If the passage is based on genuine Heraclitean material, as it may well be, the belief reflected is much more likely to be in a world-soul than in a world-reason. In early Greek thought (and as late as Plato's *Timaeus*) it was common to think of the universe as a living being, and it was natural to think of the principle of life (i.e., essentially, breath) as being drawn in from the surrounding air" (329). Nevertheless, Minar does not ultimately pursue this possibility of a living, breathing, material *logos*. Also worthy of note is Hoffman, who suggests that the *logos* of Heraclitus "designates a structure in which elements were purposefully assembled into a composition. . . . Heraclitus simply took a word that signified the ordered arrangement of language, and expanded its signification to include the ordered arrangement of the world. Thus he did give the world a special significance, but he did not depart radically from it [*sic*] previous meaning" (2006, 15). In many ways, this sense Hoffman argues for is preferable to the prevailing views. Nevertheless, it still lacks the signature Heraclitean wit. Moreover, while "composing" connotes a material activity, "composition" as Hoffman discusses it lacks this kind of material physicality. Hoffman's sense of the term suggests a static, formal structure—indeed, a precursor to the Platonic forms (2006, 17).

33. See note 13, above.

34. Translation amended.

35. *Alētheia* is commonly translated as truth, a practice Heidegger critiques throughout his work, and explains instead as the most essential term for the revealing that was the basic mode of being for the Greeks. Revealing, disclosing, bringing forth, coming into appearance are his preferred terms for parsing *alētheia*, which necessarily invokes the problematic notion of correspondence.

36. In particular, this ability of being able to "argue opposites" is discussed at *Rhet.* 1355a.

Rhetoric and Royalty

1. While Schiappa (1990) first makes the argument that *rhetorikē* is a Platonic invention, its use as a term by Alcidamas suggests a more widespread usage in Athenian intellectual culture by the fourth century.

2. Kennedy is especially useful for laying out the sequence of ancient commentators on the status of Homer as a rhetorician.

3. Knudson offers extensive argument that Homer's *Iliad* shows evidence of a *technē* of rhetoric. I am grateful for an anonymous referee's suggestion of her work. Here, my argument departs from hers in arguing that Odysseus possesses a kind of knowledge that is not yet identical to a fully developed art of rhetoric, but that still displays many characteristics of one.

4. See Kennedy 1957, 23–35, for a nontheoretical account of rhetoric in Homer.

5. Here I mean the more specific sense of *epistēmē* that Aristotle (and sometimes Plato) intends and not all Greek uses of *epistēmē.*

6. Exceptions include Doherty 1991 and 1995, especially 65–86. Doherty focuses on the implied feminine audience of Odysseus' speech here, especially in relation to the implied audiences of the poem as a whole, and notes the strangeness of the episode and Arete's importance as an audience member. However, her analysis focuses on the importance of gender in the speeches as the poet's break from a larger cultural norm, while mine addresses the significance of the issue of fidelity and identity in Odysseus' rhetoric. Stanford also briefly notes the effect of the speech on Arete (394). Dimock argues that the catalogue of women is a sort of "survey of the possible fates of womankind" (153) and is motivated by Odysseus' learning that he is the cause of his mother's death. The list shows that women's "chief glory is to be descended from and married to and to produce great men" (150) and so reveals to Odysseus the importance of his own fate in his mother's fate and fame.

7. For the former, see Krischer; for the latter, see Edwards 1980. A notable exception is to be found in Sammons, who argues that Homer uses the device of the catalogue for rhetorical purposes that draw attention to his own poetic skill—for example, his ability to offer a divine point of view on a multiplicity of characters from past mythology. According to Sammons, while the catalogue form—understood as a list with sometimes accompanying elaborative description—sometimes seems to detract from the character's narrative, the form may also be used by Homer to evoke other poems with which his own epic might be compared or to add to the pragmatic purposes of the narrative (8–18).

8. Translations of the *Rhetoric* are my own.

9. Greek edition used is Murray and Dimock 1995.

10. Reece notes the erotic elements here, and points out the similarities between Nausikaa's actions here and those of Penelope at I.333; XVI.415; XVIII.209; and XXI.64 (115). Woodhouse offers an extensive discussion of what this encounter with Odysseus means for Nausikaa as she approaches womanhood (54–65).

11. Reece gives further evidence for the ambiguity of the Phaiakians' hospitality (101–21).

12. Of course, Homer also has reason to avoid retelling the tale for the sake of maintaining *his* audience's interest.

13. Karp argues for the presence of some of these rhetorical techniques more generally in Homer.

14. Doherty (1991) notes similarities between Penelope and Arete, including their fidelity to their husbands, in contrast to other female figures in the *Odyssey* (172–73). It therefore seems especially likely that Arete might be more sympathetic to the faithful Penelope than to the apparently unfaithful Odysseus.

15. See Gantz, 173, and Hesiod fragment 30 in Merkelbach and West, 19–20.

16. Sammons notes that the speech takes on the coloration of the voice of Iphimedeia in its emphasis on themes of merely youthful threats to characterize their desire to overthrow the gods (87–88).

17. See Gantz, 380; Diodorus Siculus 4.10.6; Apollodorus *Library* 2.4.11. Note that at *Odyssey* XI.520 Herakles speaks of Zeus as his father.

18. I am grateful to Stephanie Nelson for pointing this out.

19. See Gantz, 733–34 (Gantz refers to *Odyssey Scholia*, 3F170).

20. Sammons notes the ways in which this omission distances Odysseus' poetry from that of the narrative voice of the whole epic (90).

21. Doherty (1991) also notes the omission of Clytemnestra (157–58).

22. Doherty (1991) notes the rhetorical elements in Odysseus' brevity here as well (148).

23. Hesiod *Th.* 947–49. Hesiod has Zeus make Ariadne immortal and ageless for Dionysus. See Gantz, 114–15, for a fuller description of various accounts. In some accounts, Theseus is absolved of responsibility and Dionysus' action is primary.

24. Diodorus Siculus 4.66.3, 4.65.5–7; Apollodorus *Library* 3.6.2, 3.7.5. See Gantz, 524–28.

25. In contrast, Doherty (1991) suggests that Odysseus deliberately holds out on the rest of his story in order to make Alkinoos curious (148).

26. See Karp on Athena's deliberate omissions of the truth (252).

27. Sammons suggests that Odysseus does not return to the catalogue of women when Alkinoos asks him to continue because Alkinoos finds the *kleos*-song of warriors a more fitting form for a bard (83–84). However, Alkinoos' request for the discussion of male heroes occurs in the political context of ambiguity as to whether Arete or Alkinoos holds the authority to send Odysseus home with honor; here the poetic form cannot be wholly separated from the political question.

28. Again, my interpretation here need not exclude other functions of the speeches—for example, the significance of the encounter with Achilles for Odysseus' own attitude towards life, death, and fame.

29. On the links between rhetorical ability in speech and philosophical practice in Alcidamas, see McCoy.

30. Of course, Odysseus' shift is also compatible with showing two sides of his own concerns, that is, hope and fear as to whether Penelope has been faithful in his absence. Still, that he exhibits one side to Arete and another to Alkinoos shows facility in moving between different parts of himself and reshaping his self-presentation in the exercise of *ethopoiēia*.

31. As Byre has argued, even Odysseus' account of the Cyclops seems oriented towards this single-minded goal of persuading Arete and Alkinoos that Odysseus both desires and deserves to return to Ithaka.

32. Thanks to Anna Besch, Stephanie Nelson, Stephen Scully, and Philip Freeman for helpful comments on previous drafts of this paper. Special thanks to Arthur Madigan, SJ, for recommending relevant passages in Aristotle to help me better to articulate a sense of proto-technical rhetoric. Any errors, of course, remain my own. Thanks also to two anonymous referees and to Robin Reames for inviting the paper. The very earliest

version was written during a National Endowment for the Humanities fellowship at Boston University in the late 1990s, and then set aside in a drawer for many years. It bears a limited resemblance to this one, but I am grateful for the support of the NEH at that time. Thanks also to John McCoy, who helped me to think through some examples of proto-technical knowledge in music, an area about which he knows much more than I do.

Mētis, Themis, and the Practice of Epic Speech

1. George Grote has been identified by G. B. Kerferd as the originator of one of two major traditions of the interpretation of pre-Socratic philosophy that took shape during the nineteenth century, the other having its roots in the work of G. W. F. Hegel; see Kerferd, 4–14. In keeping with his reformist political agenda, Grote's *History of Greece,* a multivolume work that appeared between 1846 and 1899, promoted a view of Athens based in reasoned public deliberation. He saw the sophists as promoting a scientific point of view that contributed to public reason, and also accounts for the resistance to their thought: "When positive science and criticism, and the idea of an invariable sequence of events, came to supplant in the more vigorous intellects the more mythical creed of omnipresent personification, an inevitable schism was produced between the instructed few and the remaining many" (Grote 1899, 359). For a fuller account of Grote, see Whedbee 2004.

2. For a longer account of the debate about whether early rhetoric owed more to "mythopoetic" orality or literate "rational reflection," see Haskins 2001. For alternate figurations of the relationship between *muthos* and *logos,* see Vernant 1988 and Hoffman 2003.

3. Detienne and Vernant provide an extensive general study of *mētis* in Greek myth, to which a number of the insights of this chapter are indebted.

4. "Scepter and *themis*" is a common formula in the *Iliad,* found at 9.99 and elsewhere.

5. See for example Hom. *Il.* 11.779; *Od.* 9.262, 14.56.

6. *Dikē* is often invoked in a similar way to *themis,* as when Odysseus, compelled to narrate a false story to his wife, complains that travelers feel pain when they must recount their sad journeys, "for it is just," meaning simply that this is the way it must be. But often *dikē* is more a property of decisions than a tradition, like *themis.* Justice can have a man as its source, whereas *themis* cannot. Sometimes, in Homer, we find justice plus the genitive: the justice of divine kings, of suitors, or of old men. See *Od.* 4.691, 18.275, 24.255. And while *dikē* can take the dative, *themis* must take the dative (for example, *themis* to strangers, see *Il.* 11.779) and never the genitive. *Dikē* would seem to be the quality in the *basileus* and in his decisions that compel his *themis,* given to him by the gods, to be enacted by his subjects.

7. On this passage, also see Walker, 5–6.

8. For the full account, see Detienne and Vernant, 11–26.

9. See Hom. Il. 1.311; Od. 21.274.

10. See Hom. *Il.* 1.343, 3.109–10, 18.250.

11. To some extent, the present-ing of the past is embedded in the poetics of the very language of Greek epic; lying is the root meanings of the word truth (*alētheia*). The Greek word for truth is *a-lētheia* which is constructed from *lēthe* (oblivion, hiddeness) plus the alpha privative. Thus for archaic Greeks truth was what was dis-covered, un-hidden or revealed. It was not a particular content of language but an effect of language–the effect of dis-covering, of bringing a thought out of the shade of oblivion into the light

of consciousness. As the effect of dis-covery, truth has no place in a world where everything can be seen. A thing must be first concealed in order to be unconcealed. To see the truth implies a former blindness to it. The cunning persuader, informed by *mētis*, not only sees what his audience fails to see, he sees *that* they fail to see. He produces the effect of truth not only by showing them what they have not seen, but by showing them that they have been blind. The blindness of Homer and Tiresias perhaps illustrated that these greatest technicians of *mētis* are aware of the limitations of their vision. *Mētis* teaches the speaker how to use *themis* to rule in the land of the blind by bringing to light those aspects of the present that argue for his position. On this line of thinking, see Detienne 1999, 48–52.

12. For general treatments of speeches in Homeric epics, see Griffin and Roisman.

13. Walker's treatment of the "embassy to Achilles" (14–15), while it does not analyze the passage in quite these terms, generally supports this point.

14. The model of "gift-exchange" as a mechanism of social structuration first developed in the anthropological writings of Bronislaw Malinowski and Marcel Mauss. It was used by classicists to create a picture of the archaic Greek culture that produced the Homeric epics in Finley (57–65, 125–31), Redfield, Donlan (1980 and 1982), Seaford (1994 and 2004), and Tandy. Historians of ancient Greek rhetoric have imported the model of "gift-exchange" into their understanding of preclassical speech arts even more recently. See Mifsud and Fredal. Michael Svoboda's essay in this volume continues this line of inquiry.

15. Cicero calls Isocrates "*magister rhetorum omnium*" (*De Or.* II.94). On the "rivalry" between Plato and Isocrates, and the historical prominence of Isocrates, see Jaeger 1943, 46–47; Marrou, 79–80 and 89–91; and Benoit, 60–71. Tarik Wareh systematically shows the tremendous debt that Plato and Aristotle owe to the Isocrates school of rhetoric.

16. In addition, see Too 1995; Poulakos 1997; Mirhady, Papillon, and Too 2000; Haskins; Johnstone, 146–61; and Papillon 2010.

17. See for example *Soph.* 19.

18. See for example Jaeger 1943, 46–47; Marrou, 79.

19. See Haskins 2004, 31 and 42–46; Johnstone, 155.

20. Jane Sutton discusses the relationship between kairos and *mētis*, in addition to reviewing other literature on the term (413–17).

It Takes an Empire to Raise a Sophist

1. See Havelock 1963 and 1982; Ong 1967 and 1982. See also Lentz. A skeptical review of the orality/literacy hypothesis is provided by Nails 1995, 139–91.

2. Any study of pre-Platonic texts on *logos* or *logon techne* must, in response to Schiappa's (1990 and 1999) argument that *rhētor-ikē* was coined by Plato, choose whether to find other terms or to follow convention in referring to the practice or profession of an art of speaking as "rhetoric." I use other terms when discussing sophist practices.

3. After noting the pivotal contribution made by George Grote (1851–56), this review concentrates on works published in the last fifty years.

4. That is, to account for the extant observations. See Lloyd's use of this phrase (especially 203).

5. See also Robinson (2008) and Curnow.

6. Although he does not cite sources for the added details, in his recounting of this story Marrou refers to "the spate of proceedings for the recovery of goods that developed after the explusion of tyrants . . . at Agrigentum (471) and . . . at Syracuse (463), and the ensuing annulment of the confiscations they had decreed" (53). Diodorus Siculus recounts a succession of revolutions in Sicily at this time, at Syracuse in particular, but

he does not mention a sudden rise in legal proceedings as an outcome (*Library* 11.67–68, 72–73, 76).

7. Apocryphal stories can be read as efforts to address perceived absences and inconsistencies in a received tradition. The following anecdote on Socrates' health, from the third-century C.E. *Attic Nights* of Aulus Gellius, more likely reflects the perceived disconnect between Thucydides' account of the Athenian plague and the absence of any comment on the plague in the Socratic writings of Plato and Xenophon: "His temperance also is said to have been so great, that he lived almost the whole period of his life with health unimpaired. Even amid the havoc of that plague which, at the beginning of the Peloponnesian war, devastated Athens with a deadly species of disease, by temperate and abstemious habits he is said to have avoided the ill-effects of indulgence and retained his physical vigour so completely, that he was not at all affected by the calamity common to all" (II.I.4–5; Rolfe, vol. 1: 123). In a similar fashion, I am suggesting that the first stories of Corax and Tisias reflect early attempts to make economic and social sense of their success—not necessarily true, but probable in some necessary way.

8. For this view, Jarratt cites Marrou; Kennedy 1980, 18–19; and Kerferd, 15.

9. Havelock 1957; Guthrie 1971; Enos; McComiskey 2002; Robinson 2008; and Johnstone.

10. See especially 442–44. See also Meiggs, 285–88.

11. See also Robinson 2008, 26.

12. This portion of Guthrie's history was published separately as *The Sophists* (1971).

13. See the discussion of the "rhetoric of *banausia*" in Nightingale, 55–59.

14. See the accounts offered by Guthrie 1971, 35–39; Kerferd, 24–28; Romilly 1992, 4–7; and Munn, 78–83.

15. For this analysis, Fredal draws on anthropological and sociological analyses of "gift exchange" by Arjun Appadurai, Mary Douglas, A. W. Gouldner, and Marcel Mauss. But within the present volume, David Hoffman explains how a "practice" of speech might function under these often conflicting demands of custom.

16. The wide availability of goods is noted by Pericles in the "Funeral Oration" as recorded by Thucydides (2.38).

17. See, for example, the discussions in Guthrie 1971, 51–54; Kerferd, 1; Jarratt, 10–12; and Romilly 1992, ix–x.

18. Of the twenty-seven dialogues generally accepted as genuine, nine involve discussions with sophists or include a lengthy discussion of their views or social roles: *Euthydemus, Gorgias, Lesser Hippias, Ion, Meno, Protagoras, Sophist, Theaetetus, Thrasymachus* (book 1 of *Republic*).

19. "Some were also saved for the sake of Euripides. For the Sicilians, it would seem, more than any other Hellenes outside the home land, had a yearning fondness for his poetry" (29.2; Perrin 1916a, 309).

20. See Guthrie 1971, 262–64; see also Schiappa 2003b, 52 and 126.

21. This anecdote comes from Plutarch, *Lives: Pericles* (36.3; Perrin 1916b, 105).

22. A fragment from a fourth-century Platonist, Heraclides Ponticus (*Laws*, fr. 21), as relayed by Diogenes Laertius (IX. 50), is the source of this claim that Protagoras drafted the constitution. See Guthrie 1971, 264; O'Brien, 4.

23. Tandy provides a very succinct summary of his book in his introduction, 2–6.

24. See also Hammond's discussion of Athens' efforts, in 450 and 447, to standardize currency throughout the empire (1986, 306).

25. Two Athenians are included in Sprague's collected translations of the B fragments: Antiphon and Critias. Because we know of at least three people named

Antiphon and two named Critias, we cannot be certain that the two sets of fragments are about just two men. Plus, Athenians occupied a peculiar position within the dual economic system of their empire. See Levin, 241–70; Morrison, 126; Nails 2002, 241–70; and Fredal, 152n9. Sprague's edited collection of translations of the Deils-Kranz fragments includes texts on Protagoras, Xeniades, Gorgias, Lycophron, Prodicus, Thrasymachus, Hippias, Antiphon, Critias, Anonymous Iamblichi, and Euthydemus. One may question whether Antiphon and Critias were considered sophists in the same sense as the others.

26. See also Henderson's "Introductory Note" for the play (1998a, 220–23).

27. See Todd 2005, 99; and Gagarin 2005, 300–302.

28. Todd 2005, 99–102.

29. See opening scenes from both dialogues: *Protagoras* 314e–316b and *Gorgias* 447a–d.

30. Carol Poster's contribution to this volume—"Gorgias' 'On Non-Being': Genre, Purpose, and Testimonia"—paints a much more complex picture of Gorgias, arguing that his career cannot be reduced to just one role: sophist, philosopher, or rhetorician. Likewise, the "great sophists" played different roles, both for themselves and for their interlocutors, in the dual economies in the different cities they visited.

31. For the debt to the sophists, see, for example, Marrou, 49; Guthrie 1971, 38; Kerferd, 17; and Romilly 1992, 6.

32. "The polis came into existence when a newly institutionalized political and economic center undertook to exclude the peripheral members of the community from the economic mainstream" (Tandy, 5).

33. See passages 39, 87, 147, 224–26, 295–96.

34. See translator's note on passage 39 (Norlin, 208), but see passages 240–41 on the money (*chremata*) fathers are willing to pay.

35. "This pattern of exploitation finally led in Athens to Solon's sixth-century legislative reforms, which canceled debts and outlawed debt bondage" (Tandy, 4–5).

36. See Isocrates' review of Athenian history: *Antidosis*,§§ 63–65, 232–35, 283–85, 295–300, 306–8, 315–19.

37. See discussions of the "help friends, harm enemies," ethic in Blundell 1989 and Dover 1994.

38. Harvey Yunis sums up the transition this way: "Even when rhetoric achieved fully independent disciplinary status in the fourth century, its roots in the rhetorical situation of Athenian democracy"—and its empire, we would add—"remained evident" (Yunis 1998, 234).

Afterword

1. By "rhetorical theory" I mean a set of descriptive, explanatory, and pedagogical beliefs about the art of public speaking known in classical Greece by the label *rhētorikē technē*. Such a theory can be distinguished from theories of *logos* and, in Isocrates, from *philosophia*, though they all can be appreciated as parts of the same family tree.

2. Giving credit where credit is due, Carol Poster made an important foray into the scholarship concerning Heraclitus and *logos* in 2006 and 2008, which Reames acknowledges and builds upon.

3. The one nit I would pick with McCoy appears in her first footnote, where she casually mentions Alcidamas' use of the word *rhētorikē* as challenging my argument that the term is a fourth-century invention. I have repeatedly critiqued that exact surmise, since Alcidamas' text was almost certainly written years—probably decades—after Plato's *Gorgias* (Schiappa 1990, 461–63; 1999, 20–21n; 2003b, 221–22).

4. I describe a pragmatic approach to definitions as prescriptive rules of the form "X counts as Y in context Z" in Schiappa 2003a.

5. Though the speech analyzed by Gaines is *set* in 400 B.C.E., the prosecution of Andokides was a famous case, and it is possible that the surviving text was a later rhetorical exercise (Dover 1968, 192n).

6. Poster says in footnote 13 that Isocrates uses the word *rhētorikē* twice, but such a statement is misleading. The term referenced is used only once (in *Nicocles* 8); the second occurrence is when Isocrates quotes himself in *Antidosis* 256. The Greek word is *rhētorikous*, a masculine adjectival form meaning "oratorical." To refer to a discrete art of rhetoric requires the feminine form (*rhētorikē*) either modifying *technē* or standing alone as a substantive. Since *Nicocles* certainly appears after Plato's *Gorgias*, it is possible that Isocrates was taking advantage of the semantic field opened up with the word *rhētorikē*, but in a manner that in context contrasts "oratorical" with what Isocrates says is the more important ability to deliberate in one's own mind. The fact that Isocrates never explicitly refers to *rhētorikē* suggests that he prefers his own words for describing his educational program (Timmerman and Schiappa).

7. My sincere thanks to John T. Kirby and Wilfred E. Major for their feedback to drafts of this afterword.

Appendix A

1. See Schenkeveld for discussion of the use of *akouein* to describe a putative "pupil's" relationship to an older figure.

2. Pythagoras, Parmenides, and so forth are also portrayed as conducting such embassies. In a later period, this tradition continues with the appointments to the Museum in Alexandria, embassies, and post of *ab epistulis* often reflecting general distinction rather than specific technical skill (Lewis).

3. As this is not found in the Aristotelian corpus, it may reflect a lost Aristotelian work, an intermediary source, or simply an inaccurate citation from memory on part of Cicero.

4. Bibliography on dates of Platonic dialogues is, of course, extensive. My own discussion of issues concerning Platonic chronology is Poster (1998).

5. See Williams (1931) for discussion of comic evidence for date of embassy.

6. The dramatic date of the dialogue appears to be 402 B.C.E., but given the uncertainties of both Platonic dramatic and compositional chronology, this does not decisively place Gorgias in Thessaly in 402, any more than *Apology* 19e places Gorgias in Athens in precisely 399. As Plato's interests were rather obviously more in people's ideas than in biographical details such as dates and times, it would be a category mistake to read him as a careful chronicler of specific historical facts; this is not to dismiss his evidence as mendacious, but rather to avoid reading it as more precise than it was intended. Thus, conservatively, from Plato we may conclude that Gorgias' activities in Athens and Thessaly were both widely known in the period ca. 405–399 B.C.E.

7. See Swain for the point that Philostratus is not engaged in straightforward biography, but rather a historical discussion of a certain model of display oratory, and while not deliberately creating fiction, he should not be read as concerned primarily with the accuracy of minute historical detail (that is, he would have been more concerned with stylistic influence than precisely the number of hours and the contexts in which admirers would have been in contact with Gorgias). Moreover, he was writing over five hundred years after the events in question, and the reliability of his sources is not guaranteed.

8. There is no clear evidence as to whether the actual teaching of Gorgias consisted of a series of model orations, as suggested by Cole (1991), lectures on rhetorical theory, or some more interactive activities. The Platonic dialogues seem to contrast Gorgias' habit of long speeches with Socratic dialogue; this may not reflect Gorgianic pedagogical practice but instead simply Gorgias' reputation for display oratory.

9. Penella notes that Gorgias, being considered the founder of the type of sophistic Philostratus was advocating, is being invoked as a historical precedent for both sophistic and philosophical discourse. Rather than distinguishing among historians, philosophers, and sophists as occupying separate disciplinary spaces, Penella points out, Philostratus emphasizes a unified Panhellenic paideia of which sophistic and Platonism were integral parts.

Appendix C

1. The antecedent for "him" in the prepositional phrase "before him" (πρὸ αὐτῆϲ) has not survived in the text as we currently have it.

2. For this translation, see *Liddell, Scott, Jones Ancient Greek Lexicon*, s.v., τεχνογράφος.

Bibliography

Adam, James. 1908. *Religious Teachers of Greece.* Edinburgh: T & T Clark.

Adomenas, Mantas. 1999. "Heraclitus on Religion." *Phronesis* 44 (2): 87–113.

Anderson, Graham. 1986. *Philostratus: Biography and Belles Lettres in the Third Century A.D.* London: Croom Helm.

——. 1993. *The Second Sophistic: A Cultural Phenomenon in the Roman Empire.* London: Routledge.

Assman, Jan. 2003. *The Mind of Egypt: History and Meaning in the Time of the Pharaohs.* Trans. Andrew Jenkins. Cambridge, MA: Harvard University Press.

Azoulay, Vincent. 2014. *Pericles of Athens.* Princeton, NJ: Princeton University Press.

Baca, Damián, and Victor Villanueva. 2010. *Rhetorics of the Americas: 3114 B.C.E. to 2012 C.E.* New York: Palgrave Macmillan.

Bakker, Egbert J. 1997. *Poetry in Speech: Orality and Homeric Discourse.* Ithaca, NY: Cornell University Press.

Ballif, Michelle. 2001. *Seduction, Sophistry, and the Woman with the Rhetorical Figure.* Carbondale: Southern Illinois University Press.

——, ed. 2013. *Theorizing Histories of Rhetoric.* Carbondale: Southern Illinois University Press.

——, ed. 2014. Special Issue: Untimely Historiographies. *Rhetoric Society Quarterly* 44 (3).

Barnes, Jonathan. 1982. *The Presocratic Philosophers.* 2nd ed. New York: Routledge.

——, trans. 1984. *The Complete Works of Aristotle.* Rev. ed. Princeton, NJ: Princeton University Press.

——. 1987. *Early Greek Philosophy.* London: Penguin.

Bartlett, Robert, and Susan Collins, trans. 2011. Aristotle's *Nicomachean Ethics.* Chicago: University of Chicago Press.

Bateson, Gregory. 1935. "Culture Contact and Schismogenesis." *Man* 35: 178–83.

——. (1936) 1958. *Naven.* Stanford, CA: Stanford University Press.

Benoit, William L. 1991. "Isocrates and Plato on Rhetoric and Rhetorical Education." *Rhetoric Society Quarterly* 21 (1): 60–71.

Bergk, Theodor. 1887. *Griechische Literaturgeschichte.* Ed. Rudolf Peppmüller. Vol. 4. Berlin: Weidmannsche Buchhandlung.

Blundell, Mary Whitlock. 1989. *Helping Friends and Harming Enemies: A Study in Sophocles and Greek Ethics.* Cambridge, MA: Harvard University Press.

Bourdieu, Pierre. 1977. *Outline of a Theory of Practice.* Trans. Richard Nice. Cambridge, UK: Cambridge University Press. Originally published as *Esquisse d'une théorie de la pratique, precédé de trois études d'ethnologie' kabyle.* Paris: Seuil, 1972.

Brown, Peter. 1992. *Power and Persuasion in Late Antiquity: Towards a Christian Empire.* Madison: University of Wisconsin Press.

Brownson, Carleton L., trans. 1921. *Hellenica Books VI and VII, Anabasis Books I–III.* Loeb Classical Library. Cambridge, MA: Harvard University Press.

Buchheim, Thomas. 1989. *Reden, Fragmente und Testimonien. Gorgias von Leontinoi. Philosophische Bibliothek* 404. Hamburg: F. Meiner.

Burkert, Walter. 2013. "Parmenides' Proem and Pythagoras' Descent." In *Philosophy and Salvation in Greek Religion*, ed. Vishwa Adluri, 85–116. Trans. Joydeep Bagchee. Berlin: De Gruyter.

Burnet, John, 1892. *Early Greek Philosophy*. 1st ed. London: Adam and Charles Black.

——, ed. 1901. *Phaedrus*. In *Platonis opera*, vol. 2: 223–95, Scriptorum classicorum bibliotheca Oxoniensis. Oxford: Clarendon Press.

——. 1908. *Early Greek Philosophy*. 2nd ed. London: Adam and Charles Black.

——. 1930. *Early Greek Philosophy*. 4th ed. London: Adam and Charles Black.

Bury, R. G., trans. (1935) 1961. "Against the Logicians." In *Sextus Empiricus with an English Translation*, vol. 2. Loeb Classical Library. Cambridge, MA: Harvard University Press.

Butler, Harold Edgeworth, trans. 1920. *Institutio Oratorio by Quintilian*. Loeb Classical Library. Cambridge MA: Harvard University Press.

Buxton, Richard. 1999. *From Myth to Reason? Studies in the Development of Greek Thought*. Oxford, UK: Oxford University Press.

Byre, Calvin. "The Rhetoric of Description in the Odyssey 9.116–41: Odysseus and Goat Island." *Classical Journal* 89 (4): 357–67.

Carey, Christopher. 2000. "Old Comedy and the Sophists." In *The Rivals of Aristophanes: Studies in Athenian Old Comedy*, ed. F. David Harvey and John Wilkins, 419–36. London: Duckworth Publishing.

——, ed. 2007. *Lysiae Orationes cum Fragmentis*. Oxford: Clarendon Press.

Certeau, Michel de. 1984. *The Practice of Everyday Life*. Trans. Steven Rendall. Berkeley: University of California Press. Originally published as *L'invention du quotidien-Arts de faire*. Paris: Gallimard, 1980.

Charlton, William. 1985. "Greek Philosophy and the Concept of an Academic Discipline." *History of Political Thought* 6 (1/2): 47–61.

Cherniss, Harold. 1935. *Aristotle's Criticism of Presocratic Philosophy*. Baltimore: Johns Hopkins University Press.

——. 1951. "The Characteristics and Effects of Presocratic Philosophy." *Journal of the History of Ideas* 12 (3): 319–45.

Clark, Gillian, trans. 1989. *On the Pythagorean Life by Iamblichus*. Trans. Gillian Clark. Liverpool UK: Liverpool University Press.

Clay, Jenny Strauss. 2007. "Hesiod's Rhetorical Art." In *A Companion to Greek Rhetoric*, ed. Ian Worthington, 447–57. London: Blackwell.

Clinton, Kevin. 1982. "The Nature of the Late Fifth-Century Revision of the Athenian Law Code." In *Studies in Attic Epigraphy, History, and Topography: Presented to Eugene Vanderpool*. Hesperia Supplements 19, 27–37. Princeton, NJ: American School of Classical Studies at Athens.

Cole, Thomas. 1991. *The Origins of Rhetoric in Ancient Greece*. Baltimore: Johns Hopkins University Press.

——. 2007. "Who Was Corax?" In *The Attic Orators*, ed. Edwin Carawan, 37–59. New York: Oxford University Press.

Collobert, Catherine. 2002. "Aristotle's Review of the Presocratics: Is Aristotle Finally a Historian of Philosophy?" *Journal of the History of Philosophy* 40 (3): 281–95.

Consigny, Scott. 2001. *Gorgias: Sophist and Artist*. Columbia: University of South Carolina Press.

Cooper, Guy L., III, and Karl Wilhelm Krüger. 1998. *Attic Greek Prose Syntax.* Ann Arbor: University of Michigan Press.

Copleston, Edward. 1807. *Advice to a Young Reviewer with a Specimen of the Art.* Oxford, UK: J. Parker and J. Cooke.

——, 1965. *Principium Sapientiae: The Origins of Greek Philosophical Thought.* New York: Harper Torchbook.

Cornford, Francis M. 1912. *From Religion to Philosophy: A Study in the Origins of Western Speculation.* New York: Longmans, Green and Co.

Covino, William A. 1994. *Magic, Rhetoric, and Literacy: An Eccentric History of the Composing Imagination.* Albany: State University of New York Press.

Curd, Patricia. 2011. "New Work on the Presocratics." *Journal of the History of Philosophy* 49 (1): 1–37.

Curnow, Trevor. 2008. "Minor Sophists." In *The Sophists: An Introduction,* ed. Patricia O'Grady, 153–63. London: Duckworth.

Cysarz, Dirk, et al. 2004. "Oscillations of Heart Rate and Respiration Synchronize During Poetry Recitation." *American Journal of Physiology: Heart and Circulatory Physiology* 287 (2): H579–H587.

Dakyns, Henry Graham, trans. 1890. *The Works of Xenophon in Four Volumes.* Vol. 3. London: Macmillan and Co.

Darcus, Shirley M. 1979. "Logos of Psyche in Heraclitus." *Rivista storica dell'antichita* 9: 89–93.

Darnell, Donald K., and Wayne Brockriede. 1976. *Persons Communicating.* Englewood Cliffs, NJ: Prentice-Hall.

De Brauw, Michael. 2010. "The Parts of the Speech." In *A Companion to Greek Rhetoric,* ed. Ian Worthington, 187–202. Malden, MA: John Wiley and Sons.

De Sélincourt, Aubrey, trans. 1972. Herodotus *The Histories.* Rev. ed. New York: Penguin.

Denniston, John Dewar, and Kenneth James Dover. 1950. *The Greek Particles.* London: Gerald Duckworth & Co., Ltd.

Detienne, Marcel. 1999. *The Masters of Truth in Archaic Greece.* Trans. Janet Lloyd. New York: Zone Books. Originally published as *Les Maîtres de vérité dans la grèce archaïque.* Paris: Librarie general française, 1967.

——, and Jean-Pierre Vernant. (1974) 1978. *Cunning Intelligence in Greek Culture and Society.* Trans. Janet Lloyd. Atlantic Highlands, NJ: Humanities Press.

Diels, Hermann. 1951–52. *Die Fragmente der Vorsokratiker.* 3 vols. 6th ed. Revised by Walther Kranz. Berlin: Weidmann.

Dimock, George. 1989. *The Unity of the* Odyssey. Amherst: University of Massachusetts Press.

Dodds, Eric R. 1973. *The Ancient Concept of Progress and Other Essays.* Oxford, UK: Clarendon Press.

Doherty, Lillian. 1991. "The Internal and Implied Audiences of *Odyssey* 11." *Arethusa* 24: 145–76.

——. 1992. "Gender and Internal Audiences in the Odyssey." *American Journal of Philology.* 113 (2): 161–77.

——. 1995. *Siren Songs: Gender, Audiences, and Narrators in the* Odyssey. Ann Arbor: University of Michigan Press.

Donlan, Walter. 1980. *The Aristocratic Ideal in Ancient Greece: Attitudes of Superiority from Homer to the End of the Fifth Century B.C.* Lawrence, KS: Coronado Press.

——. 1982. "The Politics of Generosity in Homer." *Helios* 9 (2): 1–16.

Dover, Kenneth J. 1968. *Lysias and the* Corpus Lysiacum. Berkeley: University of California Press.

———. (1974) 1994. *Greek Popular Morality in the Time of Plato and Aristotle.* Rpt. Indianapolis, IN: Hackett Publishing Co.

Drerup, Englebert. 1902. "Die Anfänge der rhetorischen Kunstprosa." *Jahrbücher für classische Philologie,* Supplementband 27: 219–351.

Economist. 2013. "Unreliable Research: Trouble at the Lab." 19 October.

Edwards, Mark W. 1980. "The Structure of Homeric Catalogues." *Transactions of the American Philological Association* 110: 81–105.

Edwards, Michael. 1994. *The Attic Orators.* London: Bristol Classical Press.

Einarson, Benedict, and Phillip H. de Lacy, trans. 1967. *Moralia by Plutarch.* Vol. 14. Loeb Classical Library. Cambridge, MA: Harvard University Press.

English, Robert B. 1913. "Heraclitus and the Soul." *Transactions and Proceedings of the American Philological Association* 44: 163–85.

Enos, Richard Leo. (1993) 2012. *Greek Rhetoric before Aristotle.* Rev. ed. Anderson, SC: Parlor Press.

Evelyn-White, Hugh G., trans. 1914. Hesiod: *The Homeric Hymns and Homerica. Theogony.* Loeb Classical Library. Cambridge, MA: Harvard University Press.

Festugiere, A. J., trans. 1945. *Corpus Hermeticum.* Vol. 2. Ed. A. D. Nock. Paris: Belles lettres.

Fine, John V. A. 1983. *The Ancient Greeks: A Critical History.* Cambridge, MA: Harvard University Press.

Finley, Moses I. 1965. *The World of Odysseus.* Rev. ed. New York: Viking Press.

Forde, Steven. 1989. *The Ambition to Rule: Alcibiades and the Politics of Imperialism in Thucydides.* Ithaca, NY: Cornell University Press.

Forster, Edward Seymour, and David J. Furley, trans. 1955. *On Sophistical Refutations, On Coming-to-be and Passing Away, and On the Cosmos by Aristotle.* Loeb Classical Library. Cambridge, MA: Harvard University Press.

Foster, Edith. 2010. *Thucydides, Pericles, and Periclean Imperialism.* Cambridge, UK: Cambridge University Press.

Fowler, Harold N., trans. (1914) 1982. *Euthyphro, Apology, Crito, Phaedo, Phaedrus by Plato.* Loeb Classical Library. Cambridge, MA: Harvard University Press.

———, trans. (1928) 2006. *Theaetetus, Sophist by Plato.* Loeb Classical Library. Cambridge, MA: Harvard University Press.

———, and Walter R. M. Lamb, trans. (1925) 1962. *Statesman, Philebus, Ion by Plato.* Loeb Classical Library. Cambridge, MA: Harvard University Press.

Frankel, Hermann. 1938. "Heraclitus on God and the Phenomenal World." *Transactions and Proceedings of the American Philological Association* 69: 230–44.

Fredal, James. 2008. "Why Shouldn't Sophists Charge Fees?" *Rhetoric Society Quarterly* 38 (2): 148–70.

Freese, J. H. 1926. *Aristotle: Art of Rhetoric.* Loeb Classical Library. Cambridge, MA: Harvard University Press.

Gadamer, Hans-Georg. 1998. *The Beginning of Philosophy.* Trans. Rod Coltman. New York: Continuum.

Gagarin, Michael. 1994. "Probability and Persuasion: Plato and Early Greek Rhetoric." In *Persuasion: Greek Rhetoric in Action,* ed. Ian Worthington, 46–68. New York: Routledge.

———. 2005. *Cambridge Guide to Ancient Athenian Law.* New York: Cambridge University Press.

Gaines, Robert N. 1993. Review of *Protagoras and Logos: A Study in Greek Philosophy and Rhetoric,* by Edward Schiappa. *Quarterly Journal of Speech* 79: 500–503.

Gallop, David, trans. 1972. "Hippias." In *The Older Sophists,* ed. Rosamond Kent Sprague, 94–105. Columbia: University of South Carolina Press.

Gantz, Timothy. 1993. *Early Greek Myth: A Guide to Literary and Artistic Sources.* Baltimore: Johns Hopkins University Press.

Gemelli Marciano, M. Laura. 2008. "Images and Experience: At the Roots of Parmenides' *Aletheia.*" *Ancient Philosophy* 28 (1): 21–48.

Gencarella, Stephen Olbrys. 2007. "The Myth of Rhetoric: *Korax* and the Art of Pollution." *Rhetoric Society Quarterly* 37 (3): 251–73.

Gigon, Olof. 1935. *Untersuchungen zu Heraklit.* Leipzig: Dietrerich.

Gill, Christopher. 1996. *Personality in Greek Epic, Tragedy, and Philosophy: The Self in Dialogue.* New York: Oxford University Press.

Glasson, T. F. 1952. "Heraclitus' Alleged Logos Doctrine." *Journal of Theological Studies* 3 (2): 231–38.

Glenn, Cheryl. 1997. *Rhetoric Retold: Regendering the Tradition from Antiquity Through the Renaissance.* Carbondale: Southern Illinois University Press.

Gomme, Arnold W. 1945–70. *A Historical Commentary on Thucydides.* 5 vols. Oxford, UK: Oxford University Press.

Graham, Daniel W., trans. 2010. *The Texts of Early Greek Philosophy.* New York: Cambridge University Press.

Gray, V. J. 1985. "Xenophon's *Cynegeticus.*" *Hermes* 113 (2): 156–72.

Grene, David, trans. 1987. *The History by Herodotus.* Chicago: University of Chicago Press.

Griffin, Jasper. 2004. "The Speeches." In *The Cambridge Companion to Homer,* ed. Robert Fowler, 156–68. Cambridge, UK: Cambridge University Press.

Grimaldi, William M. A. 1988. *Aristotle, Rhetoric II: A Commentary.* New York: Fordham University Press.

Gros, Étienne, ed. and trans. 1840. *Philodemi Rhetorica ex herculanensi papyro lithographice Oxonii excusa, restituit, Latine vertit.* Paris: Firmin Didot Fratres.

Grote, George. 1846–56. *History of Greece from the Time of Solon to 403 B.C.* 8 vols. London: J. Murray.

Grube, George M.A., trans. 1997. *Republic.* In *Plato: Complete Works.* Ed. John M. Cooper. Rev. C. D. C. Reeve. Indianapolis, IN: Hackett Publishing Co.

Gulick, Charles Burton, trans. 1930. *The Deipnosophists of Athenaeus of Naucratis.* 7 vols. Loeb Classical Library. Cambridge, MA: Harvard University Press.

Guthrie, William K. C. 1957. "Aristotle as a Historian of Philosophy." *Journal of Hellenic Studies* 77 (1): 35–41.

———. 1962. *The Earlier Presocratics and the Pythagoreans.* In *The History of Greek Philosophy,* vol. 1. Cambridge, UK: Cambridge University Press.

———.1965. *The Presocratic Tradition from Parmenides to Democritus.* In *A History of Greek Philosophy,* vol. 2. Cambridge, UK: Cambridge University Press.

———. 1971. *The Sophists.* In *A History of Greek Philosophy,* vol. 3. Cambridge, UK: Cambridge University Press.

Hackforth, Reginald, trans and comm. 1952. *Phaedrus by Plato.* Cambridge, UK: Cambridge University Press.

Haidt, Jonathan. 2012. *The Righteous Mind.* New York: Vintage.

Hamberger, Peter. 1914. *Die rednerische Disposition in der alten Τέχνη ῥητορική (Korax—Gorgias—Antiphon).* Rhetorische Studien 2. Paderborn: Ferdinand Schöningh.

Hammond, Martin, trans. 2009. Thucydides, *History of the Peloponnesian War.* New York: Oxford University Press.

Hammond, Nicholas G. L. 1986. *A History of Greece to 322 B.C.* 3rd ed. New York: Oxford University Press.

Hanson, Victor D. 2005. *A War Like No Other.* New York: Random House.

Harloe, Katherine, and Neville Morley, eds. 2012. *Thucydides and the Modern World: Reception, Reinterpretation, and Influence from the Renaissance to the Present.* Cambridge, UK: Cambridge University Press.

Harrison, E. L. 1964. "Was Gorgias a Sophist?" *Phoenix* 18 (3): 183–92.

Hart, Roderick P., and Don M. Burks. 1972. "Rhetorical Sensitivity and Social Interaction." *Speech Monographs* 39 (2): 75–91.

Hart, Roderick P., Robert E. Carlson, and William F. Eadie. 1980. "Attitudes toward Communication and the Assessment of Rhetorical Sensitivity." *Communication Monographs* 47 (1): 1–22.

Haskins, Ekaterina V. 2001. "Rhetoric between Orality and Literacy: Cultural Memory and Performance in Isocrates and Aristotle." *Quarterly Journal of Speech* 78 (2): 158–78.

——. 2004. *Logos and Power in Isocrates and Aristotle.* Columbia: University of South Carolina Press.

Havelock, Eric. 1957. *The Liberal Temper of Greek Politics.* New Haven, CT: Yale University Press.

——. 1963. *Preface to Plato.* Cambridge, MA: Harvard University Press.

——. 1982. *The Literate Revolution in Greece and Its Cultural Consequences.* Princeton, NJ: Princeton University Press.

Hawthorn, Geoffrey. 2014. *Thucydides on Politics: Back to the Present.* Cambridge, UK: Cambridge University Press.

Heath, Malcolm. 2004. *Menander: A Rhetor in Context.* Oxford, UK: Oxford University Press.

Heidegger, Martin. 1979. *Heraclitus Seminar 1966/67.* Trans. Charles H. Seibert. Tuscaloosa: University of Alabama Press.

——. 1984. "Logos (Heraclitus, Fragment B 50)." In *Early Greek Thinking,* trans. David F. Krell and Frank A. Capuzzi, 59–78. New York: Harper and Row.

——. 1998. *Parmenides.* Trans. Andre Schuwer and Richard Rojcewicz. Bloomington: Indiana University Press.

——. 2000. *Introduction to Metaphysics.* Trans. Gregory Fried and Richard Polt. New Haven, CT: Yale University Press.

——. 2008. *Basic Concepts of Ancient Philosophy.* Trans. Richard Rojcewicz. Bloomington: Indiana University Press.

Heitsch, Ernst. 2002. *Platon Werke I 2: Apologie des Sokrates, Übersetzung und Kommentar.* Göttingen: Vandenhoeck & Ruprecht.

Henderson, Jeffrey. 1998a. "Introductory Note." In *Knights by Aristophanes,* trans. and ed. Jeffrey Henderson, 220–23. Loeb Classical Library. Cambridge, MA: Harvard University Press.

——, trans. 1998b. *Knights by Aristophanes.* Loeb Classical Library. Cambridge, MA: Harvard University Press.

Hendrickson, George L., trans. 1939. *Brutus by Cicero.* Loeb Classical Library. Cambridge MA: Harvard University Press.

Hesk, Jon. 2001. "New Model Rhetoric: Review of *The Beginnings of Rhetorical Theory in Classical Greece,* by Edward Schiappa." *Classical Review* 51: 60–61.

Hicks, Robert D., ed. and trans. 1972. *Diogenes Laertius: Lives of Eminent Philosophers.* 2 vols. Loeb Classical Library. Cambridge, MA: Harvard University Press.

Hoffman, David C. 2003. "*Logos* as Composition." *Rhetoric Society Quarterly* 33 (3): 27–53.

——. 2006. "Structural *Logos* in Heraclitus and the Sophists." *Advances in the History of Rhetoric* 9 (1): 1–32.

Hornblower, Simon. 1987. *Thucydides.* Baltimore: Johns Hopkins University Press.

Hubbard, Thomas K. 1986. "Parabatic Self-Criticism and the Two Versions of Aristophanes' *Clouds.*" *Classical Antiquity* 5 (2): 182–97.

Hudson-Williams, H. L. 1948. "Thucydides, Isocrates, and the Rhetorical Method of Composition." *Classical Quarterly* 42 (3/4): 76–81.

Inge, W. R. 1956. *Christian Mysticism.* 7th ed. New York: Meridian Books.

Inwood, Brad, trans. 1992. *The Poem of Empedocles: A Text and Translation with an Introduction.* Toronto: University of Toronto Press.

Ioannidis, John. 2005. "Why Most Published Research Findings Are False." *PLOS Medicine* 2 (8): e124. DOI:10.1371/journal.pmed.0020124.

Jackson, Robin, Kimon Lycos, and Harold Tarrant, trans. 1998. *Commentary on Plato's* Gorgias *by Olympiodorus.* Leiden, Netherlands: Brill.

Jaeger, Werner. 1943. *Paideia: The Ideals of Greek Culture.* Vol. 3. Trans. Gilbert Highet. New York: Oxford University Press.

——. 1947. *The Theology of the Early Greek Philosophers.* Trans. Edward S. Robinson. Oxford, UK: Clarendon Press.

——. 1948. *Aristotle: Fundamentals of the History of His Development.* Trans. Richard Robinson. Oxford, UK: Clarendon Press.

Jarratt, Susan C. 1991. *Rereading the Sophists: Classical Rhetoric Refigured.* Carbondale: Southern Illinois University Press.

Jebb, Richard Claverhouse. 1893. *The Attic Orators from Antiphon to Isaeus.* 2 vols. London: Macmillan.

Johnstone, Christopher Lyle. 2009. *Listening to the Logos: Speech and the Coming of Wisdom in Ancient Greece.* Columbia: University of South Carolina Press.

Jones, Horace Leonard, trans. 1929. *Strabo Geography.* Cambridge, MA: Harvard University Press.

Kagan, Donald. 2003. *The Peloponnesian War.* New York: Viking.

Kahn, Charles. 1979. *The Art and Thought of Heraclitus: An Edition of the Fragments with Translation and Commentary.* Cambridge, UK: Cambridge University Press.

Kaptchuck, Ted J., et al. 2010. "Placebos without Deception: A Randomized Controlled Trial in Irritable Bowel Syndrome." *PLOS One* 5 (12). DOI:10.1371/journal.pone.0015591.

Karp, Andre J. 1977. "Homeric Origins of Ancient Rhetoric." *Arethusa* 10 (2): 237–58.

Kassel, Rudolf, ed. 1976. *Aristotelis ars rhetorica.* Berlin: Walter de Gruyter.

Kennedy, George A. 1957. "The Ancient Dispute over Rhetoric in Homer." *American Journal of Philology* 78: 23–35.

——. 1963. *The Art of Persuasion in Greece.* Princeton NJ: Princeton University Press.

——, trans. 1972. "Gorgias." In *The Older Sophists,* ed. Rosamond Kent Sprague. Columbia: University of South Carolina Press.

——. 1980. *Classical Rhetoric and Its Christian and Secular Tradition from Ancient to Modern Times.* Chapel Hill: University of North Carolina Press.

——, trans. 1991. *Aristotle On Rhetoric: A Theory of Civic Discourse.* New York: Oxford University Press.

——. 1994. *A New History of Classical Rhetoric.* Princeton, NJ: Princeton University Press.

——. 1998. *Comparative Rhetoric: An Historical and Cross-Cultural Introduction.* New York: Oxford University Press.

——, trans. 2007. *Aristotle On Rhetoric.* 2nd ed. New York: Oxford University Press.

Kerferd, George B. 1981. *The Sophistic Movement.* Cambridge, UK: Cambridge University Press.

Kingsley, Peter. 1995. *Ancient Philosophy, Mystery, and Magic: Empedocles and Pythagorean Tradition.* Oxford, UK: Clarendon Press.

——. 1999. *In the Dark Places of Wisdom.* Point Reyes, CA: Golden Sufi Center.

——. 2002. "Empedocles for the New Millennium." *Ancient Philosophy* 22 (2): 333–413.

——. 2003. *Reality.* Point Reyes, CA: Golden Sufi Center.

Kirby, John T. 1992. "Rhetoric and Poetic in Hesiod." *Ramus* 21 (1): 34–60.

Kirk, Geoffrey S. 1954. *The Cosmic Fragments of Heraclitus.* London: Cambridge University Press.

——. 1962. *The Presocratic Philosophers.* Cambridge, UK: Cambridge University Press.

——, John E. Raven, and Malcolm Schofield. 1983. *The Presocratic Philosophers: A Critical History with a Selection of Texts.* 2nd ed. Cambridge, UK: Cambridge University.

Knudsen, Rachel Ahern. 2014. *Homeric Speech and the Origins of Rhetoric.* Baltimore: Johns Hopkins University Press.

Krischer, Tilman. 1971. *Formale Konventionen der homerischen Epik,* Setemata 56. München: Beck.

Kühner, Raphael, and Bernhard Gerth. 1898. *Ausführliche Grammatik der griechischen Sprache, Zweiter Teil: Satzlehre.* Hannover: Hahnsche Buchhandlung.

Lamb, Walter R. M., trans. 1967. *Lysis, Symposium, Gorgias by Plato.* Loeb Classical Library. Cambridge, MA: Harvard University Press.

Larson, Sean. 2014. "Rhetorical Ethics in the Comedy of Aristophanes." PhD diss., University of Minnesota.

Lattimore, Richmond, trans. 1951. *The Iliad of Homer.* Chicago: University of Chicago Press.

——, trans. 1967. *The Odyssey* by Homer. New York: Harper and Row.

Lattimore, Steven, trans. 1998. *Thucydides: The Peloponnesian War.* Indianapolis, IN: Hackett.

Lawson-Tancred, Hugh C. 1991. *Aristotle, The Art of Rhetoric.* London: Penguin Press.

Leeman, Anton D., and Harm Pinkster. 1981. *M. Tullius Cicero De oratore libri III: Kommentar, 1. Band: Buch I, 1–165.* Wissenschafliche Kommentare zu griechischen und lateinischen Schriftstellern. Heidelberg: Carl Winter Universitätsverlag.

Lentz, Tony. 1989. *Orality and Literacy in Hellenic Greece.* Carbondale: Southern Illinois University Press.

Levin, Donald Norman, trans. 1972. "Critias." In *The Older Sophists,* ed. Rosamond Kent Sprague, 241–70. Columbia: University of South Carolina Press.

Lewis, Naphtali. 1981. "Literati in the Service of Roman Emperors: Politics Before Culture." In *Coins, Culture, and History in the Ancient World: Numismatic and Other Studies in Honor of Bluma L. Trell,* ed. Lionel Casson and Martin Price, 149–66. Detroit: Wayne State University Press.

Lipson, Carol S., and Roberta Binkley, eds. 2004. *Rhetoric Before and Beyond the Greeks.* Albany: State University of New York Press.

——, eds. 2009. *Ancient Non-Greek Rhetorics.* West Lafayette, IN: Parlor Press.

Litwa, M. David, trans. 2016. Hippolytus: *Refutation of All Heresies.* Writings from the Greco-Roman World, v. 40. Atlanta, GA: Society for Biblical Literature.

Lloyd, Geoffrey E. R. 1978. "Saving the Appearances." *Classical Quarterly,* 28 (1): 202–22.

Lombardo, Stanley, and Karen Bell, trans. 1997. *Protagoras.* In *Plato: Complete Works,* ed. John M. Cooper. Indianapolis, IN: Hackett Publishing Co.

Long. Anthony A. 2015. *Greek Models of Mind and Self.* Cambridge, MA: Harvard University Press.

Lunsford, Andrea A., ed. 1995. *Reclaiming Rhetorica: Women in the Rhetorical Tradition.* Pittsburgh, PA: University of Pittsburgh Press.

MacDowell, Douglas M., ed. and comm. 1962. *Andokides: On the Mysteries.* Oxford, UK: Clarendon Press.

Mackin, James A., Jr. 1991. "Schismogenesis and Community: Pericles' Funeral Oration." *Quarterly Journal of Speech* 77 (3): 251–62.

MacMahon, J. H., trans. 1868. *The Refutation of All Heresies by Hippolytus.* Edinburgh: T & T Clark.

Major, Wilfred E. 2013. *The Court of Comedy: Aristophanes, Rhetoric, and Democracy in Fifth-Century Athens.* Columbus: Ohio State University Press.

Malafouris, Lambros. 2013. *How Things Shape Mind: A Theory of Material Engagement.* Cambridge, MA: MIT Press.

Malinowski, Bronislaw. (1922) 1991. *Argonauts of the Western Pacific: An Account of Native Enterprise and Adventure in the Archipelagoes of Melanesian New Guinea.* London: Routledge.

Mansfield, Jaap. 1994. "The Rhetoric in the Poem of Parmenides." *Filosofia, Politica, Retorica* 1994: 1–11.

Mao, LuMing, ed. 2013. Special Issue: Comparative Rhetoric. *Rhetoric Society Quarterly* 43 (3).

Marchant, E. C., trans. 1923. *Memorabilia by Xenophon.* Loeb Classical Library. Cambridge, MA: Harvard University Press.

Marcovich, M. 1967. *The Fragments of Heraclitus: Greek Text with a Short Commentary.* Merida, Venezuela: Los Andes University Press.

Marrou, Henri-Irénée. 1956. *A History of Education in Antiquity.* Trans. George Lamb. Madison: University of Wisconsin Press. Originally published as *Histoire de l'Education dans l'Antiquité.* Paris: Seuil, 1948.

Mauss, Marcel. 1925. *Essai sur le don, forme archaique de l'echange.* Paris: Presses universitaires de France. Trans. Ian Cunnison as *The Gift: Forms and Functions of Exchange in Archaic Societies.* New York: Norton & Co., 1967.

McComiskey, Bruce. 1994. "Sophistic Rhetoric and Philosophy: A Selective Bibliography." *Rhetoric Society Quarterly* 24 (3/4): 25–38.

——. 2002. *Gorgias and the New Sophistic Rhetoric.* Carbondale: Southern Illinois University Press.

McCoy, Marina Berzins. 2009. "Alcidamas, Isocrates, and Plato on Speech, Writing, and Philosophical Rhetoric." *Ancient Philosophy* 29 (2): 45–66.

McDiarmid, John B. 1953. "Theophrastus on the Presocratic Causes." *Harvard Theological Review* 61: 85–156.

Meiggs, Russell. 1972. *The Athenian Empire.* New York: Oxford University Press.

Mensch, Pamela, trans. 2014. Herodotus, *Histories.* Ed. James Romm. Indianapolis, IN: Hackett.

Merkelbach, Reinhold, and Martin L. West, eds. 1967. *Fragmenta Hesiodea.* London: Oxford University Press.

Mifsud, Marilee. 2007. "On Rhetoric as Gift/Giving." *Philosophy and Rhetoric* 40 (1): 89–107.

Miller, Edward L. 1981. "The Logos of Heraclitus: Updating the Report." *Harvard Theological Review* 74 (2): 161–76.

Minar, Edwin. 1939. "The Logos of Heraclitus." *Classical Philology* 34 (4): 323–41.

Mirhady, David C., trans. 2000. Isocrates 1. *Ad Demonicus*. In *Isocrates I*, trans. David C. Mirhady and Yun Lee Too, 1–11. Austin: University of Texas Press.

——. 2007. "Introduction." In *Influences on Peripatetic Rhetoric: Essays in Honor of William W. Fortenbaugh*, ed. David C. Mirhady, 1–18. Leiden: Brill.

——, Terry Papillon, and Yun Lee Too. 2000. "Introduction to Isocrates." In *Isocrates I*, trans. David C. Mirhady and Yun Lee Too, 1–11. Austin: University of Texas Press.

Morley, Neville. 2013. *Thucydides and the Idea of History*. London: I. B. Tauris.

Morrison, John S., trans. 1972. "Antiphon." In *The Older Sophists*, ed. Rosamond Kent Sprague. Columbia: University of South Carolina Press.

Mourelatos, Alexander. 1965. "Heraclitus Fr. 114" *American Journal of Philology* 86 (3): 259.

Mourelatos, Alexander P. D. 2008. *The Route of Parmenides*. Rev. ed. Las Vegas, NV: Parmenides Publishing.

Muir, John V., trans. 2001. *Alcidamas: The Works and Fragments*. London: Bristol Classic Press.

Munn, Mark. 2000. *The School of History: Athens in the Age of Socrates*. Berkeley: University of California Press.

Murray, A. T., and George E. Dimock, trans. 1995. *Homer: The Odyssey*. Vol. 1. 2nd ed. Cambridge, MA: Harvard University Press.

Nails, Debra. 1995. *Agora, Academy, and the Conduct of Philosophy*. Boston: Kluwer Academic Publishers.

——. 2002. *The People of Plato: A Prosopography of Plato and Other Socratics*. Indianapolis, IN: Hackett Publishing Co., Inc.

Nightingale, Andrea Wilson. 1995. *Genres in Dialogue: Plato and the Construct of Philosophy*. New York: Cambridge University Press.

Norlin, George, trans. 1929. *Isocrates II*. 3 vols. Loeb Classical Library. Cambridge, MA: Harvard University Press.

——, and LaRue Van Hook, trans. 1968. *Isocrates*. 3 vols. Cambridge, MA: Harvard University Press.

Nutton, Vivian. 2004. *Ancient Medicine*. New York: Routledge, 2004.

O'Brien, Michael J., trans. 1972. "Protagoras." In *The Older Sophists*, ed. Rosamond Kent Sprague. Columbia: University of South Carolina Press.

O'Grady, Patricia, ed. 2008. *The Sophists: An Introduction*. London: Duckworth.

Ong, Walter J. 1967. *The Presence of the Word: Some Prolegomena for Cultural and Religious History*. New Haven, CT: Yale University Press.

——. 1982. *Orality and Literacy: The Technologizing of the Word*. New York: Methuen & Co.

Osborne, Catherine. 1987. *Rethinking Early Greek Philosophy: Hippolytus of Rome and the Presocratics*. London: Duckworth.

Palmer, John. 2013. *Parmenides and Presocratic Philosophy*. New York: Oxford University Press.

Papillon, Terry L. 1996. "Isocrates and the Use of Myth." *Hermathena* 161: 9–21.

——. 1997. "The Identity of Gorgias in Isocrates' *Helen*." *Electronic Antiquity* 3 (6): 1–18.

——. 1998. "Isocrates and the Greek Poetic Tradition." *Scholia* 7: 41–61.

——, trans. 2004. *Isocrates II*. Austin: University of Texas Press.

——. 2007. "Isocrates." In *Blackwell's Companion to Greek Rhetoric,* ed. Ian Worthington, 58–74. London: Blackwell.

——. 2010. "Isocrates." In *A Companion to Greek Rhetoric,* ed. Ian Worthington, 58–74. Chichester UK: Wiley-Blackstone.

Patton, Kimberley C. 2004. "'A Great and Strange Correction': Intentionality, Locality, and Epiphany in the Category of Dream Incubation." *History of Religions* 43 (3): 194–223.

Penella, Robert J. 1979. "Philostratus' Letter to Julia Domna." *Hermes* 107 (2): 161–68.

Perelman, Chaïm. 1982. *The Realm of Rhetoric.* South Bend, IN: University of Notre Dame Press.

——, and Lucie Olbrechts-Tyteca. (1958) 1969. *The New Rhetoric.* Trans. John Wilkinson and Purcell Weaver. South Bend, IN: University of Notre Dame Press.

Perrin, Bernadotte, trans. 1916a. *Nicias by Plutarch.* Loeb Classical Library. Cambridge MA: Harvard University Press.

——. 1916b. *Pericles by Plutarch.* Loeb Classical Library. Cambridge MA: Harvard University Press.

Poster, Carol. 1994. "Persuasion in an Empty Ontology: The Eleatic Synthesis of Poetry, Philosophy, and Rhetoric." *Philosophy and Rhetoric* 27 (4): 277–99.

——. 1996. "Being and Becoming: Rhetorical Ontology in Early Greek Thought." *Philosophy and Rhetoric* 29 (1): 1–21.

——. 1998. "The Idea(s) of Order of Platonic Dialogues and Their Hermeneutic Consequences." *Phoenix: Journal of the Classical Association of Canada* 52 (3/4): 282–98.

——, trans. 1999. *Clouds by Aristophanes.* In *Aristophanes 3,* ed. David Slavitt and Palmer Bovie, 85–192. Philadelphia: University of Pennsylvania Press.

——. 2006. "The Task of the Bow" *Philosophy and Rhetoric* 39 (1): 1–21.

——. 2008. "Evidence, Authority, and Interpretation: A Response to Jason Helms." *Philosophy and Rhetoric* 41: 288–99.

Poulakos, John. 1995. *Sophisitical Rhetoric in Ancient Greece.* Columbia: University of South Carolina Press.

Poulakos, Takis. 1997. *Speaking for the Polis: Isocrates' Rhetorical Education.* Columbia: University of South Carolina Press.

Price, Jonathan J. 2001. *Thucydides and Internal War.* Cambridge, UK: Cambridge University Press.

Radermacher, Ludwig. 1951. *Artium scriptores (Reste der voraristotelischen Rhetorik).* Wien: Rudolf M. Rohrer.

Rebhorn, Wayne, ed. 2001. *Renaissance Debates on Rhetoric.* Ithaca, NY: Cornell University Press.

Redfield, James. 1975. *Nature and Culture in the* Iliad*: The Tragedy of Hector.* Chicago: University of Chicago Press.

Reece, Steve. 1993. *The Stranger's Welcome: Oral Theory and the Aesthetics of the Homeric Hospitality Scene.* Ann Arbor: University of Michigan Press.

Reinhardt, Tobias. 2007. "Techniques of Proof in 4th Century Rhetoric: Ar. Rhet. 2.23–24 and Pre-Aristotelian Rhetorical Theory." In *Influences on Peripatetic Rhetoric: Essays in Honor of William W. Fortenbaugh,* ed. David C. Mirhady, 87–104. Leiden: Brill.

Richardson, Lewis F. 1939. *Generalized Foreign Politics: a Study in Group Psychology.* Cambridge, UK: Cambridge University Press.

Robb, Kevin. 1993. "*Asebeia* and *Sunousia:* The Issues Behind the Indictment of Socrates." In *Plato's Dialogues: New Studies and Interpretations,* ed. Gerald Press, 77–106. Lanham, MD: Rowman and Littlefield.

Robinson, Steven R. 2008. "The Political Background of the Sophists at Athens." In *The Sophists: An Introduction,* ed. Patricia O'Grady, 21–29. London: Duckworth.

Robinson, Thomas. 1991. *Heraclitus.* Toronto: University of Toronto Press.

Roegholt, Lubbertus Patroclus. 1893. *Ps. Lysiae oratio contra Andocidem.* Groningae: Hoitsema Fratres.

Rohde, Erwin. 1925. *Psyche.* Trans. W. B. Hillis. London: Kegan Paul.

Roisman, Hanna M. 2007. "Right Rhetoric in Homer." In *A Companion to Greek Rhetoric,* ed. Ian Worthington, 429–46. Malden, MA: Blackwell.

Rolfe, John C., trans. 1927. Aulus Gellius *Attic Nights.* 3 vols. Loeb Classical Library. Cambridge, MA: Harvard University Press.

Romilly, Jacqueline de. 1958. "*Eunoia* in Isocrates or the Political Importance of Creating Good Will." *Journal of Hellenic Studies* 78: 92–101.

——. 1963. *Thucydides and Athenian Imperialism.* Trans. Phillip Thody. Oxford, UK: Blackwell.

——. 1992. *The Great Sophists in Periclean Athens.* Trans. Janet Lloyd. Oxford, UK: Clarendon Press.

Ross, William David. 1958. *Aristotelis topica et sophistici elenchi.* Oxford: Clarendon Press. Rpt. with corrections. Oxford: Clarendon Press, 1970.

Rubinstein, Lene. 2000. *Litigation and Cooperation: Supporting Speakers in the Courts of Classical Athens. Historia:* Einzelschriften, 147. Stuttgart: Franz Steiner Verlag.

Sahlins, Marshall. 2004. *Apologies to Thucydides: Understanding History as Culture and Vice Versa.* Chicago: University of Chicago Press.

Sammons, Benjamin. 2010. *The Art and Rhetoric of the Homeric Catalogue.* Oxford, UK: Oxford University Press.

Sansone, David. 2012. *Greek Drama and the Invention of Rhetoric.* Malden, MA: Wiley-Blackwell.

Schenkeveld, Dirk M. 1992. "Prose Usages of Ἀκούειν 'To Read'." *Classical Quarterly* 42 (1): 129–41.

Schiappa, Edward. 1985. "Dissociation and the Arguments of Rhetorical Theory." *Journal of the American Forensics Association* 22 (1): 72–82.

——. 1990. "Did Plato Coin *Rhētorikē*?" *American Journal of Philology* 111 (4): 457–70.

——. 1997. "Interpreting Gorgias's 'Being' in *On Not-Being* or *On Nature.*" *Philosophy and Rhetoric* 30 (1): 13–30.

——. 1999. *The Beginnings of Rhetorical Theory in Classical Greece.* New Haven, CT: Yale University Press.

——. 2003a. *Defining Reality: Definitions and the Politics of Meaning.* Carbondale: Southern Illinois University Press.

——. (1991) 2003b. *Protagoras and Logos: A Study in Greek Philosophy and Rhetoric.* 2nd ed. Columbia: University of South Carolina Press.

——, and Jim Hamm. 2007. "Rhetorical Questions: An Introduction." In *A Companion to Greek Rhetoric,* ed. Ian Worthington, 3–15. London: Blackwell.

Schirren, Thomas. 2009. "91. Textaufbau und Redeteilschemata (partes orationis)." In *Rhetorik und Stilistik/Rhetoric and Stylistics. Ein internationales Handbuch historischer und systematischer Forschung/An International Handbook of Historical and Systematic Research,* ed. Ulla Fix, Andreas Gardt, and Joachim Knape, vol. 2: 1515–28. Berlin: Walter de Gruyter.

Schneider, Valentin. 1901. "Ps. Lysias κατ' Ἀνδοκίδου ἀσεβείας (VI)." *Jahrbücher für classische Philologie,* Supplementband 27: 352–72.

Scotti, Angelo Antonio, and Josephus Genuensis. 1855. *Philodemi De rhetorica libri IV pars altera.* Herculanensium Voluminum quae supersunt. Vol. 11. Neapoli: Ex Regia Typographia.

Seaford, Richard. 1994. *Ritual and Reciprocity: Homer and Tragedy in the Developing City-State.* Oxford: Clarendon Press.

——. 2004. *Money and the Early Greek Mind: Homer, Philosophy, Tragedy.* New York: Cambridge University Press.

Seddon, Keith, trans. 2005. Cebes *Tablet.* In *Epictetus' Handbook and the Tablet of Cebes,* 185–200. New York: Routledge.

Shanske, Darien. 2006. *Thucydides and the Philosophical Origins of History.* New York: Cambridge University Press.

Sloterdijk, Peter. 1987. *Critique of Cynical Reason.* Trans. Michael Eldred. Minneapolis: University of Minnesota Press.

Solmsen, Felix. 1934. T[heodorus] von Byzanz, Rhetor [Nr. 38]. *Paulys Real-Encyclopädie der classischen Alternumswissenschaft.* Neue Bearbeitung. Zweite Reihe [R–Z]. Zeinter Halbband Thapsos-Thesara: Cols. 1839–47. Stuttgart: Metzler.

Sosower, Mark L. 1987. *Palatinus Graecus 88 and the Manuscript Tradition of Lysias.* Amsterdam: Adolf M. Hakkert.

Snell, Bruno. 1953. *The Discovery of the Mind.* Oxford: Basil Blackwell.

Spengel, Leonardus. 1840. *Das vierte Buch der Rhetorik des Philodemos in den herkulanischen Rollen. Abhandlungen der Philosophisch-philologischen Classe der königlich Bayerischen Akademie der Wissenschaften.* Dritten Bandes, Erste Abtheilund, 209–303. München: auf Kosten der Akademie.

Sprague, Rosamond Kent, ed. 1972. *The Older Sophists: A Complete Translation by Several Hands of the Fragments in* Die Fragmente Der Vorsokratiker, *edited by Diels-Kranz. With a New Edition of Antiphon and of Euthydemus.* Columbia: University of South Carolina Press.

Stahl, Hans-Peter. (1966) 2003. *Thucydides: Man's Place in History.* English ed. Swansea: Classical Press of Wales.

Stanford, William B., ed. and comm. 1992. *Odyssey I–XII* by Homer. Vol. 1. 2nd ed. Scarborough, UK: Thomas Nelson and Sons.

Stevenson, J. G. 1974. "Aristotle as Historian of Philosophy." *Journal of Hellenic Studies* 94: 138–43.

Stroebe, Wolfgang, Tom Postmes, and Russell Spears. 2012. "Scientific Misconduct and the Myth of Self-Correction in Science." *Perspectives on Psychological Science* 7 (6): 670–88.

Sudhaus, Siegfried, ed. 1892–1896. *Philodemi volumina rhetorica.* Bibliotheca scriptorum Graecorum et Romanorum Teubneriana. 2 vols. and Suppl. Lipsiae: B. G. Teubneri.

Sutton, Jane. 2001. "Kairos." In *Encyclopedia of Rhetoric,* ed. Thomas Sloane, 413–17. New York: Oxford University Press.

Swain, Simon. 1991. "The Reliability of Philostratus's *Lives of the Sophists.*" *Classical Antiquity* 10 (1): 148–63.

Tandy, David W. 1997. *Warriors into Traders: The Power of the Market in Early Greece.* Berkeley: University of California Press.

Tannen, Deborah, ed. 1993. *Gender and Conversational Interaction.* Oxford, UK: Oxford University Press.

——. 1994. *Talking From 9 to 5.* New York: William Morrow & Co.

——. 2001. *I Only Say This Because I Love You.* New York: Random House.

Tattersall, Ian. 2012. *Masters of the Planet: The Search for Our Human Origins.* New York: Palgrave Macmillan.

Tell, Håkan. 2009. "Wisdom for Sale? The Sophists and Money." *Classical Philology* 104: 13–33.

Theobald, Michael. 2003. *Studien zum Römerbrief.* Wissenschaftliche Untersuchungen zum Neuen Testament 136. Tübingen: Mohr Siebeck.

Timmerman, David M., and Edward Schiappa. 2010. *Classical Greek Rhetorical Theory and the Disciplining of Discourse.* Cambridge, UK: Cambridge University Press.

Todd, Stephen C., trans. 2000. *Lysias.* Austin: University of Texas Press.

——. 2005. "Law and Oratory at Athens." In *Cambridge Guide to Ancient Athenian Law,* ed. Michael Gagarin, 97–111. New York: Cambridge University Press.

——, trans. and comm. 2007. *A Commentary on Lysias, Speeches 1–11.* New York: Oxford University Press.

Too, Yun Lee. 1995. *The Rhetoric of Identity in Isocrates: Text, Power, Pedagogy.* Cambridge, UK: Cambridge University Press.

——, trans. 2000. Isocrates 2. *Ad Nicocles.* In *Isocrates I,* trans. David C. Mirhady and Yun Lee Too, 157–68. Austin: University of Texas Press.

Usher, Stephen, trans. 1974. *The Critical Essays of Dionysius of Halicarnassus.* Vol. 1. Loeb Classical Library. Cambridge, MA: Harvard University Press.

——. 1992. "Early Rhetoric: Review of *The Origins of Rhetoric in Ancient Greece,* by Thomas Cole." *Classical Review* 42 (1): 58–60.

——. 1999. *Greek Oratory: Tradition and Originality.* Oxford, UK: Oxford University Press.

Ustinova, Yulia. 2009. *Caves and the Ancient Greek Mind.* New York: Oxford University Press.

Uždavinys, Algis. 2008. *Philosophy as a Rite of Rebirth: From Ancient Egypt to Neoplatonism.* Wiltshire, UK: Prometheus Trust.

Van Hook, Larue, trans. 1945. *Isocrates III.* 3 vols. Loeb Classical Library. Cambridge, MA: Harvard University Press.

Vernant, Jean-Pierre. 1983. "The Formation of Positivist Thought in Archaic Greece." In *Myth and Thought among the Greeks,* trans. Janet Lloyd and Jeff Fort, 343–74. London: Routledge. Originally published as *Mythe et pensée chez les Grecs.* Paris: La Découverte, 1965.

——. 1988. "The Reason of Myth." In *Myth and Society in Ancient Greece,* trans. Janet Lloyd, 203–60. New York: Zone Books. Originally published as *Mythe et société en Grèce ancienne.* Paris: La Découverte, 1974.

Versnel, H. S. 2002. "The Poetics of the Magical Charm: An Essay in the Power of Words." In *Magic and Ritual in the Ancient World,* ed. P. Mirecki and M. Meyer, 104–58. Leiden: Brill.

Vickers, Brian. 1988. *In Defence of Rhetoric.* Oxford, UK: Clarendon Press.

Vidal-Naquet, Pierre. 1998. *The Black Hunter: Forms of Thought and Forms of Society in the Greek World.* Trans. Andrew Szegedy-Maszak. Baltimore: Johns Hopkins University Press. Originally published as *Le chasseur noir: Formes de pensée et formes de société dans le monde grec.* Paris: La Découverte, 1991.

Vitanza, Victor J., ed. 1994. *Writing Histories of Rhetoric.* Carbondale: Southern Illinois University Press.

——. 1997. *Negation, Subjectivity, and the History of Rhetoric.* Albany: State University of New York Press.

Vries, Gerrit Jacob de. 1969. *A Commentary on the* Phaedrus *of Plato.* Amsterdam: Adolf M. Hakkert.

Walker, Jeffrey. 2000. *Rhetoric and Poetics in Antiquity.* New York: Oxford University Press.

Walters, Frank D. 1994. "Gorgias as Philosopher of Being: Epistemic Foundationalism in Sophistic Thought." *Philosophy and Rhetoric* 27 (2): 143–55.

Wardy, Robert. 1996. *The Birth of Rhetoric: Gorgias, Plato and Their Successors.* New York: Routledge.

Wareh, Tarik. 2012. *The Theory and Practice of Life: Isocrates and the Philosophers.* Washington, DC: Center for Hellenic Studies.

Waterfield, Robin, ed. and trans. 2000. *The First Philosophers: The Presocratics and the Sophists.* New York: Oxford University Press.

Wender, Dorothea, trans. 1973. *Hesiod and Theognis.* New York: Penguin Books.

Whately, Richard. 1819. *Historic Doubts Relative to Napoleon Buonaparte.* London: Fellowes.

Whedbee, Karen E. 2003. "The Tyranny of Athens: Representations of Rhetorical Democracy in Eighteenth-Century Britain." *Rhetoric Society Quarterly* 33 (4): 65–85.

——. 2004. "Reclaiming Rhetorical Democracy: George Grote's Defense of Cleon and the Athenian Demagogues." *Rhetoric Society Quarterly* 34 (4): 71–95.

——. 2008. "Making the Worse Case Appear the Better: British Reception of the Greek Sophists prior to 1850." *Rhetoric and Public Affairs* 11 (4): 603–30.

Williams, B. H. Garnons. 1931. "The Political Mission of Gorgias to Athens in 427 B.C." *Classical Quarterly* 25 (1): 52–56.

Williams, Bernard. 1993. *Shame and Necessity.* Berkeley: University of California Press.

Wilson, William, trans. 1869. *The Writings of Clement of Alexandria.* Edinburgh: T & T Clark.

Winkelman, Michael. 2004. "Shamanism as the Original Neurotheology." *Zygon* 39 (1): 193–217.

Woodhouse, William J. 1969. *The Composition of Homer's* Odyssey. Oxford, UK: Clarendon Press.

Wright, Wilmer Cave, trans. 1922. *The Lives of the Sophists by Philostratus.* London: William Heinemann.

Yunis, Harvey. 1998. "The Constraints of Democracy and the Rise of the Art of Rhetoric." In *Democracy, Empire, and the Arts in Fifth-Century Athens,* ed. Deborah Boedeker and Kurt A. Raaflaub, 223–40. Cambridge, MA: Harvard University Press.

——, ed. 2011. *Plato. Phaedrus.* Cambridge, UK: Cambridge University Press.

Zeyl, Donald J., trans. 1997. *Gorgias.* In *Plato: Complete Works,* ed. John M. Cooper, 791–869. Indianapolis IN: Hackett Publishing Co.

Contributors

ROBERT N. GAINES is professor of communication studies at the University of Alabama. He was formerly editor of *Advances in the History of Rhetoric* and currently serves as translator in the Philodemus Project. His rhetorical scholarship has appeared in *Advances in the History of Rhetoric, Cronache Ercolanesi, Hermes: Zeitschrift für klassische Philologie, Rheinisches Museum für Philologie, Rhetoric and Philosophy, Rhetoric Society Quarterly, Rhetorica,* and *Transactions of the American Philological Association.*

DAVID C. HOFFMAN is associate professor of communication in the School of Public Affairs at Baruch College, City University of New York. He has published research on classical and eighteenth-century rhetoric in such journals as *Rhetoric and Public Affairs, Rhetorica, Argumentation and Advocacy,* and *Rhetoric Society Quarterly.*

MARINA MCCOY holds the Fitzgibbons Chair of Philosophy in the Philosophy Department at Boston College. She is the author of *Plato on the Rhetoric of Sophists and Philosophers* (2008) as well as numerous articles on the relationship between rhetoric and philosophy in journals including *Ancient Philosophy, Philosophy and Rhetoric, Arethusa,* and *International Philosophical Quarterly.* She has recently served as a referee for manuscripts for Oxford University Press, Ancient Philosophy, and Phoenix, and is a board member for the Institute for Philosophy in Public Life, based at the University of North Dakota.

TERRY L. PAPILLON is dean of the college and professor of Classics at the University of the South and editor of the online classics journal *Electronic Antiquity.* He received his B.A. in classics from St. Olaf College in Northfield, Minnesota, and his Ph.D. in classical philology from the University of North Carolina at Chapel Hill. He has taught at UNC Chapel Hill, the University of Minnesota–Duluth, Marquette University, and Virginia Tech. He has published articles on Greek rhetoric and two books: *Rhetorical Studies in the Aristocratea of Demosthenes* (1998) and *Isocrates II* (2004).

CAROL POSTER, now retired, recently served as Goss Distinguished Professor of Writing at Fort Hays State University and as associate professor at York University in Toronto. She has published essays on ancient philosophy and rhetoric. She is coeditor of *Letter Writing Manuals from Antiquity to the Present* (2007) and recipient of, among others, the Gildersleeve Prize (*American Journal of Philology*) and the Kneupper Award (*Rhetoric Society Quarterly*).

ROBIN REAMES is assistant professor of English at the University of Illinois at Chicago. She works on ancient and contemporary rhetorical theory. She received her Ph.D. in rhetoric from Carnegie Mellon University in 2009 and has published articles in *Rhetorica, Philosophy and Rhetoric,* and *Journal of Communication and Religion.* Her current book project is on Plato's rhetorical theory.

THOMAS RICKERT is professor of English at Purdue University. He is the author of essays on ancient and contemporary rhetorical theory, as well as the monographs *Acts of*

Enjoyment: Rhetoric, Žižek, and the Return of the Subject (2007) and *Ambient Rhetoric: The Attunements of Rhetorical Being* (2013). He serves as an editor for the Janice Lauer Series in Rhetoric and Composition with Parlor Press and for the online journal *Enculturation.*

EDWARD SCHIAPPA is John E. Burchard Professor of Humanities and head of the Comparative Media Studies and Writing Program at the Massachusetts Institute of Technology. He has published ten books on the history of rhetoric and rhetorical theory, and his work has appeared in *Philosophy and Rhetoric, Quarterly Journal of Speech, Rhetoric Review, Argumentation, Communication Monographs, Communication Theory,* and *American Journal of Philology.* He has served as editor of *Argumentation and Advocacy* and was awarded the National Communication Association's Douglas W. Ehninger Distinguished Scholar Award in 2000 and the Rhetorical and Communication Theory Distinguished Scholar Award in 2006, and he was named a National Communication Association Distinguished Scholar in 2009.

MICHAEL SVOBODA is assistant professor of writing at George Washington University. He earned his interdisciplinary Ph.D. from Penn State University after closing the bookstore he had owned and operated off-campus for seventeen years. The results of his work in two quite different research programs—ancient Greek rhetoric, philosophy, and history; and environmental rhetoric—have been published as articles, reviews, and review essays in *Rhetoric Society Quarterly, Rhetoric Review, Rhetorica, Review of Communication, Techné: Research in Philosophy and Technology, Quarterly Journal of Speech, Plagiary, Philosophy and Rhetoric,* and *Bulletin of Science, Technology, and Society.*

Index